I0138954

THE BOSTON POLICE
STRIKE OF 1919

THE BOSTON POLICE STRIKE OF 1919

Politics, Riots, and the Fight for Unionization

Willard M. Oliver

ROWMAN & LITTLEFIELD
Lanham • Boulder • New York • London

Published by Rowman & Littlefield
An imprint of The Rowman & Littlefield Publishing Group, Inc.
4501 Forbes Boulevard, Suite 200, Lanham, Maryland 20706
www.rowman.com

86-90 Paul Street, London EC2A 4NE

Copyright © 2023 by The Rowman & Littlefield Publishing Group, Inc.

All rights reserved. No part of this book may be reproduced in any form or
by any electronic or mechanical means, including information storage and
retrieval systems, without written permission from the publisher, except by a
reviewer who may quote passages in a review.

British Library Cataloguing in Publication Information Available

Library of Congress Cataloging-in-Publication Data

Names: Oliver, Willard M., author.
Title: The Boston police strike of 1919 : politics, riots, and the fight
   for unionization / Willard M. Oliver.
Description: Lanham, MD : The Rowman & Littlefield Publishing Group, Inc.,
   2023. | Includes bibliographical references and index. | Summary: "At
   5:45 p.m. on September 9, 1919, nearly every patrolman on the Boston
   Police Department abandoned their posts, leaving the city victim to four
   days of crime, looting and mob violence. This is the story of what led
   to the strike and the political ramifications of the greatest tragedy in
   American policing"-- Provided by publisher.
Identifiers: LCCN 2022061060 (print) | LCCN 2022061061 (ebook) | ISBN
   9781538144114 (cloth) | ISBN 9781538144121 (epub)
Subjects: LCSH: Police Strike, Boston, Mass., 1919. | Boston (Mass.).
   Police Department.
Classification: LCC HV8148.B72 O38 2023 (print) | LCC HV8148.B72
   (ebook)
   | DDC 331.892/8136320974461--dc23/eng/20230512
LC record available at https://lccn.loc.gov/2022061060
LC ebook record available at https://lccn.loc.gov/2022061061

To Maria Ilaria Oliver, my first grandchild.
You give life new meaning.
Welcome to the family!

There is no right to strike against the public safety by anybody, anywhere, any time.

—Governor Calvin Coolidge

Contents

Prologue
September 8 and 9, 1919

Patrolman John Franklin McInnes entered the Court Square Police Station just before 5:30 p.m. on the evening of September 8, 1919, where he would learn whether or not he still had a job with the Boston Police Department. Earlier that morning he had been found guilty of violating Section 19, Rule 35, of the Boston police regulations. He had not used excessive force on a suspect and had not harmed anyone. He had not taken graft, not even a free cup of coffee. What he had been found guilty of was joining the recently created Boston Policemen's Union Number 16,807 of the American Federation of Labor (AFL).

A small crowd had gathered outside the entrance of the stately, although

Patrolman John F. McInnes, president of the Boston Policemen's Union.
Photo courtesy of the Boston Public Library, Arts Department.

somewhat decrepit-looking, police station. They were interested in what was happening with the Boston police.[1] Some jeered, some cheered, but they were not overly vocal about it either way. The public was well aware of the situation because it had been reported on for several weeks in the local newspapers—a confrontation between the new police union and the police commissioner, Edwin Upton Curtis, had been brewing for weeks. On the same day that the American Federation of Labor allowed police officers to affiliate with their organization, Commissioner Curtis had issued a general order amending Rule 35 to ban the officers from affiliating with any outside organizations, except for police department–sanctioned veterans organizations.[2] The patrolmen ignored the rule, formed their union, and elected their fellow officers to lead the way. Patrolman John F. McInnes had overwhelmingly been voted their choice for president.

McInnes, a tall, imposing man, entered the locker room to don his uniform and equipment for the 5:45 p.m. roll call where he would learn his fate. His assumption was that he would be fired. However, despite that gloomy possibility, he was warmly greeted by his fellow officers, who were also preparing for the evening roll call. He realized that if he and the other 18 members of the union's leadership were not fired from the police force, he would soon be heading to his usual street intersection of Devonshire and Water Streets. There, he would relieve the dayshift patrolman directing traffic. Since Boston still had no stoplights in the city, McInnes's job was a necessity for alleviating traffic congestion and was greatly appreciated by the growing number of motorists in the city—not to mention the pedestrians. However, if he were fired, he would be returning to his locker to grab his personal belongings before heading to Fay Hall for the union meeting. Around 5:35 p.m., ready for duty in his policeman's uniform, he headed to the roll-call room.

Born on March 28, 1874, McInnes was 45 years old at the time of the growing unrest over unionization. He was a lifelong Bostonian who was born and raised in South Boston by a father who worked as a mason. John grew up learning the trade, and although he had the skills, he decided it was not to be his future. Instead, he enlisted in the US Army at the age of 16 and was sent west to the Wyoming and Dakota territories. When America went to war with Spain, McInnes was sent with the 9th Massachusetts Infantry to Cuba, where he participated in both the Battle of San Juan and the Siege of Santiago.[3]

When his enlistment was up after the war, McInnes returned home to Boston and settled down into a mason's job. He married Miss Mary G. Sullivan, and they started a family. Perhaps the longing for adventure was not quite out of his system, or perhaps he was just looking for a steady income, but he joined the Boston Police Department on October 14, 1907, as a reserve officer in Division 11.

McInnes continued in that position until America entered World War I. During the war he served as a commander in roles as diverse as "an intelligence officer, an instructor of infantry, an officer in the 157th Colored Brigade, and an investigator and provost marshal."[4] When the war ended, he returned to the position of Boston patrolman and directed traffic at Devonshire and Water Streets. The fact that McInnes was a veteran of two wars was among the reasons he had been elected president of the union.

Just before arriving at the roll-call room, he saw the two attorneys representing him and the Policemen's Union, James H. Vahey and John P. Feeney. They had come to discuss the situation with the man in charge of the Court Square police station, Captain Sullivan, and after entering the station, they had been routinely cheered by the men. McInnes was certainly glad to see them, for he appreciated their words of encouragement.[5] It had seemed such a long road to get where they were, and now that they had reached this culminating point, McInnes could not help but feel a little unsure of himself. The presence of the attorneys bolstered his spirits.

The issue had been developing for decades, but the previous police commissioner, Stephen James O'Meara, a good Irish cop who was well loved by everyone, had done little to better the policemen's lot. Their pay had been locked into place when the state had taken over control of the Boston Police Department. Although they had received a pay raise nearly 20 years earlier, and one more recently that year, it was always too little, too late. The cost of living increase had not put the officers ahead, especially during World War I; it just left them not as far behind. In addition, the barracks they were required to live in while on duty was nearly half a century old and had fallen into disrepair. Coupled with the long hours and long workweeks, with only one day off a week, the men wanted change. They had tried for nearly 20 years by working through the Boston Patrolman's Social Club, but they had been mostly ignored. Now, with the backing of the AFL, they were on the brink of change, but the recently appointed commissioner did not appear to support their endeavors.

At a few minutes before 5:45 p.m., McInnes entered the roll-call room, and a burst of cheers greeted him by the nearly 40 officers in attendance. There were handshakes, slaps on the back, and lots of verbal support. If McInnes had any doubts, they quickly vanished. Finding an empty chair, he sat and waited.

Promptly at 5:45 p.m., Captain Sullivan and the station command staff entered the room. All rose to attention, then took their seats again. The captain did not waste any time. Announcing that there was a new general order issued by the police commissioner, he read it aloud. "Boston, Sept. 8, 1919, General Order No. 122. Police Commissioner Edwin U. Curtis, having heard the several complaints charging the following named patrolmen," (at which point Captain Sullivan read off the names of 19 officers, including that of John F. McInnes)[6] "with violation of Section 19 of Rule 35 of the Rules and Regulations of the Police Department, finds the said," (he again read off the 19 officers' names) "respectively guilty of the charge preferred against each one of them."[7] This information was already 12-hour-old news, so everyone now sat silently, listening for the final determination. "Police Commissioner Curtis suspends the sentence to be imposed on each one upon said finding of guilty, and pending the imposition of said sentence, and by virtue of Rule 40 of the Rules and Regulations of the department, suspends from duty each of the following named patrolmen," and once again, he read off the names of the officers.[8] When McInnes's name was read this time, the room burst into cheers.

McInnes was momentarily stunned, for he had fully expected to be fired, but he was only suspended. Still, he knew the outcome was the same. He would not be directing traffic that evening. McInnes stood up, walked up to the captain, and surrendered his devices and insignia. The captain then said he would like to see him for a moment in his office. McInnes followed Sullivan out, and roll call continued. The conversation with Sullivan was brief and fell into the category of fatherly advice. When he left the captain's office, roll call was over, and the men of the station house broke out into more cheers. As McInnes left the station, they followed him out with a rousing rendition of the song "Hail, Hail, the Gang's All Here." McInnes sang heartily along himself.

When McInnes exited Police Station 2, he found the crowd had swelled to well over 100 people and included many reporters, who began asking questions, particularly about what happened and what would come next for the Policemen's Union. McInnes only told them he had been suspended. When asked to comment on the roll call, the only thing he said was that Captain Sullivan was a "fine fellow" and that he would "stand by him even if the whole city was against him."[9]

McInnes then headed over to Fay Hall. He had work to do. He had been there earlier in the day, meeting with the Boston Policemen's Union leadership at 2:30 p.m. in advance of the decision. They had recessed at 4:15 p.m. so McInnes and the other officers needing to report for roll call could do so. All the other officers took a break as well, for Fay Hall had turned unbearably hot. The temperature had risen to 92 degrees that afternoon.[10]

McInnes was cheered when he entered the hall.[11] Everyone there already knew the outcome, and there was much discussion. He began conversing with the union's lawyers, as well as with the representative from the AFL. He also met with the rest of the Policemen's Union leadership, all save those who were on duty, although a few of those stopped by to confer as well.

The questions that needed to be answered were whether they should call for a strike vote and, if so, how they should proceed. It did not take long to answer the first question, because there was clearly a strong sentiment among the men to declare a strike; therefore, a vote would be necessary.[12] That left another question: If the strike vote were favorable, when would they go on strike? Some argued for right after the vote, whereas some wanted to do it later in the week, but it was decided that the time would be 5:45 p.m. on Tuesday, September 9, 1919. This would occur at the evening roll call and, symbolically, at the same time the 19 officers learned they were suspended. They had less than 24 hours to make their decision.

Balloting did not begin until just before 10 o'clock that night.[13] The hall was filled with every police officer not on duty, and they had made the necessary preparations for collecting the ballots in a nearby wastepaper basket that was set atop a table. Patrolmen Philip S. Corbett served as the warden of the ballot box, such as it was.[14] Corbett was 31 years old and had been a Boston patrolman for four and one-half years. He was of medium height and build—a strikingly handsome man with chestnut hair and dazzling blue eyes. Before joining the department, Corbett had been a machinist and railway brakeman and had served in the US military during World War I, having only returned to police duty less than a year prior.

Corbett kept the balloting process orderly, and he had three additional patrolmen to help him keep it that way.[15] Each man was given a slip of paper upon which he was to write either "Yes" or "No," then proceed to the front of the hall and deposit his vote in the wastepaper basket. Most of the men began shouting aloud, "Here's a strike!" as they dropped their vote into the ballot box.[16] Corbett would then hold off the next balloter until the name of the previous patrolman had been checked off.[17]

The men in the hall, either waiting to vote or having already done so, often broke out in cheers or song. The ebullient mood began to wane, but around one o'clock in the morning, when the evening shift, now off duty, made their way to the hall, the cheering and singing broke out once more.

The voting continued to go strong until well past 2 a.m., but it began to die off again as the morning hours approached.[18] "In the early hours," the *Boston Evening Globe* reported later that day, "the score or more of men sitting about the big hall conversed in lowered tones, and the place appeared more like a hospital or other public institution than a hall where a strike vote was being polled."[19]

The vote lasted well into the morning, for it had been decided that it was more important to give every member of the Boston Policemen's Union the opportunity to vote on the strike, since many might not have had the chance before going on midnight duty. For that reason, and to ensure that the count was accurate, they did not release the final, official tally until 10 a.m. that morning. A statement was prepared by the union's leadership in consultation with their lawyers and the AFL representative. For the first time, official union letterhead was used to release the news to the media. It announced that the vote to strike had received 1,134 "yes" votes, 2 "no" votes, and one slip of paper was left blank.[20]

When Boston mayor Andrew James Peters was told of the final vote and was asked if he was prepared for the police to go on strike, he told reporters:

> Police Commissioner Curtis assured me that he was in a position to give the people adequate protection. Governor Coolidge said he was fully prepared to render support to the police commissioner in any measures which might be instituted by the police commissioner. I am relying on these promises.[21]

When Police Commissioner Edwin Upton Curtis was told of the final vote and was asked if he was prepared for the police to go on strike, he bluntly stated, "I am prepared for all eventualities," then paused and added, "I am ready for anything."[22] Whether they were ready or not no longer mattered, for regardless, at roll call that evening, the police who were supposed to go on duty would not do so, while those on duty would leave the station without replacement.

At 5:45 p.m. on the evening of September 9, 1919, the city of Boston would effectively be without a police force.

1882 Map depicting "old Boston" from the 1600s and "new Boston" in 1880. Photo courtesy of the Boston Public Library, Leventhal Map & Education Center.

1

America's First Police Department

The Boston Police Department, established in 1838, is generally credited with being the first modern police department in the United States.[1] That year, a bill passed in the General Court authorized the city to appoint police officers for a full-time day patrol. The year differs from the modern-day patch Boston police officers wear on their uniforms, for their shoulder patch is inscribed with "Boston Police A.D. 1630," and the inscription on their badge is "Bostonia Condita A.D. 1630."[2] This suggests the department originally saw creation in 1630, most likely based on the development of the town's first night watch.[3] The year of the Boston night watch's establishment, however, is also somewhat in question. Most documentation states Boston created its first night watch in 1635, while the Boston Police Department's website lists 1631, despite the fact that the date on their patch and badge is listed as 1630.[4]

Still more confusing with regard to the Boston Police Department's date of origin is the fact that the old badge police officers wore was once inscribed with "First in the Nation 1854." In that year Boston consolidated all of the entities responsible for public safety into one force, including both the night watch and the day patrol.[5] The Boston Police Department no longer mentions the year 1854, perhaps because that would make the Boston Police Department second in the nation after the New York City Police

1

Department, which is generally credited as having been established in 1845.[6]

The debate over the founding year of the Boston Police Department is perhaps an academic one, but it highlights the reality that the Boston Police, like so many others, was not created out of whole cloth. Rather, modern-day police departments are the creation of a slowly evolving system, developed over time, and based on the needs of their communities and the institutional capabilities of the government regarding public safety.

This evolution of the Boston Police Department tells us that the department started in either 1838 or 1854 was an American creation, while the Boston Police Department developed in 1630, 1631, or 1635 had begun life as an English institution. Any study of the American Boston Police Department necessitates an understanding of the English form of policing. Knowledge of how the English developed their own system of policing helps us appreciate the development of the American system of policing, especially as it pertains to the Boston Police Department prior to 1919. To truly start at the beginning, specifically with the development of the modern police department, it is best to understand the development of societies, and the best place for that comes from American anthropologist Jared Diamond's book *Guns, Germs, and Steel: The Fates of Human Societies* (1997).

In his Pulitzer Prize–winning book, Diamond classifies societies into four developmental categories: bands, tribes, chiefdoms, and states.[7] These are the stages that societies tend to progress through and, when successful at each stage, they typically continue growing and evolving into the next stage. The first and most rudimentary form of society, beyond the family itself, is the band. As described by Diamond, bands only number in the dozens, are based on kin relations, and tend to be nomadic. The resolution of any conflicts is handled through informal measures because "there are no formal institutions, such as laws, police, and treaties, to resolve conflicts within and between bands."[8] In their decision-making and leadership, bands tend to be egalitarian, and members of the band treat each other with the principle of equality, in part because they are family but also as a means of survival.

As bands develop, they grow into tribes. Tribes typically number in the hundreds, are still widely kin-based, and the people begin establishing fixed settlements. While bands exist as hunters and gatherers, tribes begin to cultivate their food, whether growing crops or herding animals. Tribes, like bands, remain egalitarian in nature, and they still "lack a bureaucracy, police force, and taxes."[9] Conflicts continue to be resolved through informal means of social control, although now a head of the tribe (which Diamond calls the "big-man") may be the one settling disputes among people within a tribe or those across tribes.

Chiefdoms are the next stage of societal evolution and become "considerably larger than tribes, ranging from several thousand to several tens of thousands of people."[10] Chiefdoms expand beyond just maintaining one village and tend to grow into multiple villages. This necessitates a more centralized form of decision-making and leadership and thus can no longer be egalitarian. What replaces it is typically a hereditary system that resolves its conflicts through centralized and more formal mechanisms. This is often a responsibility retained by the chief himself as a means of maintaining order. While there is typically no formal police department established, there are usually formal methods of self-policing that are used to maintain order or, in cases of greater need, armed men representing the chief. Thus, the first signs of police-like forces tend to appear in chiefdoms, but they are more militaristic in nature.

The last form of society is the one most people live under today: the modern state. States typically number over 50,000 in population and can range from city-states to nation-states. They are fixed settlements that exist as cities, counties, and provinces, or, like the United States, a conglomeration of states. The society has a highly centralized system that has developed bureaucratic means of control, is generally class-oriented, and maintains a monopoly on the use of force. "Internal conflict resolution within states," Diamond explains, "has become increasingly formalized by laws, a judiciary, and police."[11] Thus, the first signs of a modern police force tend to appear in the last evolution of societies and states.

England's chiefdom phase, as described by Diamond, was most assuredly its Feudal Era, which ranged from AD 700 to approximately AD 1300.[12] The "chiefs" in this case were the feudal lords who asserted ownership over the land and maintained centralized control over the "tuns" and "vills" (towns and villages) of the time period through barons and knights. Everyone living on the lord's land was wholly reliant on the lord's graces for what they had, and they paid their lord through taxes.

As in most chiefdoms described by Diamond, there were no formal police departments; rather, a system of formalized self-help typically developed during this time period to maintain order. During England's Feudal Era in the early Middle Ages, the self-help system that developed came to be known as the frankpledge system. In this system a group of 10 families, living in close proximity to one another, were designated as a "tithing" (also spelled as "tything").[13] The term derived from the tithe, the annual amount given in produce or earnings to the church. In this case the 10 families in the tithing became a surety for one another; they pledged to hold all other members of the tithing accountable for the behaviors of the group. If anyone stepped out of line or committed a crime, it was up to the tithing to resolve the issue.

The system then went higher with the "hundred," a collection of 10 tithings. If there were disputes within a tithing that the families were not able to resolve, or if there were disputes or crimes committed across two or more tithings, then the hundred became responsible for finding a resolution. The head of the hundred, elected by the group, became the hundred-head or the *gerefa*, an Anglo-Saxon word for chief. This entire collective effort toward self-help served as a means for people to pledge themselves to each other for purposes of protection. This is why, in the 12th century, it came to be referred to as the "Frankpledge system."[14] Each year all freemen over the age of 12 were required to make a frankpledge before the gerefa, swearing by oath to uphold their allegiance to the people within their tithing and hundred.

The system was effective to a degree because the tithings consisted mainly of people related to one another. This generally meant that they were already altruistic in their communal inter-actions with one another. Although this was a formalization of the informal means of social control, it provided a framework by which the people, still largely egalitarian because of their clan connections, were able to maintain order. In addition, the frankpledge system prevented the feudal lords from having to use their own resources to assert control over the people for pur-poses of law and order. That only came about when the lord's property was the subject of a dispute or crime.

Representing their interests, the lords, of course, always had armed men at their disposal through the military. During this era, however, another position developed to represent the lord's interests outside of himself or his military. A reeve was appointed to oversee an area typically occupied by a hundred, and, in time, the reeve came to replace the position of gerefa altogether.[15] At first the shire-reeve had limited duties, mostly associated with the court system. As their powers grew, the reeves came to represent the king's interest in the shire, so in addition to court-related duties such as issuing writs, they also became responsible for the collection of taxes and duties. Still further, they oversaw the more formal hundred court, served as a witness for sales and bartering exchanges in order to main-tain fair trade, and became the oath takers for the frankpledge system. Moreover, when it came to law enforcement duties, the shire-reeves were responsible for dealing with crimes against the king, raising the hue and cry—notifying men in the immedi-ate vicinity that a crime has just been committed—and pursuing the offenders. Collectively, these duties are not too different from the modern sheriffs in towns and cities today in America.

With the Norman conquest of England in AD 1066 and the growth of towns and cities that followed, England began its transition from a chiefdom to a state. In time, "newly devel-oped techniques of royal, baronial, and ecclesiastical adminis-tration gave the local community its structure," and the taxes laid upon the villages and towns provided the developing state the ability to fund more centralized control.[16] The reeve served as the means by which government asserted much of its control over the people, but soon additional measures became necessary. London passed an ordinance in 1233 mandating "that local people keep watches and have constables," to provide the city with an added measure of public safety.[17] Toward the end of the 13th century, this mandate applied to all towns when King Edward I issued the Statute of Winchester in 1285, that decreed, "The king commandeth, that from henceforth all watches be made as it hath been used in times past."[18] The night watch, charged with closing the city gates at dusk, were authorized to arrest any who tried passing into the town during the hours of darkness and to "forthwith deliver him to the sheriff"[19] when there was a suspicious stranger. In addition, the statute also mandated that "in every hundred and franchise two constables shall be chosen."[20] The constables were in charge of inspecting the arms of the night watchmen and overseeing their deployment.

Not long after the establishment of the night watch, a daytime patrol, known as the ward, was also adopted and became well entrenched within the English system by the early 14th century. This combined system of the shire-reeve, constables, and watchmen, including both the night watch and the day ward, became the mechanism by which England's government oversaw public safety, and it served as the early form—actually the only form—of policing for the next 500 years. Throughout its existence, the constable-and-watch system was never highly respected in England, for most considered it grossly ineffective. John Fielding, writing in the 18th century, made note that "the watchmen . . . hardly ever tried to stop any villains,"[21] while modern scholars have explained, "It was common for the illiterate, elderly, infirm, lazy, or simply corrupt to be working as constables."[22] As far back as the late 16th century, the asinine Constable Dogberry and his night watchmen were written as buffoons in Shakespeare's play *Much Ado About Nothing*. In one scene, when the aristocratic Conrade calls Constable Dogberry an ass, Dogberry accepts the title as one of nobility, imploring his masters to "remember that I am an ass; though it be not written down, yet forget not that I am an ass."[23] Despite the ridicule at the time, little changed or altered the performance of the constables, watch, and ward.

When America first colonized at the beginning of the 17th century with the founding of Jamestown in 1607, Boston was one of the earliest towns to form. Named after the town in the English county of Lincolnshire, Boston was established on September 7, 1630.[24] Because the town was in fact an English colony, the English system of the constable, watch, and ward was established there. The first night watch in American history, instituted by the court in Boston, began its duties on April 12, 1631.[25] The night watch formed at sunset and initially consisted of an officer and six men in a kind of military guard tasked with patrolling the Boston Neck, the thin strip of land that gave access to the then-peninsular city. As John Winthrop noted in his journal that year, "We began a court of guard upon the neck between Roxbury and Boston, whereupon should be always resident an officer and six men."[26]

Three years later, in 1634, the court created the position of constable, and William Cheseborough was the first person appointed to the position. That same year, on September 1, 1634, the local leaders decided they would create their own town government because, according to Winthrop, the court "had become so oppressive."[27] Two years after forming, the town government officially assumed command of the Boston Watch, made effective on February 27, 1636.[28] The town charged the Boston night watch to "see that all disturbances and disorders in night shall be prevented and suppressed."[29] In order to achieve this, the watch had "authority to examine all persons, whom they have reason to suspect of any unlawful design, and to demand of them their business abroad at such time, and wither they are going."[30] The method by which they carried out these duties was to "walk the rounds in and about the streets, lanes, wharves, and principal inhabited parts of the city or town, to prevent danger by fire, and to see that good order is kept."[31] They carried with them a rattle on their rounds, sounding the alarm by spinning it at the first sign of trouble. This is why the locals came to refer to them as "the rattle watch."[32]

The most serious danger against which the night watch stood guard was not so much criminal activity but fires. Any fire, no matter how small, posed the deadliest hazard to the all-wooden cities of the day. That danger was soon learned all too well for, in 1652, Boston suffered a series of deadly fires. The response to this was to give the night watch a bell so they could sound the fire alarm throughout the city. In addition, the watch's hours, originally sunset to sunrise, changed to the more fixed hours of 10 p.m. to 5 a.m., and those became the times when they lit and extinguished the streetlamps.[33]

The recruitment for the watch was typically in the form of a draft. All men over the age of 18 were liable to have to serve. The exceptions included those already in a position of service such as justices of the peace, ministers, and sheriffs. If a person who was drafted refused to serve, they were required to find their own replacement. This generally meant the ranks of the night watch were filled with incompetents who had no interest in the position, if they even presented themselves for duty.

The constable-and-watch system established in Boston fared little better than that in England. Despite changes in the way these men were paid or the move to make it mandatory that all able-bodied men serve on the watch, the fact that many simply ignored the call or paid for a replacement did not create an effective force or one that was well respected. When those who could afford to avoid service on the watch made their payment, as Benjamin Franklin complained, the money was not used to hire a suitable replacement. Franklin elaborated, "Those who chose never to attend paid [the constable] six shillings a year to be excus'd, which was suppos'd to be for hiring substitutes; but was in reality much more than was necessary for that purpose, and made the constableship a place for profit."[34] Franklin further charged, "The constable, for a little drink, often got such raga-muffins about him as a watch, that respectable housekeepers did not choose to mix with" and "walking the rounds, too, was often neglected, and most of the nights spent in tippling."[35] A commentary in one 1808 newspaper put it more bluntly when it stated, "Since substitutes have been allowed, that patrol is com-posed principally of the most worthless part of the community . . . it is like setting wolves to guard the sheep."[36] To remedy this situation, Franklin, writing in 1788, in no less than his own auto-biography, advocated for a paid police force by levying taxes on property. Unfortunately for Franklin, that did not happen for another 50 years—long after he was gone.

Even into the early 19th century, public safety did not advance much beyond the "rattle watch" of the early 17th century, as evidenced in New York City in the early 1800s by the group of constables and "roundsmen" popularly known as the "leatherheads" (for the tight-fitting leather helmets they wore).[37] They, too, were not well respected by the adults of New York City, and it has been said they often provided hours of amusement for the youth. "Youthful and exuberant New Yorkers considered an evening out was not spent in the Orthodox manner unless they played some rough practical jokes on the poor, old, inoffensive Leatherheads," wrote retired police chief George Walling, reminiscing about the early days.[38]

> It is recorded of such a staid young man as Washington Irving ... [of "Legend of Sleepy Hollow" and "Rip Van Winkle" fame] was in the habit of upsetting watch-boxes if he caught a "Leatherhead" asleep inside; and on one occasion, so it is said, he lassoed the box with a stout rope, and with the aid of companions dragged it down Broadway, while the watchman inside yelled loudly for help.[39]

It was, in truth, so common to find the night watchmen asleep during Washington Irving's day that New Yorkers often quipped, "While the city sleeps, the watchmen do too."[40]

It was the same in Boston, for as legal historian Lawrence Friedman explained, "There was a constant chorus of complaints about the constables and watchmen."[41] He notes one example in which a series of burglaries were occurring in Boston in August 1789, in which a commentator quipped it was "high time the watchmen were overhauled; they have been asleep since New Year's."[42] Of those in charge of the watchmen, it was said they were "men in their prime, aged from ninety to one hundred years, and the crew only average about fourscore, and so we have the advantage of their age and experience, *at least the robbers do.*"[43] The complaints went unanswered until the next century.

Boston tried to make things better when it passed an ordinance making the first town selectman the "Superintendent of Police," who soon became the mayor himself. By 1811 the designation for watchman became that of "police officer."[44] In addition, an 1801 statute required a continuous watch; thus, beginning that year, they paid the night watchmen. The city did not suffer for finding recruits because of the consistent pay, which was 50 cents a night.[45] They also tried to regulate the position by requiring at least one member of a household to serve on the watch, and to increase the quality, they were required to be married, taxpayers, and voters. Still, at the dismal rates of pay, the quality of the recruits remained low, and even when the rates were higher, too many recruits had full-time jobs during the day and simply used the night watch to catch up on their sleep and receive pay while doing so. Although Boston was a growing city, "fiscal conservatism held down the numbers as well as the pay of watchmen."[46] According to police historian Roger Lane, about 80 were hired each year, working two shifts of 36 each, and they were supposed to take turns patrolling the city, all except South Boston, which, because it was separated from the peninsula by water, received no watchmen.[47]

Boston's population continued to expand and included approximately 16,000 people when Massachusetts joined the union on February 8, 1788; the town grew to nearly 25,000, at which time the ordinance of 1801 attempted to improve the force. By 1822 the population stood at 49,000 people, but the number of night watchmen had changed little in this time period. The growth of the town and demand by the people for an improved night watch motivated the act to incorporate the town, turning the town into a city. On March 4, 1822, the citizens ratified the act; while this may have addressed Boston's growth, it did not directly address the problem of public safety.[48]

After Josiah Quincy became the mayor of the city in 1823, his first act for addressing the policing problem was to create a new office called Marshal of the City.[49] Appointed annually by the mayor, the position became a highly political position soon devoid of most policing responsibilities and came to be more readily focused on issues of public health. Still, because the marshal served at the will and pleasure of the mayor, anytime the mayor needed something done, it became easier to turn to the marshal. When the city issued dog licenses in 1825 and banned the use of firearms in the city, it became the marshal's responsibility to enforce them. As the responsibilities grew, the lines between the constables, night watch, and the marshal began to blur.

Mayor Quincy generally used the marshal to try to literally clean up the city by having him address more of the health-related issues, while he used the peace officers to crack down on vice.[50] The red-light district of Boston, the West End at the time, became the district of his focus, and it was there, he said, where there "shall at least be a struggle for the supremacy of the law."[51] Immediately, Quincy revoked all West End liquor licenses, then set about using the peace officers to arrest all violators of any vice. His goal was not so much to eradicate vice from the city but to drive it underground, making it less visible to the public. He later explained in a report:

> These measures did not originate in any theories, or visions of ideal purity . . . but in a single sense of duty and respect for the character of the city; proceeding upon the principle that if in great cities the existence of vice is inevitable, that its course should be in secret, like other filth, in drains, and in darkness; not obtrusive, not powerful, not prowling publicly in the streets.[52]

Although Quincy was the mayor, he acted as the marshal in that he was often seen leading and directing the peace officers. His cleansing of the city, both literally and figuratively in regard to vice, proved mostly successful. His actions through the marshal's office helped to build more drains and sewers and clean up privies and refuse off the city streets, while the use of his special peace officers demonstrated the ability to crack down on vice and drive it underground. Still, his active use of the powers of government proved controversial, for a marshal using the police to enforce the laws was something rather unique to Boston, and most of America for that matter. "These means," as

Mayor Quincy saw it, "are better than armies of constables and watchmen."[53] He also proudly noted that with the exception of the marshal, "this state of things has been effected without the addition of one man to the ancient arm of the police."[54]

The so-called "ancient arm of the police" was certainly dated, for by 1829, when Quincy stepped down as mayor, little had changed. The Boston police still only numbered 24 constables and 80 watchmen, "of whom never more than *eighteen* are out at a time."[55] This was the number of men despite the fact the city had grown to approximately 60,000 citizens. The new mayor, General Harrison Gray Otis, however, took the opposite perspective of his predecessor and, rather than expand and focus, he began drawing down and foregoing active enforcement. Otis hired no new watchmen, removed the constables from the West End, and reduced the salary of the marshal. When he decided not to run for a second two-year term as mayor, the city breathed a collective sigh of relief.

The next mayor, Alderman Charles Wells, came from the ranks of the city. His full-time occupation was working as a carpenter. Mayor Wells, listening to the will of the people, began restoring the constables, returning the salary of the marshal to its previous level and hiring additional watchmen; however, he effectively only restored the system to what it had been previously. Again, nothing had really changed except for the population of the city. This lack of progress proved disastrous for what was about to come, a series of mob violence and riots over a three-year period, from 1834 to 1837.[56]

On the sweltering hot evening of July 28, 1834, a woman appeared at the house of Edward Cutter of Charlestown, Massachusetts. Dressed only in a nightgown and with a closely shorn head, she seemed distraught and deranged. She muttered incoherently and babbled. Cutter guessed, correctly, that she was from the Ursuline convent located just a few hundred yards up the hill, which was then called Mount Benedict (also called Convent Hill and Ploughed Hill). Soon, a carriage came to the house, and the mother superior of the convent identified the mysterious woman as Sister Mary John. She explained that the sister was suffering from "brain fever," due in part to the "suffocating heat and the stress of a heavy academic workload."[57] The so-called "mysterious woman" was then returned to the convent.[58]

In an already highly anti-Catholic Boston, it did not take long before rumors began to spread across town about the mysterious woman who was being held captive against her will in the Ursuline convent. Rumors spread through small group discussions developed into organized meetings, letters to the editor, calls for the city to do something, and placards demanding action: "To the Selectmen of Charlestown!! Gentlemen: It is currently reported that a mysterious affair has lately happened at the Nunery in Charlestown, now it is your duty gentlemen to have this affair investigated immediately, if not the Truckmen of Boston will demolish the Nunery Thursday night—August 14."[59] They did not wait that long.

The "Boston Truckmen" were stevedores and cartmen working the wharves who "took it upon themselves to 'police' the mores of the community when the local authorities proved unable to cope with the problem."[60] They had already taken down several brothels over the previous 10 years, including the one infamously known as the Beehive.[61] When they heard about the woman held against her will, they began agitating for some action to be taken by the city. The selectmen did visit the convent the morning of August 11, and afterward conveyed that the woman was, in fact, free to leave at any time. However, that did not put an end to the rumors, and that evening a group of angry citizens gathered at the convent doors. They called for the release of the mysterious lady, and the mother superior told them to leave by threatening retaliation. "The Bishop has twenty thousand of the vilest Irishmen at his command, and you may read your riot act till your throats are sore, but you'll not quell them."[62]

That did not go over well, and although they left, they returned in force and began setting fire to tar barrels. The fire department was called, but rather than put out the fires, they joined the spectators, which had grown to an angry mob of some 2,000 people. "No local peace officers were present, officially," explains police historian Lane, "and those from Boston were not requested."[63] Emboldened, the crowd burned the convent to the ground.

The mayor of Boston at the time, Theodore Lyman, was concerned that the burning of the Catholic convent would generate mob violence between Catholics and Protestants in Boston, so he began working on a response. "The city council spent over $1,500 on special constables, ordinarily a full year's appropriation," reports Lane, and "Mayor Lyman arranged for both the *posse comitatus* and the militia."[64] On the afternoon of August 12, 1834, he deployed them to surround Faneuil Hall, the city arsenal, the Cathedral of the Holy Cross, and the Catholic church in Charlestown. A crowd formed that evening at the arsenal, but seeing it guarded, they moved on to the cathedral, then to city hall. Frustrated, the mob went to Charlestown, saw that the Catholic church was guarded, went back up to the unguarded convent, and proceeded to destroy all that remained.

While the burning of the Ursuline convent demonstrated the extent of anti-Catholicism in Boston, it also showed just how far mobs were willing to go in their collective and violent actions. In terms of the police, however, it demonstrated just how poorly prepared the city stood against mob violence, thus sending a signal to the community that should another event anger the people, they need not fear interference from their peace officers. That soon came in the form of a public frenzy against the abolitionists.

William Lloyd Garrison had started his career in the newspapers and out of this became an abolitionist who called for an end to slavery through his newspaper *The Liberator* and through the New England Anti-Slavery Society, formed in 1832. Garrison became a target of much hate and derision for espousing these views, and he received numerous death threats. In the South, bounties were offered for his capture "dead or alive."[65] Local anger spilled over on October 21, 1835, when Garrison agreed to speak before the Boston Female Anti-Slavery Society. It was reported in the *Boston Commercial Gazette* that "an assemblage of fifteen hundred or two thousand highly respectable gentlemen" had gathered in protest, tearing down the sign that announced the speech.[66] Mayor Lyman, present at the meeting (although an anti-abolitionist himself), feared that a riot might be in the offing, asked the ladies to leave the hall, and had Garrison taken away through a back entrance. The so-called gentlemen, however, found him in his flight, and "they tied and roughly handled Garrison, and began pulling him through the streets."[67] Two citizens rescued Garrison, and he was escorted to the local jail for his protection. Deprived of their prize, the mob hung Garrison in effigy. As historian Lane highlights, "the mob was neither beaten nor cowed," and the tensions in Boston over the issue of slavery continued to mount.[68]

The following year, on July 30, 1836, another riot revolved around whether two women of African descent were fugitive slaves or free Black people. On that day, Eliza Small and Polly Ann Bates sailed into Boston Harbor with papers saying they were free women. Matthew Turner, a slave agent for John B. Morris, stopped the boat on which they were passengers and made the claim they were fugitive slaves. The captain agreed to detain the women while Turner sought an arrest warrant. Word spread and Freemen began gathering on the pier, which in turn caused a crowd to form. A hearing was set for August 1, and many free Black people and white abolitionists were present in the courtroom; there were also several hundred more outside. The question centered on the right of the captain to detain the women, and with the answer being no, they were ordered released. Turner, however, asked if he would then need another warrant for him to detain them, and the shout of "Go! Go!" was heard.[69] The courtroom erupted into pandemonium as it was flooded with people who managed to rescue the two women, who were then ferried away to Canada. This time, the people became aware of how ineffective the peace officers were in protecting the courtroom or tracking down the escapees.

Things came to a head one year later with the Broad Street Riot, which took place on June 11, 1837. This riot was a nativist clash between the Anglo volunteer firefighters and the Irish. Fire Engine Company 20 put out a fire in Boston Neck and upon their return stopped off at a pub that was open in violation of the Blue Laws that Sunday. When the rowdy firefighters left the bar, in the words of then-mayor Samuel Eliot "in a more or less bellicose mood," the streets were filled with Irishmen on their way to a funeral procession.[70] The firefighters arrogantly pushed their way through the crowd, which sparked a fight. The firefighter in charge, realizing they were outnumbered, ordered the men back to the fire station. The Irishmen, with their blood up, attacked the firehouse, and a brawl ensued. More firefighters were called to the scene, and more Irishmen joined in the fight. Eventually, the Irishmen were outnumbered, and they fled back to their homes, but the firefighters and other men who joined in, an estimated 800 men with the crowds growing to over 10,000, pursued them. The skirmish became a riot when the homes of the Irishmen were entered and destroyed. Soon, Broad Street "seemed to be having a snowstorm" for "featherbeds were ripped up and their contents scattered to the winds in such quantities" that by the end, parts of the street were "buried ankle-deep in feathers."[71] What ultimately dispersed the crowd was not the peace officers of Boston, but Mayor Eliot calling on the National Lancers, a local cavalry company, and the state militia. Once again, a Boston riot proved the ineffectiveness of the almost nonexistent peace officers.

The Broad Street Riot was the final straw. "Prompted by Mayor Eliot," police historian Roger Lane explains, "the city government determined that it was necessary both to reorganize the fire department and to provide a stronger police."[72] Over the next three months, Mayor Eliot and the city council focused their attention on the fire department. Once those reforms were completed, Mayor Eliot addressed the council on September 18 and reminded them he had not forgotten his call for police reform. "The police [force] of this city," the mayor explained, "has consisted of a small number of constables, and is rather adapted to circumstances as they were half a century ago."[73] The city council formed a committee to look into the problem and were in full agreement with the mayor after their deliberations. The committee was apparently somewhat aware of the creation of the world's first modern police department in England, the London Metropolitan Police, which was established in 1828, for they called for a similar force in Boston. The new Boston Police force, they declared, "is intended, as far as may be," to emulate "the system of London, [where] a similar patrol is established, and is found to be of advantage in various ways beside the enforcement of laws."[74] They would be a "special city police" under municipal control, preventive in nature, with full-time daytime patrols, and the officers would be paid a regular wage, starting at the rate of two dollars a day. Most importantly, however, they would be a proactive force with the power to arrest. As Lane explains:

> They would not, like the watch, be confined by custom to watching for fires and fights and other overt disturbances. They would not, like the sheriffs and constables, rely largely upon the complaints of the injured. The police would prevent trouble by actively seeking it out on their own, before it had time to reach serious proportions.[75]

On April 15, 1838, the General Court passed a bill allowing the City of Boston to appoint police officers. These new officers, supervised by the marshal, were directed to enforce the law within the city limits, and they were granted the power of arrest. The only powers they did not receive were the civil powers afforded to the constables. The Boston Police Department, separate from the watch, became the first modern police department in the United States. Little attention was paid to this significant event, for no mention appeared of the General Court's action in the newspapers. Mayor Eliot set about hiring the men who would serve in the new department and made six appointments in the month of May.

It was an inauspicious start.

Boston Police officers in front of Police Station No. 4, Lagrange Street, circa 1880s.
Photo courtesy of the Boston Public Library, Arts Department.

2

The Boston Police Department

Having won reelection to office in 1839, Mayor Samuel A. Eliot informed the city council and the people of Boston on the status of the recently formed police in his inaugural address.[1] In addition to creating the new police force, hiring additional officers, and deploying them on the city streets, he also increased the pay for both the constables and night watchmen. Still, unlike the London Metropolitan Police that began with a force of 1,000 uniformed police officers, the Boston Police began with only six officers who did not wear uniforms. Despite this, Mayor Eliot proudly stated that in creating the police, "Great pains have been taken, and, it is believed, not without good effect, to prevent the violation of the laws and ordinances, especially of those the violation of which has a tendency to the breach of the peace."[2] The mayor could indeed claim "not without good effect," for there had been no additional riots since the formation of the new police force. He happily concluded, "The public peace has been uninterrupted during the past year" and "the reputation of the city has suffered no such blow as was inflicted on it in the previous years."[3]

Despite the positive spin on the absence of riots, this did not mean the public was necessarily satisfied with the actions of the new police force, especially when it came to the subject of liquor. Massachusetts had a long history of not only embracing

19

the abolitionist movement but the temperance movement as well. The state legislature, the Massachusetts General Court, had passed a law the previous year banning sales of spirits in quantities of less than 15 gallons.[4] The law was intended to curb the sale of alcohol by virtue of the expense of having to buy so large a quantity. However, it included no enforcement mechanism, for almost no town had the capacity to enforce such a law—all, that is, except Boston.

In light of the creation of the new police force, Boston had the capability of enforcing the new law, despite its lack of personnel. "For the first time," historian Roger Lane explains, "the police were called upon to act as detectives on their own initiative, to enter places without warrant . . . search the premises, and seize the evidence."[5] Many Bostonians, already not pleased with the law itself, became incensed when the police actually began enforcing it. This was most evident in the problem of public drunkenness, which "was rapidly becoming a serious problem in Boston during the 1840s," as evidence from Boston's lower criminal courts shows.[6]

Laws had been on the books since the colonial era to handle public drunkenness, but generally the laws referred only to those people who were both habitually drunk and a nuisance, and there was no penalty associated with the offense. In 1835, with the codification of the common law in Massachusetts, public drunkenness became one of the offenses punishable under the list of moral offenses that, beginning in 1838, could now be enforced.[7] Those involved in the temperance movement and many citizens who were tired of the disorder that drunkenness caused were pleased with the law's enforcement; however, many groups, especially those among the working and immigrant classes, were not. This backdrop was the setting in which bootmaker John Augustus came to earn his cognomen "the father of the American probation system," for he agreed to take some of the drunkards into his care in an effort toward rehabilitation.[8] Augustus, however, was only one man and could only take on so many charges, so it was not enough to quell the public dispute over police enforcement of the new codified laws.

Public drunkenness was not the only crime the Boston Police had not previously enforced. A similar pattern followed regarding the moral offense of prostitution, for after the creation of the Boston Police, the number of that crime's arrests also increased because the city now had the capacity to enforce the law. This new phenomenon of police enforcement divided the citizens of Boston on this issue as well, and once again, John Augustus stepped in to try to reform these women through his probation system.[9] Like public drunkenness, Augustus could only do so much while the public, divided mainly along class lines when it came to prostitution, argued over the law's enforcement.

Much of the growth in crime during this time period did indeed have to do with the police now enforcing the law. If a crime is not enforced one week but then is the following, the marked increase in crime could simply be due to change in the law's enforcement. Yet the very reason for the enforcement of the law by the newly formed police force also had much to do with societal change. Recalling Diamond's discussion on developing societies, many of the changes that move a society from a chiefdom to a state were having their effect on the city of Boston. Population growth, the loss of familial-relational egalitarianism, and the old mechanisms of social restraint's inability to control the behaviors of the populace all called for the need for change. One issue in Boston where this became most evident was in the growing number of businesses and the issue of business licenses.[10]

When Boston had a colonial government, it naturally adopted the English practice of issuing business licenses. As the town remained small, growing only gradually, the issuing of licenses was easy to both manage and control. Once the city grew, the number of businesses grew as well, in both the number of traditional businesses (e.g., liquor stores, chimney sweeps, and pawnshops) and the proliferation of new businesses (e.g., life insurance, newsboys, and banks). The problem with the growth is that keeping track of the businesses is onerous enough, but the enforcement of the laws on businesses that violate the laws and the standards the businesses are supposed to maintain upon receiving the licenses becomes untenable. Naturally, with the creation of a police force, there now existed a means by which these regulations could be enforced, whether through license checks, inspections, or investigations for suspected violations. So, while enforcement of the law increases the number of cases, the reason for the enforcement is often nothing more than a reaction to an increase in crimes and other violations.

One issue that quickly becomes apparent with any new law and its enforcement is that the agency, in this case the Boston Police, is usually woefully unprepared and does not have the capacity for such kinds of enforcement. It is one thing to regulate licenses for liquor stores or newsboys or chimney sweeps. It is a wholly different matter when it comes to life insurance companies and banks. These were people who did not commit their crimes on the streets or with the crude methods of force, but rather within businesses and with guile. They were labeled with the then–relatively new word *swindlers*. "Swindlers did not advertise themselves as swindlers," writes criminal justice historian Lawrence M. Friedman. "On the contrary, they imitated polite society; they could succeed only if they kept their criminal identity secret."[11] The men hired as police officers in Boston typically did not have the capability to investigate such crimes, for as Friedman also explains, "it took new and different techniques to fight this kind of crime."[12] As Lane tells us, this is why "there was a movement by 1845 to create a detective branch of the police, on salary, whose members would be available to the whole community and work in its interest."[13]

The position of police detective was a wholly new concept in policing at this time, although not without historic precedent. Some suggest that the first detective was Eugène-François Vidocq, a French criminal turned detective who often worked with the Paris police.[14] He served as the literary model for a number of authors, including Honoré de Balzac, Victor Hugo, and Edgar Allan Poe. It was Poe who created the first fictional detective, C. Auguste Dupin, in his 1841 short story "The Murders in the Rue Morgue," set in Paris, France.[15] Others argue that the first true detectives—those who had not been former criminals—were Henry Fielding's Bow Street Runners, located in the Bow Street district of London, England.[16] As chief magistrate of the district, Fielding organized a police force with investigatory powers in order to have cases brought before his court, rather than waiting for them to be brought by the people.[17] In either case, it is not likely that what accounted for police detectives in London or Paris had much influence on the creation of the detectives in the Boston Police. More plausible is that Poe's character, who appeared in the story "The Mystery of Marie Rogêt" in 1842 and "The Purloined Letter" in 1844, is the one that led to the first true detectives in 1845. Still, all of this is speculation, while the reality is that it probably came about from necessity—the need for experts who could deal with the more difficult crimes—combined with a change in leadership in the hiring of a man who had a flair for drama, the flamboyant Francis Tukey.

On December 11, 1845, Josiah Quincy IV began his term as mayor of Boston, continuing the family tradition, for his father, Josiah Quincy III, had served as mayor from 1823 to 1828. Like his father before him, Quincy IV was a reformer, and "crime and disorder, disease, drink, and poverty would all be met by a vigorous police, expanded for [that] purpose."[18] At the time, the Boston Police employed 12 police officers for both its day and night patrols, the latter being augmented by the 150 members of the night watch, to police a city that now numbered some 140,000 citizens. The police were, as historian Matthew Pearl explains, "ill-equipped for the challenge," so in response "Quincy and the City Council installed a take-all-prisoners city marshal, the brash Francis Tukey."[19]

Tukey had no background in policing, but rather gained the office through his friendship with Josiah Quincy. Originally from Portland, Maine, where he once worked as a mechanic after his wife died, Tukey moved to Boston. There he fashioned himself as a baker, but after ending up in a number of legal disputes, including two charges of assault, he quit the business.[20] His legal issues may have sparked his motivation to become a lawyer, for soon after his baker days, Tukey enrolled at Harvard's Law School and earned his law degree two years later. Tukey soon began interacting with high society, passing himself off as a native of Boston, and somewhere along the way became friends with the mayor. When the position of marshal came available, Tukey somehow convinced the mayor to appoint him as the new marshal, which Quincy did in June 1846. Tukey was 32 years old at the time.

Tukey took charge immediately, and his first action was the expansion of his police force. Eighteen additional officers were appointed, increasing the Boston police to 30 officers, with 22 working day patrol and eight detailed to a special night patrol. Three additional police officers were also hired, officers who "were added to serve as detectives, the first on the public payroll."[21] In addition, Tukey secured a $700 pay raise for himself by eliminating one of his deputies. When the local newspaper ridiculed this action, Tukey ordered the newsboys for those papers cited for licensing violations.

Although using the officers to check the licenses of the newsboys was no doubt an abuse of power, Tukey's increased force allowed him to begin enforcing other licensing requirements, including those for various licensed professions (e.g., domestics, services, etc.), gambling establishments, and brothels. Perhaps no other licensing enforcement gave Tukey more power, however, than the enforcement of liquor licenses throughout the city. His first enforcement of these licensing laws came through strict enforcement of the Sunday laws in the fall of 1846. Any establishment selling liquor on Sunday in violation of the law was cited for violating the terms of their liquor license. He followed this with an austere application of the public drunkenness laws and then moved on to licensing violations by the bars and pubs. Eventually, he discovered the means to enforce all of these laws at the same time.

Tukey quickly started innovating with ways to use his police officers more effectively, commencing with night raids on specific establishments known for both crime and license violations, such as a gaming resort and brothels. These raids were referred to at the time as "descents." A group of officers would descend upon a particular establishment known for past violations of the law and would make arrests for every violation present. On March 8 one particular descent on a gambling house resulted in 86 arrests. The descent, however, that proved the most brash, came on the night of April 23, 1851, and quickly came to be popularly known as "The Celebrated Ann Street Descent."[22] Tukey used nearly every officer on the force to descend on Ann Street and raided every gaming house, bar, and brothel along the entire city street. As a young police officer, and future police chief, Edward H. Savage recalled in his biography, "On the eve of the 23rd of April, this year, we make the great Police descent in Ann Street, capturing some one hundred and sixty bipeds, who were punished for piping, fiddling, dancing, drinking, and attending crimes."[23]

To support these growing raids, Tukey continually requested additional funds from the city council in order to hire additional officers. By 1851 Tukey had 40 officers on day patrol and 22 officers working nights. He also increased the number of detectives from three to five, as well as the number of night watchmen, successfully increasing their ranks from 150 to 190 men.

Tukey also developed one additional flamboyant method that instantly became popular with the people: his "show-up of rogues." These instantly drew large crowds, and it became a weekly institution from its inception.[24] The idea was for the police to round up criminals once a week to create a rogues' gallery for the police force. "Seventy-six pickpockets, burglars, panel thieves, etc.," which included 12 women, were the first group to be rounded up and "shown up to the whole of the police force."[25] Although those forced into this lineup were all known criminals, none of them was under arrest at the time, nor were any of them identified as having committed any kind of criminal activity and arrested on the spot. Rather, they were simply rounded up to show the police who the prevailing criminals in Boston were, and whom they should keep an eye on in the future. Because the spectacle had drawn such a large crowd, and the police had identified these people as criminals, the crowd began to boo and jeer those in the lineup, and when they were finally allowed to leave the rogues' gallery, they "were forced to run a gauntlet of crowing citizens who tore their clothing and marked their backs with crosses in chalk."[26]

Although Tukey proved popular with many people, his actions also turned many people against him. One particular event in 1851 demonstrated how people took sides in favor and opposition to Tukey. Boston had a long history of abolitionism, and the citizens collectively recoiled at the recent passage of the federal Fugitive Slave Act of 1850 that mandated all escaped slaves were to be returned to their southern owners, regardless of where in the United States they were captured. When Thomas Sims, an escaped slave from Georgia, was discovered stowed away onboard a ship in the Boston harbor, he became the first test case of the new law. The ship's crew confronted him, believed him a fugitive slave, and, after locking him in a cabin, called the local authorities. Sims managed to escape before US marshal Charles Devens arrived on the ship, so Devens asked Tukey for his assistance finding Sims. Tukey himself could not help, but he allowed two of his officers to be deputized by Devens in order to assist him in the search for Sims, since they were more familiar with the city than Devens. The officers were able to track down Sims and place him under arrest, although they charged him with the state violation of theft. Deven and the officers took him directly to the courthouse.

Hearing of the arrest, the Boston Vigilance Committee quickly denounced the police as "slave catchers" and "kidnappers," and soon after a crowd formed and surrounded the courthouse. The Boston police held back the crowds while the court hearings were conducted to determine Sims's fate. In the end the judge ruled that Sims, in accordance with the Fugitive Slave law, needed to be returned. Knowing this would not go over well with the agitated crowd, Tukey literally had the courthouse surrounded with a heavy chain, placing it about waist high, in order to prevent anyone from entering—or leaving—the courthouse. Once enough military protection arrived, Sims was marched to the harbor, placed aboard a ship, and eventually returned to Georgia. "While the whole affair helped the Boston force to win a reputation in some quarters as the most efficient in the country," historian Roger Lane explains, "it also made bitter enemies for the officers in general and the marshal in particular."[27]

Tukey's detractors continued to ridicule him for many other reasons as well, such as the high salary he managed to finagle, an amount only slightly less than the mayor, treasurer, and city solicitor received. His enforcement of license violations also upset many Bostonians who mostly likely would have been his supporters had he not enforced these regulations so stringently, but when common people became the target of his tough enforcement, he lost their support. For instance, when the city began issuing licenses for dogs, Tukey began strictly enforcing the ordinances against unlicensed dogs. He also enforced an unpopular ordinance during the winter, having people arrested for failing to clear the snow and ice off their sidewalks. He also spoke openly of his solution to the growing problem of "street urchins"—homeless children living on the city streets. Tukey's stance was to bind them as apprentices or domestics until they reached emancipation age. In a city that stood vehemently against slavery, that particular idea was not well received. And as city marshal, Tukey managed to insult an entire population of the city, nearly 55,000 strong, when he railed against the commission's hiring of an Irishman to serve on the police force. This was, however, in keeping with popular sentiment at the time, for the Irish had arrived en masse in 1847 because of the Irish famine, and they were typically described as "vicious, crime [and] profligate . . . who imported their vile propensities and habits from across the water."[28] Although the commission did, in fact, appoint him to the police force, Tukey steadfastly refused to assign him to a position.[29]

In January 1852, the political tides began to change, which proved the beginning of the end for Marshal Tukey. The change in politics began with the election of Benjamin Seaver, the 13th mayor of Boston selected by the citizens. Although it is said that Tukey helped him win election by marching the entire night patrol force to the polls to vote for Seaver, it was to no avail, for one of Seaver's first acts was to abolish the police night patrol, leaving nighttime duties solely to the watch. Seaver also ordered the Irishman working for the police retained and ordered Tukey to put him to work. By late spring Seaver limited enforcement of the license laws, and by summer he changed police appointments to an annual basis, giving the mayor and city council the ability to check Tukey's decisions. This was certainly a blow to Tukey, for Seaver was effectively reining in the power of the city marshal.

It was also at this time that the city decided the head of the Boston Police would no longer be the "city marshal" but rather changed the official title to "chief of police." The new position minimized the powers of the head of the Boston Police under some state laws, especially those related to liquor laws, for these statutes only mentioned marshals, constables, and sheriffs, not police chiefs. Still further, since the new position had been changed to "chief of police," all the mayor had to do was appoint someone new to the position. Seaver decided not to do so, effectively firing Tukey. "The Great Caesar fell for his ambition," one newspaper editor wrote of the powerful city marshal. "The Great Tukey, because, like the Sons of Levi, he took too much upon himself."[30] Squeezed out of the city marshal position, Tukey tried running for political office when a death opened a position on the city council. He lost the election by a narrow margin and afterward fled to California, where he restarted life as a politician.

The Tukey era of policing was significant not so much for his particular policies or personal flamboyance, but for the rapid expansion of the police and its duties and enforcement capabilities. In his short six-year tenure, Tukey had turned the first fledgling police force in the United States into one that can be recognized in modern terms. "The men on the beat," Lane explains, "gave directions, unsnarled traffic, returned lost children, aided victims of sudden accident, and escorted drunks either to the station house or home."[31] Despite this, the Tukey era proved to be one of the last progressive developments of the Boston Police Department for many decades to come.

Mayor Seaver appointed Gilbert Nurse as the first chief of police, and one of Nurse's first actions was to provide officers with new badges. As future chief Savage recalled, "Heretofore, for some years, the officers had worn leather badges, buckled round the hat, with the word Police in large silver letters, and a number in front."[32] The new badges, now worn on the left coat lapel, were "an oblong, six-pointed *brass* star, about as big as one's hand, with an unintelligible device in the centre, and looked more like a Sculpin's head than a Policeman badge."[33] Perhaps the most important change (the oddly fish-shaped badge aside) came from the state legislature, the "General Court," which, on May 23, 1853, authorized Boston to reorganize the watch and the police.

Although the night watch was now up to approximately 250 men, it remained "governed by the same simple rules published in 1821—they were to walk the rounds singly rather than in pairs, forbidden to sleep on the job, and fired for three consecutive and unexplained failures to show up for work."[34] And they were still only supervised by two men—a captain and constable. As a result of this lack of oversight, as many personal anecdotes on the night watchmen's behaviors attest, they no doubt violated even these simplest of rules. The night watch had never been effective at policing criminal behavior, as Tukey had pointed out during his tenure as city marshal, and the need for sounding the fire alarm had been reduced by the installation of an alarm box system in 1851. Their pay remained low, at one dollar a day, necessitating that they work some other job during the day, which generally explained why they often slept on duty. They were a wholly anachronistic and ineffective institution held over from the early days of the Massachusetts Bay Colony. Now that they could do something to effect organizational change, the city needed a plan.

It took nearly a year, but by the spring of 1854, the new mayor, Jerome V. C. Smith, and the city aldermen had a plan of action. The seemingly draconian plan called for the discharge of every member of both the watch and the police force, and, on the following day, the creation of an all new "Department of Police."[35] "On the 26th day of May, 1854, at precisely six o'clock p.m.," records future police chief Savage, "the Boston Watch and Police, which had lived two hundred and twenty-nine years, ceased to exist, and 'The Boston Police Department' became an *Institution.*"[36] The police officers who were discharged were all hired back, while the night watchmen who wanted full-time jobs were hired on as police officers. Although there were still some remaining positions to be filled, the new force numbered 250 police officers.[37] The city, divided into eight stations with captains and lieutenants overseeing them, maintained 24-hour coverage by dividing patrols into three shifts. The new police chief, Robert Taylor, earned $1,800 per year, captains were paid $3 a day, and patrolmen earned $2 for each shift. And by the end of the year, the ugly fish-shaped badge had been replaced with a "silver octagon oval plate, little larger than a silver dollar, with a 'five-pointed star,' on which was engraved Boston Police."[38]

In 1857 the department increased its numbers to 266 men, and the need for an additional class of officers became evident.[39] The lieutenants quickly found themselves overworked after the consolidation, for anything a captain ordered done within the division fell upon the lieutenant. However, supervision of the officers on the street during their shifts was also assigned to the lieutenants, and occasionally, when divisional detectives became overtaxed, the lieutenants were called upon for their support. This realization led to the development of the midlevel supervisory rank of sergeant; three were appointed to each division, hence one for each shift. The duties of supervising and managing the officers on patrol then fell to them, relieving the lieutenants of that duty.

The following year, the department slightly altered the badge by leaving off the star and issued, for the first time, a police uniform.[40] Unfortunately, the public criticized the uniforms, saying they made the police looking like "popinjays."[41] This is because, according to Savage, the uniform consisted of a "blue coat, Police buttons, blue pants and black vests, dress coat for Chief and Captains, and frock coat for Deputy and Patrolmen."[42] Unlike other police departments in the 1800s that adopted uniforms for their police officers, the Boston police did not rebel over this issue, but rather accepted it as part of the professionalization of the department.[43] In cities such as New York, Philadelphia, and Chicago, officers resisted the uniforms, and many quit when ordered to wear them. For some of the officers in those departments, "it conflicted with their notions of independence and self-respect," while others saw it as "expensive and fantastical," and still more claimed it to be nothing less than a "badge of servitude."[44] "Historians agree that the uniforms for the Boston police," according to police historian Eric Monkkonen, "encountered the least resistance of any pre–Civil War department."[45] As a result, by 1859, the Boston Police Department was fully uniformed, and had there been any reservations in the wearing of the uniform, as police historian Lane points out, "two years later the Civil War erased any lingering stigma attached to a uniform."[46]

The Civil War certainly wreaked havoc on the country, but so too did it devastate the Boston Police Department.[47] The turnover of officers was high, as men quit to join the military, but never was there a greater need for a strong police force than during the upheaval the war caused in Boston. And despite the attempts of the city to increase the authorized number of officers, reaching 350 by war's end, it proved difficult to maintain those levels due to the shortage of available men.

The reduced number of officers strained the department, especially at a time when certain crimes increased during the war, especially juvenile crime, as well as the demand for particular services, such as parade escorts and funeral details. Still further, the soldiers themselves placed demands on the police department, whether it was through the pursuit of military deserters or dealing with the influx of problems associated with military units entering the city. Moreover, when the United States enacted the nation's first Conscription Act, the city was awash in violence they were unprepared for from the draft riots.[48] The myriad problems the war brought to the city significantly changed the policing dynamic.

The war also changed one specific aspect of the conduct of Boston policing: the carrying of firearms. Until the Civil War the baton had been common for day patrols and the rattle-watch for night patrols. Although the department did not furnish handguns for the members of its force, many of the police officers began carrying their own weapons since the presence of so many armed soldiers made them woefully lacking in terms of personal safety. It was not until 1884, under Police Chief Edward Savage, that officers were issued a numbered Smith & Wesson .38 revolver.[49]

If the Civil War brought numerous changes to the police department, the Reconstruction era brought not only significant change to the department, it also introduced a significant amount of new problems. The ouster of Tukey and the policy change that gave the mayor and aldermen the power to make all police appointments was intended to bring some element of control over the department, allowing them to hire and fire officers at their pleasure. However, the system was fraught with problems, mostly resulting from politics. A prizewinning article written about the Boston Police Department by George H. McCaffrey explained that the "system worked very unsatisfactorily," primarily "because places on the police force were invariably bestowed as a reward for partisan activity."[50] Many of the men appointed as police officers were not interested in policing as a career but only as a means to an end, and often that means was corruption and the end was a higher political office. As such, many of the officers were incompetent when it came to police work, especially detective work, which did not bode well when crime began rising in the post–Civil War era.

The issue of police incompetence in Boston first caught the attention of the state legislature, the General Court, in 1861, when it held a series of hearings on the matter. What they found highlighted the problems of political partisanship. There was discussion of the state intervening in the management of the Boston Police Department, but there seemed to be little support for such action, especially when the politicians exploiting the spoils system in Boston had strong political ties to the state legislators conducting the investigation. After "eight years of intermittent probing and constant complaint," however, the General Court again agreed to conduct a series of hearings to consider taking action to control the Boston Police Department.[51] Once again, however, the hearings exposed the reality that most of the political corruption in the police department was a result of the political patronage system, and that any lack of enforcement on the part of the police was merely a means of collecting graft from illicit businesses. Therefore, once again, the General Court entertained a metropolitan bill that would allow the state to take control of the Boston Police Department, but still it failed because of strong political ties between the politicians that would enact such a bill and the corruption. As the lawyer representing the city pointed out in his summation, "You must remember, gentlemen, that all of these arguments against the . . . police tell equally against all self-government in Boston."[52]

Although the state did not take control of the Boston Police Department, the hearings in 1869 did become the catalyst for some amount of change. Although the politicians shied away from the exposure of the political corruption, one aspect of the investigation that became hard to ignore was the incompetence on the part of the detective bureau.[53] The post–Civil War crime wave had created a professional class of criminals that the detectives, especially the spoils system–appointed detectives, were incapable of handling.[54] Therefore, while the General Court decided not to take action, the mayor and aldermen of Boston did. On February 14, 1870, the aldermen issued a report criticizing "the present detective system," which they claimed, "more than anything else, has tended to bring the department into disrepute."[55] The report's recommendation was to abolish the detective bureau. Rather than waiting for comment on their proposal, as soon as they released the report, they voted to do just that, and along for good measure, they fired the police chief.

For the next several months, the aldermen debated the appointment of the next police chief, trying in earnest to avoid the issue associated with another spoils appointment. By April 4 they settled on Edward Savage, a career police officer who had been first appointed in 1851 and had moved up through the ranks to the position of deputy chief. Savage proved to be a good choice, for as the police chief, he deftly managed to balance his leadership of the police officers with the politics necessary to deal with the mayor and aldermen. He was also most innovative when it came to new police procedures, which led police historian Samuel Walker to write, "Chief Edward H. Savage of the Boston police was perhaps the most notable exponent of the crime prevention ideal in the mid-nineteenth century."[56] Savage found ways to effectively reform the previous police policies that had so troubled the department to the satisfaction of both city governance and his police officers. In addition, he managed to bolster police-public relations, especially through the publication of his book in 1873, considered the "first book-length history of a police department," *Police Records and Recollection: Boston by Daylight and Gaslight for Two Hundred and Forty Years.*[57] In addition to the book providing an overview of the police department's history, Savage regaled the public with sentimental tales of pauper children and other down-on-their-luck citizens who were all helped by benevolent policemen, thus gaining the public's sympathy and respect for the Boston police officer. Under Savage's leadership the department successfully avoided any additional scrutiny on the part of the state and any major changes by the mayor and aldermen. That proved not to be the case, however, after he left office in 1878.

Although Savage had the police department under control, city governance itself had changed over the eight years of his tenure, having become more politically corrupt and caught up in the spoils system.[58] Despite no reason other than to remove the weight of police appointments from the mayor and aldermen, Mayor Henry L. Pierce proposed the creation of a new police commission. The members of the commission would be nominated by the mayor and approved by the aldermen and could be removed for cause by the mayor or a two-thirds vote of the aldermen. The aldermen would retain control of the police department's appropriations and the right to determine the number of police officers, but "otherwise the commission had full and exclusive control over policy, spending, and personnel."[59] McCaffrey explained, "The control of the force was given to a board of three men appointed for five years by the mayor and confirmed by the aldermen."[60]

There was one other policy proposal placed in the police commission bill that clarified the political motivation behind the proposed changes. This bill made it mandatory for the city council to surrender their control over the licensing of liquor. Prior to this change, the aldermen had control over licensing by means of a licensing board. The liquor licensing power, however, was to now be transferred to the police commission. The commission/department that would be issuing the licenses for liquor would be the same commission/department that enforced the liquor license laws. The situation was rife with corruption, for simply put, the law had been designed, explains historian Roger

Lane, to make these new "police commissioners among the most powerful men in the city."[61] The bill, of course, passed, thus setting the stage for such flagrant corruption that no police chief, Boston mayor, or city councilman could ever prevent the state from interfering and taking over control of the Boston Police Department.

Boston Police headquarters, Pemberton Square, circa 1890s.
Photo courtesy of the Boston Public Library, Arts Department.

3

Political Control of the Boston Police Department

The newly established Boston police commission went into effect on May 15, 1878, and the first order of business for the mayor was to fill the three vacant seats. Of the first three commissioners appointed, "none of them had any previous experience with police work."[1] Henry S. Russell, Samuel R. Spinney, and James M. Bugbee were all political appointees who furthered the fears of widespread corruption and abuse within the Boston Police Department. Despite the fact that many of these concerns came true, police historian Roger Lane posits that it was not all bad. "The commission established in 1878, remained in charge of the Boston police department for seven years, during which it satisfied many of the expectations of its supporters."[2]

The new police commission set about reorganizing the department, first through a series of name changes, such as renaming the chief of police the "superintendent of police."[3] License superintendents became "inspectors," and the reestablished detective bureau members were no longer called detectives but were also dubbed "inspectors."[4] The latter, however, were only kept to six in number, because the commission did not want to see past problems with the detectives arise again with the new inspectors.

The next reform the commission aimed to achieve was the restructuring of department personnel. After looking through the available records and discussing personnel with senior level staff, they began implementing their reforms—they promoted a number of police personnel (29), demoted others (21), fired nearly an equal number (22), encouraged others to tender their resignations (11), transferred many more to other assignments (18), and forced a good many officers into retirement (31). Along with merely moving police personnel around, the commission set up new rules and regulations that came fast and furious over the next year, detailing what officers and supervisors could and, mostly, could not do. These personnel actions alone created a cascading effect in terms of altering the department's culture that had been created by Chief Savage, though not always for the better.

There were also some tangible changes to be seen in the Boston Police Department under the police commission's leadership. A two-week school for new hires was instituted, police ambulances were purchased for emergency medical situations, and new techniques of first aid and safety were taught to all officers. In addition, the department adopted new uniforms and issued firearms in 1884.

The reformed department also began dealing more effectively with rising political issues. Common services of the Boston Police Department were the police-run soup kitchens and the lodging of vagrants—some 63,000 were served in 1877. However, this outreach had become a source of contention for many of the local charities.[5] Organized charities provided their own lodging and soup kitchens for indigents and did not take kindly to the government taking over their charitable work. The police commissioners found the means for removing their hostility toward the department by instituting a work requirement for the vagrants. The new rule was that any person requesting lodging and a meal had to meet two requirements: to bathe and to work two hours for the privilege. The number of requests plummeted to less than 2,000 annual requests, thus removing the source of contention for the local charities.[6]

Perhaps the hardest reform to achieve, though, came in the department's efforts to remove the appointment of new police officers from the partisan spoils system. Despite running up against the power of the city aldermen, the annual report of the police department two years later at least claimed that "no matter what political backing a man may have, it is impossible for him to get on the force unless he is a first-class man."[7] Regardless of what they believed or wanted to believe was true, this did not necessarily make it so. While the 1878 changes did leave the police personnel decisions to the police commissioners, as police historian Lane explains, this "only prevented the city council from interfering regularly or openly."[8] It did not prevent them from interfering in other ways. The city council still retained the right to set police salaries, and those salaries could be used to leverage political concessions. The city council oversaw all contracts associated with the police department and again, not only could they be leveraged for political power, they could also be leveraged for extracurricular compensations, otherwise known as graft.

The greatest source of graft, not to mention sheer political power, came from the power to license alcohol vendors in the city. While this authority had been given to the police department, the members of the city council still had the ability to manipulate the licensing by holding such things as salaries and contracts over the heads of the police commissioners. Such actions could also be used in two different directions, for it could be used to influence the police commission to reduce the number of licenses, thus reducing the number of establishments authorized to sell alcohol, or they could increase the number of licenses they issued. "The crucial political issue," Lane explains, "was who received the permits and under what obligation."[9] The former was made even more problematic, and political, because while the majority of voters wanted open sales of alcohol, there was a significant population of prohibitionists in the city who proved hard to ignore. Though not necessarily always in their best interest to appease this minority block of voters, the Republicans did concede to gaining their support by opening up a series of hearings on the issue in 1881. This series of eight meetings over eight months did nothing more than to expose a few of the problems of the police issuing the licenses, but rather to shed light on the divisiveness of partisan politics—the police department was merely a prize to fight over. It was this very conflict, however, that proved the downfall of the city of Boston's control over their own police department.

One factor that fed the growing animosity was actually the successful reforms of the police department between 1878 and 1885. The best example of this comes with the licensing of liquor establishments. From the perspective of the police commissioners, the issuing of the licenses had become not so much a political action but a bureaucratic function. A person wishing to open a new tavern applied for a license, and the police commissioners issued the license. The efficiency of the system allowed for more establishments to open, but no one considered how these establishments were going to be used, for good or for bad. Some were respectable establishments with law-abiding employees who serviced people from the community, whereas other owners and managers were caught abusing the alcohol laws or using them as fronts for other vices, such as gambling and prostitution. The department could enforce the Sunday liquor laws or the selling of alcohol to those underage, and they could hold the threat of revoking the license over them, but for the most part, there was little interference with a licensed establishment's daily operations.

Those involved in the Boston temperance movement were obviously against the establishments up front, but many of the elite in the city who were involved in organizations concerned with the issues of moral decency saw the bureaucratic licensing of these establishments as contributing to the moral degeneracy of the city. The growth of cities in the post–Civil War era had created a populist movement that often aligned itself with the temperance movement. These populists were "already convinced that the old, rural middle class was losing out in the sweep of history" and "could not assume that his way of life was still dominant in America."[10] "He had to fight it out," explains sociologist Joseph R. Gusfield, "by political action which would coerce the public definition of what is moral and respectable."[11] Members of such newly formed organizations as the New England Society for the Suppression of Vice and the Citizens' Law and Order League of Massachusetts for the Suppression of Vice, whose leadership was filled with established businessmen, leading philanthropists, respected ministers, and presidents of the city's colleges, began using their political connections to influence change on not only the local level but at the state level as well.

At the beginning of 1885, the state legislature introduced a series of bills aimed at reform through the issuance of a new city charter for Boston. The major reforms had much to do with economics and the relationship between the city and state when it came to taxation. These reforms passed the legislature on a near-unanimous vote. To accompany these reforms, the Citizens' Law and Order League offered up a metropolitan police bill aimed at reforming the Boston Police Department in a similar manner by tying the problems of control with corruption and the temperance movement. The previous Sunday, state representative Charles Carleton Coffin had seen 26 saloons "wide open" and doing business despite the city's blue laws. While drumming up popular support for the bill, he told the people of Boston,

> I went down to the corner of Dover and Berkeley Streets last Sunday exploring—I thought I could perhaps serve the Lord that way as in any other—(laughter) and I saw plenty of drunkenness. In South Boston I saw open saloons and crowded ones, with boys and women in them. The administration of law in Boston is a farce . . . the liquor interest controls affairs in the city through the police and City Council. . . . If you, honest men and women of Boston, want yourselves and your sons and daughters relieved from the fearful dangers that surround you and them, come up . . . to the Legislature and tell the members you want it.[12]

Focusing on the corruption resulting from the licensing played to advocates of the Citizens' Law and Order League who concentrated on Sunday liquor law violations that played to the temperance movement's followers. The real purpose of the bill, however, was to wrest the power to appoint the Boston police commissioners from Boston city governance and turn it over to the state. "All verbiage brushed aside," wrote the Democratic *Boston Globe* at the time, "the question was simply whether

Boston should be permitted to manage its own local affairs or whether a foreign power should assume control."[13] "The State is not exactly a foreign power," replied the Republican *Boston Evening Transcript*, but the corrupt Boston government "necessitates legislative interference."[14]

If the bill passed, the governor would be authorized to appoint the three members of the police commission, thus giving the state control over the Boston Police Department.[15] As could be expected, the bill proved highly controversial during the debate, but when the House voted on the measure on April 16, it passed 108 to 81. Despite all parliamentary procedures employed to stop the bill from going forward, the Senate passed the bill on June 11, and soon after, the governor signed the bill into law. The Metropolitan Police Bill had become Chapter 338 of the Acts of 1885.

The phenomenon of state control of metropolitan police departments was not limited to just the city of Boston. Other states had imposed state control of city police, including "New York City in 1857, Detroit in 1865, Cleveland in 1866, New Orleans in 1868, Cincinnati in 1877," and after Boston, "Omaha in 1887," as well as "Cincinnati in 1886."[16] Police historian Fogelson points out that local versus state control was really, in fact, the difference between Democratic and Republican control of the police; the divide truly came down to politics. From the mid-19th century to its end, "in most police departments local control meant Democratic control," while the Republicans, "who generally spoke for the upper middle and upper classes, demanded state control."[17] Democrats of the time period argued for local, decentralized control as the means to avoid political corruption within the police departments, while Republicans argued that centralized control was the means of reducing such corruption.[18] The control issue also, in many ways, became a political tool by which the Republicans could break up the Democratic political machines that had become so prevalent after the Civil War. The Republicans, it seems, "regularly denounced the machine's hold over the police and exploited it to rationalize state control."[19]

Just as the establishment of the city police commission in 1878 had made various significant changes, Lane notes that, "The change from municipal to state control in 1885 made some difference."[20] And like the 1878 changes, several of the 1885 changes to state-appointed commissioners improved the police department, while others began to hamstring their effectiveness. As member of the police staff George McCaffrey explained as he wrote in praise of the changes, "Admission to the police force also was placed on a civil service basis in 1885, and a probationary period for reserve men was introduced in 1887."[21] Lane, however, highlights some of the less favorable actions: "The new commissioners abandoned such locally popular functions as the distribution of free soup and assumed such unpopular ones as the protection of property during strikes."[22] However, "fundamentally the force remained unchanged," Lane explains, because despite the state's ability to appoint the police commissioners, the Boston Police Department was still "charged with the same duties, recruited from the same classes, [and] subject to the same pressures."[23]

There is much truth in this statement, for the duties of the Boston Police Department to protect the city largely went unchanged. According to the department's fiscal year-end report on November 30, 1887, they were reported to have made 30,681 arrests. In addition, there were:

> 1,472 accidents reported; 2,461 buildings found open and made secure; . . . 37 dangerous chimneys reported; 169 dead bodies cared for; 181 defective cesspools reported; 66 defective drains reported; . . . 138 defective hydrants reported; 2,611 defective lamps reported; 4 defective sewers reported; 13,614 defective streets and walks reported; . . . 148 intoxicated persons assisted; 1,572 lost children found; 269 insane persons taken in charge; 228 missing persons reported; 151 missing persons found; . . . 7 persons rescued from drowning; 1,673 sick and injured persons assisted; . . . 51,302 street obstructions removed.[24]

All of these were the same type of duties that the police department had performed while on patrol prior to state control, and no doubt they would continue to be the types of duties designed to make the city safe. Police patrol was truly what mattered to the citizens of the city, and police patrol had gone unchanged.

Giving a speech before the National Association of Chiefs of Police in 1900, Chief Benjamin P. Eldridge quoted Theodore Roosevelt, who once said, "The duty of a patrolman is to patrol."[25] Chief Eldridge then noted the many things an officer should do while on patrol.

> He should note all removals from or into the limits of his route, and acquire such knowledge of the inhabitants as will enable him to recognize them . . . direct strangers and others, the nearest and safest way to their places of destination . . . note all cases of contagious diseases, or sudden death, where there is reasonable ground to suspect criminality . . . see the laws of the State, or ordinances of the city, are not violated, and should cause the arrest and prosecution of all persons violating same.[26]

There is good evidence that at least one patrolman of the Boston Police Department adhered to these patrol ideals, and this evidence came about through the discovery of an old police diary from 1895. The Boston Police Department had required its patrolmen at the time to maintain "a private record for his work, with day and date," and beginning in 1874, it supplied them with a pocket-sized blank diary.[27] The diary was used as a means of reconstructing his whereabouts on any given day by making note of the weather and his patrol activity. Although the patrolman's name is not recorded in the recovered diary, it is believed from some of the comments that it was the record of patrolman Stillman S. Wakeman, who joined the police department in December 1888 as a reserve officer before becoming a patrolman on February 13, 1890. Patrolmen at the time "put in long hours by today's standards: seven days a week with a fourteen day paid vacation."[28] Early in 1895, he served on night patrol in the West Roxbury Village; then in late May, he was switched to day patrol in Roslindale from 8 a.m. to 6 p.m.

Although Wakeman dutifully recorded the weather during each shift, he did not always record notes regarding his patrol activities. This may have been because many of his entries are repetitive in their description of nothing occurring on shift, such as "All is quiet on Route 10," "All is peaceful on Route 13," and "I patrol my route very thoroughly. All quiet along my lines."[29] There were some minor disturbances recorded, such as "a noise some like a pistol shot" or that he "smelled smoke," but in the case of the former he found nothing, and regarding the latter he only found a "chip heap."[30] A good portion of patrolman Wakeman's time was spent responding to citizen complaints either when they approached him on the street or they contacted the division station house. Of the criminal complaints, most dealt with larceny—stolen goods—and breaking and entering. In one case dealing with a series of larcenies, Wakeman continued to investigate the crimes until he was able to implicate several of the neighborhood boys in the crime. The patrolman also found himself responding to several cases of assault, cases that took up a disproportionate amount of his time. The police were often in charge of city licensing during this era, so

> not surprisingly, Wakeman's record of his work in West Roxbury and Roslindale shows that providing permits—especially those pertaining to construction and dog registration—was a frequent part of his day shift routine.[31]

He generally provided the blank forms to be completed, then took the form and fee back to the division station, secured the approved permit, and returned it to the applicant. On other occasions, Wakeman had to deal with the issue of expired permits or violations of the licensing laws.

One thing of note is that patrolman Wakeman always seemed to conduct his duty with fairness and was frequently very lenient with the people he dealt with on a daily basis. He often gave warnings to business owners open on Sundays and to the local drunks he knew, when they were causing problems. He also provided help where he could, such as allowing indigents to sleep in the lockup (not under arrest), assisting people with any injuries, and generally helping people solve their problems if he could. The patrolman was not always successful, for "when Wakeman failed after seven weeks to stop neighborhood dogs from killing the Will's chickens," he was criticized for his failure.

Still, Wakeman dutifully noted the man's words: "You are nothing but a boy & don't know your business."[32]

After reviewing patrolman Wakeman's diary, Alexander von Hoffman concludes, "The 1895 patrolman's diary demonstrates that the expansion of state authority represented by the deploying of police forces was not a simple process of subtraction in which central government usurped local prerogatives."[33] Von Hoffman sees it as being far more nuanced than that. "By deploying the police," he continues, "nineteenth-century government officials in cities such as Boston did expand the government's sphere of activity and centralize control over the urban citizenry."[34] However, he believes that "the main thrust of increasing governmental activism was not to impose control on the urban populace, but to provide it with a wide range of services."[35]

Although policing remained largely the same on patrol, the politics regarding the Boston Police Department at the state level continued to face numerous challenges. The reality was that the police commission had control over licensing, especially alcohol licensing, and this policy had clearly been a poor idea. The other difficulty was having a three-member commission that placed no one single person in charge. In other cities, such as New York City, the chairman of the three-member commission was the de facto police commissioner in charge of the department, as Theodore Roosevelt had been from 1895 to 1897.[36] The legislation in 1885, however, had not made this distinction when it came to Boston. Both of these problems were rectified in 1906, which is why McCaffrey, writing in 1912, declared, "The last important change was made in 1906, when the police commission of three members was abolished and a single commissioner, with an independent licensing board of three men, was established in its place."[37]

The new police commissioner—note the use of "single"—was to be appointed by the governor for a five-year term.[38] Dealing with one police commissioner rather than three certainly streamlined communications and both authority and responsibility for the Boston Police Department. It did not, however, resolve one issue that was creating tension between the city and the state, merely placing one person in the middle of the growing problem. "Although a state law passed in 1906 provided that he was appointed by the Governor," historian Lyons explains,

> he was as free from state control as was any member of the judiciary. The Mayor of Boston had no control over his appointments, his actions, or his removal. The Mayor and his Council, however, did have one important check on the Commissioner: they held the power of the purse. Without their approval neither the pay nor the size of the police force could be altered.[39]

Another historian, Koss, also highlights the difficult situation the police commissioner faced when he wrote, "The City of Boston maintained the power of the purse nonetheless, and the Commissioner depended upon the city government with which to run the department. In addition he could increase the size of the force only with the consent of the Mayor."[40] Lyons explains that in order for this situation to work, it would be "necessary that Mayor and Commissioner work together," but "if they did not, the act of 1906, which was designed to increase efficiency, would backfire."[41]

The problems had already begun to manifest within the Boston Police Department. Fogelson explains that while the state was in control of the Boston Police Department through the police commissioners and, after 1906, the single police commissioner, the state "did not contribute anything toward the upkeep of the police departments."[42] They did not do so since they were not financially responsible for the department. However, the city did not want to fund the department's upkeep either, because they were not in charge of the police department. As a result, the physical infrastructure of the police department was beginning to show its age. If the upkeep of the buildings was not bad enough, police officers' salaries also became trapped in that same political predicament. The state contributed nothing to police salaries because this was not their responsibility, but the city saw no reason to raise salaries for a department it did not control.

Still, as Koss explains, "These problems and restrictions notwithstanding, the Commissioner's office wielded immense power, and exercised virtually complete control over the management of the Department."[43] As a result, it mattered greatly who the governor appointed to the new five-year position of police commissioner. Whoever was appointed could make or break the department, depending on their ability to walk this fine line between state and local control. The person the governor selected for the position was Stephen O'Meara.

The first police commissioner under the new system was an unusual choice, for Stephen O'Meara was neither a professional police officer nor a politician, and he had never held a public office in his life. Police historian Reppetto also adds a few additional reasons for the unusual choice. "Stephen James O'Meara was an Irish-Catholic immigrant; that alone should have disqualified him but he had been born in Prince Edward Island, Canada."[44] Nevertheless, O'Meara was appointed on June 4, 1906, and he served in that role for the next 12 years. Perhaps historian Frederick Koss explained the impact of his appointment best when he wrote, "This de jure power of the commissioner became de facto under the leadership of the first man to fill the post, Stephen O'Meara."[45]

Born on July 26, 1854, in Charlottetown, O'Meara spent the first 10 years of his life growing up on Prince Edward Island. From there, young Stephen moved with his family to Charlestown, Massachusetts, received his basic education, and became interested in working for the newspapers. Graduating from high school in 1872, he landed a job as a staff reporter in the office of a new local newspaper called *The Boston Globe*. After gaining some experience with the infant paper, O'Meara left for the more established—and better paying—*Boston Journal*. Over the next 25 years, he climbed his way up through the journalist ranks from "reporter, to city editor, to news and managing editor, to editor and general manager" and "in 1895, he became editor, publisher and part owner of the paper."[46] O'Meara purchased majority ownership of the paper in 1899, but after three years he decided to sell the paper to Frank Munsey and retire.

During his years with the paper, O'Meara had been very active in the city and became a highly respected and well-known figure in Boston high society. He belonged to numerous social and political groups, presented speeches at even more, and was often encouraged to enter politics. Instead, O'Meara busied himself with putting his personal affairs in order and then, in 1904, left for a European vacation that was intended to last indefinitely. In the spring of 1906, while still in Europe, he received word that Governor Curtis Guild Jr. had appointed him commissioner of the Boston Police Department. Guild, a progressive Republican, knew O'Meara not only through the newspaper but as a fellow member of the Republican Club of Massachusetts. Both were friends with President Theodore Roosevelt, and no doubt the president and Guild had probably conspired to see O'Meara appointed to the police force. Although O'Meara could easily have said no, since he was retired and out of the country, he returned to Boston immediately and was sworn in as the first police commissioner under the new organization on June 5, 1906. O'Meara's new salary was $6,000.00 a year.[47]

From the start, O'Meara was highly sensitive to the charges that the police were a politically manipulated department, so he spoke to this issue often. In his first annual report that fall, he wrote,

> The first efforts of the Police Commissioner were directed to the task of convincing members of the admirable police force over which he took control that they were to be absolutely free from outside interference. The Commissioner now has faith to believe that the members of the force are convinced that not only their own conduct will count for or against them; that they may do and must do their full duty fearlessly; and that there are no hidden ambushes from which, for doing that duty, they can be attacked and injured.[48]

O'Meara was adamant about preventing political interference, and after setting higher standards for his police officers, a friend of his asked him to intercede on behalf of someone who had been rejected for the department because of his physical deficiencies. After looking into the matter, O'Meara told his

friend that the individual in question did not meet department standards and therefore could not be hired. In 1910 John
F. Fitzgerald, the mayor of Boston, also tried to have O'Meara
appoint four special policemen who did not meet the department's standards. O'Meara advised the mayor that while he had
the right to increase the size of the Boston Police Department,
it remained his right as police commissioner to determine who
would be hired.

O'Meara was proud of his record in this regard and wrote in
his sixth annual report, "In the five and a half years for which I
can answer, no appointment, promotion, or transfer of a police
officer, no expenditure of a dollar, no grant or refusal of the tens
of thousands of licenses and permits which the police commissioner controls have been influenced by a political personage or
a political consideration."[49]

Police historian White explained, "O'Meara could manage
the centralized office because of his power and popularity."[50]
The historian continued, "Not only did he enjoy support
among the rank and file, but his reputation also spread far
beyond the confines of Boston."[51] He certainly held friends in
high places, for "O'Meara counted Joseph Pulitzer, Senator
Henry Cabot Lodge and the illustrious Theodore Roosevelt as
his friends."[52]

Another reason O'Meara held such power was a result of
his actions within the department itself, for he set high standards for entry into the department. As one noted Bostonian,
Richard H. Dana, famous for his novel *Two Years Before the Mast*,
once claimed, "Boston policemen are physically finer than West
Point cadets."[53] O'Meara did the same for promotion in ranks as
well, and he centralized this power under his own office. The
other thing O'Meara took control over by bringing it into his
office was the violations of police policy and procedures and
their punishment, including dismissals. In one year, 1908, 27
policemen were convicted of wrongdoing, and 14 of them were
dismissed. "The number," O'Meara boasted in his year-end
report, "is the largest number of dismissals for various reasons
of rigid discipline with two exceptions in 55 years and probably
since the department was established."[54] In addition, O'Meara

enacted policies that tried to reduce the numbers of these kinds of infractions, especially when it came to police corruption and brutality. Many observed that his leadership proved successful in this regard. In one study of unlawful acts among police officers, Hopkins wrote of the Boston Police Department, "O'Meara trained his men to take verbal abuse or a punch in the jaw without replying in kind. That unrestraint is the spirit of crime, restraint is the spirit of law, is the hardest lesson for Americans or their police to learn."[55]

One especially important action on the part of Commissioner O'Meara was his role in forming a department-sanctioned social club for the city's police officers shortly after he began. As King explains, "O'Meara in his benevolence helped and encouraged his officers, in 1906, to form the Boston Patrolman's Social Club."[56] It certainly was a benevolent move, one most likely made as an attempt to win favor with the police officers since they considered Commissioner O'Meara to be an outsider to the Boston police. Writing as one who was serving in O'Meara's administration, McCaffrey believed, "The purpose of its founders was to promote a feeling of brotherhood in the department, among the file, and to give them an opportunity to hear prominent men speak on subjects relating to police work."[57] Writing from the historian's viewpoint, White explains that "the purpose of the organization was to provide patrol officers with an opportunity to participate in fraternal groups across precinct boundaries," and he makes the specific point that "the Boston Social Club was not a police union."[58]

Still, McCaffrey, writing in 1912, does mention that it served as a de facto police union when he critically mentions how a

line of activity of more doubtful value, into which the club has been led, is the pushing of the wants of patrolmen. It was wholly through the work of this body (as a body, however, not individually) that the legislature in 1907 granted the force one day off in fifteen; and it is this body also which is behind the present movement to have the pay raised for all ranks below that of captain.[59]

This is why Lyons asserts the Social Club was "an organization formed within the force in 1906 to give the men a bargaining agency."[60]

In many ways, both of these perspectives are true. The Boston Social Club was created to serve as a social club in lieu of a bargaining agency for the Boston police, and since it was sanctioned by the police commissioner, the club could also be controlled by the police commissioner. However, even if the officers thought of it as a quasi–police union, over the years, it "proved to be nothing more than a social club, and by 1918, the men had found it an ineffectual instrument of their will, incapable of bringing about the urgently-desired reforms."[61] As the future president of the Boston Police Union, John McInnes commented that the Boston Social Club was a "weak-kneed organization, controlled by police officials."[62]

There are those who suggest that Commissioner O'Meara's tenure was largely a successful one. Writing near the time of his tenure, Fosdick wrote that O'Meara's "success was in no small measure attributable to his uninterrupted tenure of service. In the twelve years of his commissionership he had the unique opportunity of making himself . . . an efficient police executive."[63] Not only that, but he also managed to serve his tenure under five different governors from both political parties, no small feat for a highly political state appointee.

A more contemporary view of his tenure comes from police historian Reppetto, who believes that "despite various problems O'Meara's administration was generally praised, and his police department was remarkably free from corruption and restrained in the use of force in an era when payoffs and the third degree were commonplace."[64] In fact, after investigating police corruption and brutality in the late 1920s and early 1930s, the Wickersham Commission noted the following in their *Report on Lawlessness in Law Enforcement*:

> The third degree and related types of police illegality are at a minimum in Boston. . . . The charges of brutality which have been received in Boston are relatively to other cities, not serious. . . . The tradition of the Boston police department against

lawlessness is a most important factor. . . . The tradition was established by Stephen O'Meara.[65]

There are, however, many who believe that O'Meara's tenure was not as successful as some believed. Leonard Vance Harrison, who conducted a review of the Boston Police Department from 1927 to 1933, believed that Chief O'Meara did indeed succeed, although he notes, "Admirable as was the manner in which they were reached, it must be admitted that they were largely negative."[66] He elaborates that O'Meara's job included "warding off political favor-seekers, counteracting unfair criticism, preventing injustice to members of the force, within or without the department," but that these actions were nothing more than "defensive activities of the commissioner."[67] O'Meara stuck to the traditions that had developed within the department and only took defensive actions to ensure his officers were protected from outside political influence and to defend all criticism of the department. There were no major advancements or innovative changes called for by the commissioner and so "a deep rut of conservatism was worn in this period."[68]

As Reppetto notes, one explanation for this might be because "cops had to be at least twenty-five, and the force tended to be old and a bit stodgy."[69] But it runs much deeper than that, for O'Meara was "responsible for much of the force's bureaucratic rigidity." "He established himself as a virtual autocrat," and his power grew so large that he held "unchallenged authority over the department."[70] As police historian Koss explains, "By eliminating political influence for evil, he also eliminated political influence for good."[71]

In late 1918 O'Meara began experiencing health problems, and by November 1918, he felt so poorly he was absent from his office for four weeks. He resumed work on December 7, but a week later, on December 14, 1918, O'Meara died of a cerebral hemorrhage. His sudden death set the stage for significant and rapid change within the Boston Police Department, for "in the course of perfecting the department," writes Koss, "the Commissioner also helped set the scene for the Boston Police Strike."[72]

Boston Police Department on parade, circa 1918/1919.
Photo courtesy of the Boston Public Library, Leslie Jones Collection.

4

The Great War's Impact on Boston

Boston patrolman Frank McManus of the Hanover Street Police Station was out walking patrol just after noon on January 15, 1919. A typical police officer of that time, patrolman McManus was making the rounds on his beat, looking out for the welfare of the people and for anything suspicious or out of the ordinary. Before the war he had been walking patrol nearby North End Park when he saw a woman who looked confused. He stopped to ask if she needed help, and she replied in broken English, "I have been advised to throw the children in the water and kill them for their own good and also to take away my burden."[1] McManus took her to the police station to get her the help she needed, then checked on the welfare of the two children. He found both of the babies in good health.

Just two weeks after the New Year began, as historian Stephen Puleo explains, "It was the kind of day Frank McManus had been waiting for—warm and quiet."[2] Although a bit unusual for January and a Wednesday afternoon, any police officer who's not a rookie comes to appreciate quiet shifts, although any senior officer also knows that the quiet can come to an end in a mere second or two. He made his way up Commercial Street and came to a police call box attached to a post; it was labeled "Boston Police" and was identified by a number and the manufacturer's name—Gamewell—written all over it. It was approximately half past noon and he needed "to make his regularly scheduled report to headquarters."[3]

McManus opened the blue metal door, lifted the handset, and placed it to his ear. As he began his report that all was well and quiet on his beat, he heard a "grinding, rumbling noise" and a "machine-gun-like rat-a-tat sound."[4] It came from just north of him, toward the Charles River, where the enormous molasses tank loomed over the offices of the Purity Distilling Company. According to Puleo, the company "needed the huge tank to store the molasses after it was off-loaded from steamers that transported their shipments from Cuba, Puerto Rico, and the West Indies."[5] Molasses, a dark-brown and highly viscous liquid, is derived from the processing of sugarcane and is a by-product that can be used in baking, candy, and even making rum. The molasses in this storage tank, however, had been used to support the war effort. Molasses can also be distilled into industrial alcohol, and Purity had found it could "sell the alcohol to major weapons manufacturers in the United States . . . to produce munitions for the war against Germany."[6]

When patrolman McManus's eyes looked up in the direction of the strange sounds, he "saw the top of the tank sliding off" and in "the next moment he saw the sea of molasses rush forth in all directions."[7] He stared at what was happening before him, trying to grasp the unbelievable scene, but, as the *Boston Globe* reported, "Before he could realize it, the buildings in the vicinity began to collapse."[8] McManus stood there, the call box handset in his hand, as he "watched in utter disbelief as the giant molasses tank on the wharf seemed to disintegrate before his eyes, disgorging an enormous wall of thick, dark liquid that blackened the sky and snuffed out the daylight."[9]

The patrolman pulled the handset back to his ear and called "for all the ambulances and policemen available, telling his superiors briefly what had happened and venturing that there was a great loss of life and a large number of persons injured."[10] Puleo described patrolman McManus's words to headquarters: "Send all available rescue vehicles and personnel immediately—there's a wave of molasses coming down Commercial Street!" One can only imagine what the desk sergeant on the receiving end was thinking.[11] Although it must have sounded like a joke—for even today, hearing of the Great Molasses Flood sounds humorous—it was no laughing matter.

Puleo, the author of *Dark Tide*, a history of this incredible tragedy, explained, "The molasses tore the North End Paving Yard building into kindling, ripped the Engine 31 firehouse from its foundation and nearly swept it into the harbor, destroyed the wood-framed Clougherty house, crushed freight cars, autos, and wagons, and ensnared men, women, children, horses, dogs, rats, wood, and steel."[12] With regard to the Clougherty house, the *Boston Globe* reported the next day that, "The body of Mrs. Clougherty . . . was found beneath a pile of boards and timbers. . . . Mrs. Clougherty was in the house when the explosion occurred and was apparently buried in the debris when the building collapsed from concussion."[13] After the wave of molasses had done its damage, rescuers found 21 people dead and 150 injured.[14]

Patrolman McManus survived the tragedy and managed to save and assist many people on that "warm and quiet" day. He also learned later that the sound he had been puzzling over, like hearing machine gun fire, came from "thousands of rivets" that fastened the tank's steel plates in place, when they "had torn away as the tank collapsed."[15]

The Great Molasses Flood was emblematic of the tragedy that was 1919, caused almost wholly by the effects of World War I. The year had started off well enough, for the New Year's celebration ushered in a time of joy and hope, along with a time of sadness and grief. The joy of the Great War ending and the hope of a better year to come was in direct contrast to the sadness of 116,000 Americans killed and the grief brought to the families of over 200,000 injured. What was most important, however, was the shared sentiment that people all across America, especially in Boston, now felt—they hoped that things would get back to normal.

Public sentiment in the wake of World War I had been displayed in a strong desire for things to return to normal. Award-winning historian David M. Kennedy explained that after the war, "It had been [President] Wilson's main intention to depart from the normal as little as possible, especially in economic matters."[16] And although the Republicans capitalized on this mood, even the Democrats had to agree. "They had no wish more compelling than to return to the 'normal' conditions of prewar days."[17] Since Woodrow Wilson had already served two terms as president, his fellow Democrat James Cox ran against and lost to Warren G. Harding, who campaigned on the return to "normalcy." Once elected, Harding went so far as to state in his inaugural address, "Our supreme task is the resumption of our onward, normal way."[18] The only problem with this, however, was that America, and especially Boston, had been changed by the war, and the war had changed what was normal.

Although the nation wanted "a return to normalcy," what had been customary before the war was the result of simpler times under a laissez-faire government.[19] But after World War I, the United States had stepped out onto the world stage. The Progressive era had demonstrated the government could flex its authority, while the war showed it could bring its authority to bear. Despite all the hopes of the people for a return to normal, as the idiom explains, that train had left the station, or, as historian Robert Murray put it more eloquently,

> The basic key to an understanding of the prevailing mood of 1919 is to be found not only in the misguided philosophy of a people rushing pell-mell into peace, but in the counteraction between that attitude and the course of historical events.[20]

These historical events, in addition to the Great War itself, were marked by the first tragic event of the New Year, the Great Molasses Flood. The very reason for the existence of the enormous and filled-to-the-brim storage tank had been for the war effort, and the repercussions of those actions proved to be just one minor example of the war's impact on Boston. Others included the changes in the economy regarding jobs and the cost of living, the pandemic, immigration, the first Red Scare, and race riots. And all of these had shaped the perceptions of the Boston police and their race toward the historical event that was the Boston Police Strike.

The Great War, as it was known at the time, had effectively begun on June 28, 1914, when Austro-Hungarian archduke Franz Ferdinand was assassinated by a Bosnian Serb Yugoslav nationalist. As Europe's entangling alliances unfolded over the next month, the war became real on July 28. Although the war became the first modern war, it soon devolved into the stalemate of trench warfare. The impasse was not broken until America's entry into the war as a result of President Wilson's speech to Congress in which he requested a declaration of war on April 2, 1917, and subsequent legislation passed later that month. US soldiers began arriving in France in June 1917. After 18 months of brutal fighting, the armistice came on November 11, 1918.

America's entry into the Great War had come as a result of changing sentiments. In 1914 most Americans had no desire to intervene in the war, and President Wilson spoke of neutrality and "America First." Even during his first term, in preparation for a second, the Democratic platform proudly declared, "He kept us out of war." But over the next three years, sentiments changed. As historian Randolph Borne explained, "The war sentiment, begun so gradually but so perseveringly by the preparedness advocates who came from the ranks of big business, caught hold of one after another of the intellectual groups," and "with the aid of [Theodore] Roosevelt, the murmurs became a monotonous chant, and finally a chorus so mighty that to be out of it was at first to be disreputable and finally almost obscene."[21] In the end, "a strident rank was worked up against Germany," leaving Wilson to declare, "Neutrality is no longer feasible or desirable where the peace of the world is involved."[22]

As Wilson addressed both Congress and the nation, he explained his change of heart and mind:

It is a fearful thing to lead this great peaceful people into war, into the most terrible and disastrous of all wars, civilization itself seeming to be in the balance. But the right is more precious than peace, and we shall fight for the things which we have always carried nearest our hearts—for democracy, for the right of those who submit to authority to have a voice in their own governments, for the rights and liberties of small nations, for a universal dominion of right by such a concert of free peoples as shall bring peace and safety to all nations and make the world itself at last free.[23]

Two days after the war's end, Wilson explained the machinations behind his actions when he told a friend, "It was necessary for me by very slow stages and with the most genuine purpose to avoid war to lead the country on to a single way of thinking."[24] But as he also explained the evening before his speech to Congress,

> Once lead this people into war, and they'll forget there ever was such a thing as tolerance. To fight you must be brutal and ruthless, and the spirit of ruthless brutality will enter into the very fibre of our national life, infecting Congress, the courts, the policeman on the beat, the man in the street.[25]

When it came to Boston, the Boston Police Department, and their policemen on the beat, Wilson could never have been more prescient.

As soon as Europe went to war in 1914, "America's role in the war and the postwar world was hotly debated in Boston."[26] There were many who supported the position of former president Theodore Roosevelt, including longtime senator from Massachusetts (and Roosevelt friend) Henry Cabot Lodge and throngs of Boston citizens. Knowing what was coming with President Wilson's speech on April 2, an estimated 200,000 people flooded the Boston Common at noon to demonstrate their support.[27] As the *Boston Globe* reported, this demonstration "was unorganized. Nothing was prepared. And yet more men, women and children came to see the American flag raised on the same staff that flags have been raised time and again than ever came before the Boston Common."[28]

As historian Anatole Sykley explains, from 1914 until before Wilson's speech, "Bostonians responded differently to the prospects of war."[29] The historian tells that while there were some who called for war, such as those of Irish descent who "called for war against Great Britain," most were in favor of neutrality, especially the merchant class, who,

In contrast (savvy descendants of the Yankee traders of old), plotted how to rebuild Boston's economy after years of pre-war neglect and decline by remaining neutral and trading with all sides alike, taking advantage of Boston's new massive port infrastructure, the Commonwealth Pier.[30]

The call was to stay out of the war directly but profit from it indirectly.

Before America's intervention, David I. Walsh (the Democratic governor of Massachusetts at the beginning of the war) and Republican Samuel W. McCall both "expressed concerns whether the state and Boston could afford the disruptions of war."[31] On February 10, 1917, just prior to America's entry, Governor McCall convened a meeting of 100 leaders, most of whom were from Boston, to prepare the state for what was believed to be America's eventual entry. In particular, he was concerned about home defense. "Foreseeing the absorption of the entire Massachusetts National Guard into the regular army," McCall advocated that a state guard be re-formed, akin to the one the state had during the pre–Revolutionary War days.[32] This proved to be a sound move, for three months after the declaration of war, the Massachusetts National Guard was indeed mobilized to create the 26th Infantry Division. Nicknamed the "Yankee Division," it deployed to France and saw battle in the St.-Mihiel and Meuse-Argonne offensives. The National Lancers, a Massachusetts cavalry militia troop created in 1836, had served in the hunt for Pancho Villa and also saw service with the Yankee Division—not as a cavalry unit this time but as the 102nd Machine Gun Battalion.[33] Other Massachusetts National Guards units were mobilized for coastal defense and port security.

The bill Governor McCall had requested was put before the legislature and passed as Massachusetts House Bill 1834, Acts of 1917. The state guard was formed from "retired servicemen and those not fit to fight at the front" and alongside the few National Guard units left behind; these new home defense guards were deployed "to guard key infrastructure such as power stations, bridges and the port area."[34] For instance, A Company out of Newton, a small town just west of Boston, had been mobilized under the 11th Infantry of the Massachusetts State Guard. Each of the guardsmen was given a two-year enlistment, and as they later conceded, "We were a poor deluded set of enthusiasts."[35] As one of them wrote in 1920, all they did during those years was, "Drill—drill—drill—month after month—Sudbury, Framingham, and Boxford—when we might have been off having a good time somewhere else."[36]

In Roxbury, closer into the city of Boston, five companies were mobilized to form the Roxbury Unit under the 10th Infantry of the Massachusetts State Guard. Company D was mustered into service on June 5, 1917, and they, too, spent much of their time in "regular drills."[37] However, they were given the added duty of securing "subscriptions to over $30,000 U.S.A. 2nd Liberty Loan 4% Bonds" and participating in parades, flag raisings, and memorial services.[38]

When the war ended, members of the state guard continued to serve. If their purpose had been somewhat vague during the war, it seemed to grow even more amorphous after Armistice Day. Again, as a member of A Company explained,

> Original two-year enlistments were continuously running out. The ranks thinned, but we were asked to recruit and carry on in spite of the fact that there seemed to be no place to carry to and no honor in carrying anywhere.[39]

Still, many of the members, like those in the Roxbury Unit, served as honor guards for the returning soldiers, both the living and the dead.

When the war ended on November 11, 1918, the headline of the *Boston Globe* read in big bold letters, "Whole World in Delirium of Joy."[40] The editors wrote inside those pages that "It is victory, victory at last. The old day is over, its long, dreadful night of war is past. A new day dawns."[41] Again, despite the hopes for a better New Year and a return to normalcy, historian Jonathan R. White noted, "Although the war was over, 1919 was a year of tension, fear, and change."[42]

One of the most significant impacts of World War I on the home front was its effect on American wages and the cost of living. Europe's entry into World War I appears to have had little impact on the American dollar initially, but by 1916 inflation was beginning to rise; between the time when America did finally enter the war and its end, the value of the dollar had dropped to unprecedented rates.[43] A comparison of the value of the American dollar just before the war commenced in 1914 with the dollar of 1919 finds that the purchasing power was cut approximately in half. One hundred dollars in 1913 was worth approximately $45 in 1919. This was because, as Murray explains, "Food costs had increased 84 percent, clothing 114.5 percent, and furniture 125 percent."[44] That meant for the "average American family in 1919 the cost of living was 99 percent higher than it had been five years before."[45]

On Armistice Day, when the war came to an end, people celebrated in the streets. But it seems that the following day, as Murray notes, "telephone wires were hot with calls canceling war contracts" and "many industries, particularly the war industries, were caught short and were faced with the necessity of making a rapid conversion."[46] Industries in America cannot turn on a dime, and it took months, even years in some cases, to retool manufacturing from a wartime footing to one of peaceful production. It was a situation no one had adequately prepared for, but America's industrial sector rose to the challenge. However, in their brutal conversion, many workers lost their jobs because the skill sets needed had changed.

It was "actually, the professional classes, salaried clerks, civic officials, police, and others in a similar category," who were, as historian Robert Murray explains, "worse off economically than at any time since the Civil War."[47] This had much to do with the fact that World War I saw the free market economy respond faster to the changes and so was able to raise private wages, while the wages of public government employees, like that of the Boston police officer, were fixed by law.[48] In addition, those industrial workers who toiled under the protection of organized labor managed to see their wages rise. This is why the power of the unions rose during World War I, made evident by their soaring membership rolls. For instance, one of the largest union organizations, the American Federation of Labor, saw its numbers skyrocket "from about 500,000 in 1900 to 4,169,000 in 1919."[49]

The story was the same throughout Boston. The city had managed to gain heavily from the war industry because of its manufacturing capabilities, its port, and its geographic location. More specifically, munitions manufacturing was centered in Boston and, as historian Lyons explains, "shipyards all along the coast worked night and day."[50] "Large numbers of unskilled workers were attracted to the vicinity of Boston by wages; Lyons notes that the wage scale, "with generous overtime rates, often reached $100 a week."[51] The total for a year typically amounted to over $3,000 and for many, over $5,000.

A new recruit starting with the Boston Police Department in 1857 had received $2 a day.[52] A new recruit starting in 1918 received the exact same pay. In that year patrolmen were on a graduated pay scale, ranging from the lowest pay of a recruit at the beginning of their career to the maximum pay after six years of service.[53] Recruits started at $2 a day while on probation or as "reserve men," as they were called, and were paid approximately $730 their first year.[54] In their second year the wage would rise to $2.25 a day, amounting to approximately $1,000 annually, until they maxed out in their sixth year at an annual salary of $1,400.[55] This had been the case since 1913. While the patrolmen had been authorized in 1898 to receive $1,400 per year, most did not do so until it became mandatory in 1913, just prior to the Great War.[56] Throughout the war in Europe and during America's intervention, they had received no raise. As Gilbert and Sullivan had their sergeant of police sing in the musical *The Pirates of Penzance*, "A policeman's lot is not a happy one." Lyons echoed this sentiment for the Boston patrolman when he wrote, "Their unhappy lot was continually emphasized as the officers came in contact with flush factory workers thronging the city."[57]

To be sure, this was not an unfair wage in 1913 prior to the war, for those working in Boston's industries made about the same, if not a little less. Even in 1916 the police had not been left that far behind, but during the years 1917 and 1918, finances had become deplorable. "Inflation and the cost of living had increased much faster than wage growth," Farmer explains, and "from 1913 to May of 1919, the cost of living had risen by 76 percent, while police wages had risen just 18 percent."[58] By the end of the war, the industrial worker was making as much as four to five times as much as a police officer. And still worse, police officers were expected to pay for their own uniforms and equipment out of their salaries, estimated to come to approximately $200 per year.[59] All of this was combined with the prices of everything continuing to rise. As one example of so many, if an officer needed to take public transit to get to work, the fares in 1916 had been five cents. After the war began, demand for services rose and the cost of doing business increased, so in August 1918, the rate rose to seven cents, in December 1918 to eight cents, and in July 1919 to ten cents.[60] There was simply no getting ahead for the patrolman in Boston town.

Still further, while working conditions for all wage earners in 1919 were much worse than they are today, they were often brutal for the police officer. "Depending on duty assignments," explains Farmer, "officers worked between 72 and 98 hours per week, and were required to sleep in the station house, in cases where they were needed."[61] More specifically, Lyons's research found that the Boston "policeman worked an average of about 87 hours a week. Those on day duty worked 75 hours; those on night duty, 87; those on wagon duty, 98."[62] This is in spite of the fact that they were required to work every day of the week, only being allowed two weeks off from duty each year.

World War I brought to America what was considered "the most severe pandemic in recent history," the 1918 flu pandemic.[63] Soldiers returning home from Europe brought this highly unique and deadly virus with them, and due to close quarters among soldiers, the virus spread. Army doctors later came to understand the spread of the flu in America when they wrote in a 1928 report, "A progressive increase in cases reported as influenza beginning with the week ending August 4, 1918, and of the influenzal pneumonia cases beginning with the week ending August 18."[64] This, however, was no ordinary flu, for as pandemic historian John M. Barry explains, "Normally influenza chiefly kills the elderly and infants, but in the 1918 pandemic, roughly half of those who died were young men and women in the prime of their life, in their twenties and thirties."[65] In many of those cases, the patient died within 48 hours of developing symptoms. The total number of deaths caused by the flu are not truly known. "The lowest estimate of the pandemic's worldwide death toll," Barry details, "is twenty-one million, in a world with a population less than one-third today's," while "epidemiologists today estimate that influenza likely caused at least fifty million deaths worldwide, and possibly as many as one hundred million."[66]

The situation in Boston began only slightly later than the army report's beginning date. In fact, it is known that two sailors who reported sick on August 27, 1918, had the first cases of the flu in the city. They were living in the bay at Commonwealth Pier, in what the US Navy called a "receiving ship." "The name was a misnomer," explains Barry, for "it was actually a barracks where as many as seven thousand sailors in transit ate and slept in what the navy itself called 'grossly overcrowded' quarters."[67] By the next day, eight more sailors reported to sick call, and on August 29, 58 more became ill.[68]

At the time, it was believed to be just a routine flu, so many who may have been exposed left the ship and brought the flu into the city proper. "On September 3 a civilian suffering from influenza was admitted to the Boston City Hospital," records Barry, and "on September 4 students at the Navy Radio School at Harvard, in Cambridge across the Charles River from Boston proper, fell ill."[69] Boston historian Sykley picks up the story when he noted that "in September 1918 three civilians died in Boston" and "by the end of 1918 a thousand Bostonians were dead."[70]

In addition to naval personnel, the army workforce from nearby Camp Devens also brought the tragedy to Boston. Located approximately 35 miles northwest of the city, there were 45,000 soldiers stationed at the camp, having recently returned from the war.[71] "On September 7, a soldier from D Company, Forty-second Infantry, was sent to the hospital," writes Barry, and "the next day a dozen more men from his company were hospitalized."[72] Then the numbers exploded—on a single day in September, 1,543 soldiers at Camp Devens reported to sick call with influenza; the army had ceased to be able to adequately respond.[73]

Dr. Roy, a physician at Camp Devens, wrote later that month to a colleague from Surgical Ward No. 16 and tried to explain the situation.

> Camp Devens is near Boston, and has about 50,000 men, or did have before this epidemic broke loose. It also has the base hospital for the Division of the Northeast. This epidemic started about four weeks ago, and has developed so rapidly that the camp is demoralized and all ordinary work is held up till it has passed. All assemblages of soldiers taboo. These men start with what appears to be an attack of la grippe or influenza, and when brought to the hospital they very rapidly develop the most viscous type of pneumonia that has ever been seen. Two hours after admission they have the mahogany spots over the cheek bones, and a few hours later you can begin to see the cyanosis extending from their ears and spreading all over the face, until it is hard to distinguish the coloured men from the white. It is only a matter of a few hours then until death comes, and it is simply a struggle for air until they suffocate. It is horrible. One can stand it to see one, two or twenty men die, but to see these poor devils dropping like flies sort of gets on your nerves. We have been averaging about 100 deaths per day, and still keeping it up. There is no doubt in my mind that there is a new mixed infection here, but what I don't know. My total time is taken up hunting rales, rales dry or moist, sibilant or crepitant or any other of the hundred things that one may find in the chest, they all mean but one thing here—pneumonia— and that means in about all cases death.[74]

By October things were out of control, and city resources could no longer handle the influx of the sick, dying, and dead. Thousands were becoming ill, and just like at Camp Devens, there were hundreds dying from the flu each day.[75] The city began ordering the closure of schools and theaters and all other such public gathering places.[76] People were told to avoid crowds and use a handkerchief when coughing, and the wearing of masks was encouraged, although not mandated in Boston. The city also outlawed spitting on sidewalks and those "people who spat on the street were arrested," keeping the police busy with arrests that could rise to "sixty in a single day,"[77] as well as having to deal with not only the invalid sick, but the dead as well.

In addition to managing the physical aspects of the pandemic, individuals were faced with a mental toll that was difficult to handle. The struggles of dealing with so many dead, the inability to properly grieve, and the isolation caused by the prohibition from social gatherings all affected the people of Boston greatly. As professor Geoff Ward has explained, pandemics cause these psychological struggles because "These are moments of extreme precariousness, where people are suddenly uncertain about their fate, economic prospects and the social order."[78] In addition to the pandemic creating such uncertainties that everyone had to face, the populace were challenged by shifting societal changes resulting from both immigration to and emigration within America, especially those who came to Boston.

Immigration to the United States had reached its peak in the 19th century during the 1880s, when 5.2 million immigrants came to America.[79] However, at the beginning of the 20th century, in 1907 alone, nearly 1.3 million new immigrants arrived, which far surpassed all past records. According to the US World War One Centennial Commission, when World War I broke out in 1914, there were concerns "about how the immigrant population would react to the war, since most recent arrivals had direct ties to countries involved in the fighting."[80] At the beginning of the war, most immigrants to America were coming from eastern and southern European countries such as Germany, Austria-Hungary, Italy, Romania, and Greece, all of which were aligned with either the Allied or the Central Powers. As a result, it is not surprising that the commission also added "These concerns deepened when the United States entered the war in April 1917."[81]

Concern for those immigrants who had arrived from countries aligned with the Central Powers was the impetus for a series of congressional acts aimed at controlling the threat, including the Espionage Act of 1917, and the Sedition and Alien Acts, both of 1918.[82] The first was to control the enemy within by targeting those interfering with the military or plotting treason and insurrection. The second was to curtail anti-American speech; it forbade the use of "disloyal, profane, scurrilous, or abusive language" about the US flag, military, and government.[83] And the third was created to allow the government to deport any alien who violated either of the other acts.

Government scrutiny turned on those immigrants who had become involved in social movements that were considered antithetical to American values, freedom, and its capitalist system, namely those labeled anarchists, radicals, communists, socialists, labor organizers, and unionizers.[84] Italian anarchists were targeted "more fervently than any other group" for their activities, because, as Puleo explains, they "believed that capitalism and government were responsible for the plight of the working class and the poor."[85] The wartime Congressional Acts were actively applied most vigorously to any Italian even remotely associated with one or more of these groups.

In addition to the issues of immigration during World War I, the war also served as the prime motivation for a mass migration of Black Americans during those years, one that has come to be known as the Great Migration.[86] As Isabel Wilkerson so eloquently writes in her book on the subject, *The Warmth of Other Suns*,

> It was during the First World War that a silent pilgrimage took its first steps within the borders of this country. The fever rose without warning or notice or much in the way of understanding by those outside its reach.[87]

The discrimination against Black people in the South under the Jim Crow laws and the lure of war manufacturing jobs in the North brought on by the wartime shortage of labor led to the beginnings of the Great Migration. Like the high prevalence of European immigrants in America, it created more conflict among the many racial and ethnic groups.

The effects of immigration were felt across the nation as well as being present in Massachusetts, and most assuredly Boston. Boston historian Jack Tager writes,

> An important factor to consider was the dramatic transformation of the state's population mix in the first two decades of the twentieth century. From 1900 to 1919 the state's economy was bustling and vigorous, and this industrial prosperity lured newcomers seeking work.[88]

In Boston most of the industrial workers were immigrants to the city—the 1920 census showed that 73 percent of the city's entire population were either immigrants or their native-born children.[89] These people were, of course, also among the city's poorest who labored "at the bottom rungs of the work scale."[90]

This changing societal dynamic can be seen in some of the areas of Boston, such as the oldest and most historic area, the North End. Although initially one of the predominant neighborhoods in the city, by the mid-1800s "the economic conditions of the North End had deteriorated, as successive waves of German and then Irish poor had settled there," writes historian Puleo, so that "by 1850, the North End had become Boston's first slum neighborhood."[91] By the late 1800s and into the first two decades of the 20th century, more than 4 million southern Italians and Sicilians had come to America, and in Boston most moved into the North End because of poverty. They could do so because as the Irish had become more accepted in Boston, they moved out, so the Italians moved in.[92]

In addition to the large numbers of Italian immigrants in those early decades, Black immigration into Boston also rose significantly, "reaching its peak during and after World War I."[93] According to Wilkerson, when the Black migrants arrived in Boston, they primarily moved into the Roxbury area located southwest of the North End, for that neighborhood already had a well-established Black community.[94] They then began seeking out economic opportunities brought on by the war.[95] The presence of so many Black people in Boston during the war was accepted, for Boston had a long history of abolitionism, and the industries located there were in great need of labor. However, when the war ended and the soldiers began returning home with the intent of returning to their jobs, the Black people in Boston were, at a minimum, resented, if not outright hated.

Tucked between the Roxbury and North End neighborhoods along the Boston Common is Beacon Hill, home primarily to Boston's elite, the Boston Brahmins. The families who lived there were of the old, traditional upper class of the city, exemplified by their associations with Harvard University and the Somerset Club. They considered themselves to be a sort of Boston aristocracy, for as Cleveland Amory, a Boston Brahmin himself, once wrote in his book, *The Proper Bostonians*, "The Proper Bostonian did not just happen; he was planned."[96] The Brahmins had developed from their own exclusive society in the early 19th century; they endeavored to order all things, believed in moderation in all things, and adhered to their own sense of propriety at all cost.[97] The culture was marked by certain family names—names such as Eliot, Forbes, Boylston, Lawrence, Lodge, Cabot, and Coolidge—for lineage to the Boston Brahmin was everything. The elitist attitude of these Bostonian families in the 19th century had created a symbiotic relationship with the elites of Harvard University, both feeding and advancing their sense of superiority and entitlement.[98]

As immigration increased in Boston in the second half of the 19th century, particularly with regard to the Irish, the Brahmins rose above this lower-class ethnic group by simply keeping them out of their elitist circles.[99] They did so by banning them from their clubs, their institutions, and even, as we saw with City Marshal Tukey, from the Boston Police Department. If the Irish were not kept out of such institutions for their ethnicity, they were most certainly kept out of them for their religion, since most Irish were Catholic; the Brahmins were only affiliated with Unitarian or Episcopal churches.[100]

In order to adapt to these informal social rules, the Irish Catholics kept to themselves and worked in those occupations open to the lower classes—those jobs that did not feature the familiar business store-window sign "No Irish Need Apply," which, despite some claims, did indeed exist.[101] And by the beginning of the 20th century, as historian Handlin explains,

> The mass of Irishmen continued to occupy the low places in society they had earlier held. Their wives and daughters performed most of the city's domestic service; and men and boys of Irish ancestry constitute the bulk of unskilled workers.[102]

Even the police commissioner who replaced the beloved Commissioner O'Meara, Edwin Upton Curtis, kept Irish servants in his household.[103]

The one area in which the Irish had made some gains in the second half of the 19th century and in which they were entrenched by the 20th was municipal government. In part, this had much to do with their willingness to take on those jobs in government that did not pay well. Nevertheless, it placed them in a position to challenge, if not outright threaten, the Boston Brahmin.

What initiated the greatest change in this class struggle, however, came with the Great War. At first, it seemed to have no impact, but once American industries began benefiting from war contracts, especially after America entered the war, there was a high demand for industrial labor. And it just so happened that by 1917, the Irish had not only a lock on labor but on the labor movement as well.[104] The notion that both the Brahmin and Boston's poor would keep to themselves in a sort of harmonious stalemate was over.[105] As those first two decades of the 20th century gave way to the end of World War I, the long-standing peace between the Boston Brahmins and the Boston Irish was but one more tension that led to open conflict.

When war was first declared, the US government's concern for European immigrant anarchists dramatically increased—the concern for public safety was accompanied by a new fear on October 25, 1917, the day of the Bolshevik Revolution. It was made even more real with the signing of the Peace Treaty of Brest-Litovsk on March 3, 1918, between the Bolsheviks and Germany. This accord not only ended Russia's involvement in World War I, but also signaled an alliance between the new Russian powers—the Communist Party—with Germany and the Central Powers.[106] In light of the proverb "the friend of my enemy is my enemy," communism joined the list of growing American concerns and gave birth to what has been called the Red Scare.[107]

In 1917, when America entered the war, German intrigue had been the US government's focus of concern, but by 1919 (after the war), historian Mark Ellis writes, "Bolshevism had supplanted German intrigue as the most feared foreign subversion and it was blamed for widespread industrial unrest in 1919 and a spate of bombings."[108] The fear of communism, along with socialism, had joined the fear of the anarchists, with most of the concern centered on immigrants, especially those from countries where communism or socialism was a way of life. Although many historians now suggest the Red Scare was nothing more than a socially constructed means of immigrant fearmongering that was not rooted in reality, it would seem they would have to at least concede that the bombs they delivered were real.

The Galleanists were one group who delivered many of the bombs; they had hopes of changing the American system. The faction was named for Italian anarchist Luigi Galleani, who came to America in 1901 and had begun advocating the use of violence to overthrow those he believed were tyrants and capitalists.[109] Gathering a band of followers who took to referring to themselves after their chosen leader, they orchestrated a mail-bombing campaign in April 1919. They mailed at least 36 packages loaded with dynamite that were wrapped in plain brown paper on the outside with one side labeled "open," and green paper on the inside, featuring a label that read "Gimble Brothers—Novelty Samples." Opening the package as directed was designed to trigger the explosives with the intent of murdering the unsuspecting recipient.

The packages were mailed in late April so that hopefully they would be received on May Day, May 1, International Workers' Day. One of the first bombs was received by Georgia senator Thomas W. Hardwick's housekeeper; she opened the package as instructed, and it blew off her hands. The blast also burned the senator's wife's face, as she happened to be sitting nearby. Several other packages were opened "incorrectly," so the packages did not explode but were taken to the police when the actual contents were discovered. Many of the packages were then recovered; some were still sitting in the post office for lack of sufficient postage and had been mailed to intended recipients including several governors, senators, mayors, and New York City police commissioner Richard Enright. Business magnates J. P. Morgan Jr. and John D. Rockefeller were also intended targets. One other individual who was supposed to receive the "novelty samples" was US attorney general A. Mitchell Palmer.

Alexander Mitchell Palmer was born into a Quaker family in Moosehead, Pennsylvania, on May 4, 1872. After graduation from Swarthmore College in 1891, he studied law and was admitted to the bar in 1893. Palmer opened a law office in Stroudsburg, Pennsylvania, and ran for a seat in the House of Representatives in 1908. He served three terms and, as a faithful Democrat, President Wilson appointed him as Alien Property Custodian during World War I. In this role it was his office's mission to seize the assets of foreigners living in the United States who were considered to be enemies of the state. After the war, at the beginning of 1919, Wilson needed to fill the position of US attorney general, and he chose Palmer, who took office on March 5, 1919. The next month he was to have received one of the mail bombs, most likely as retaliation for his work as Alien Property Custodian. The bomb was intercepted and defused, but one month later, the Galleanists tried again.

"On June 2, 1919, bombs lit up the midnight sky in seven eastern cities," writes historian Beverly Gage, "a coordinated effort raising the specter of a widespread conspiracy."[110] After the Galleanists' poor showing for their bombing efforts in May, they endeavored to set off nine bombs in eight different cities by delivering much larger packages straight to the targets' residence. One was intended for Attorney General Palmer.

"Palmer had spent the night quietly at home, reading and chatting with his wife, Roberta, in the downstairs library . . . just three months into his new job as attorney general," writes historian Kenneth D. Ackerman.[111] "He and Roberta had finished a whirlwind round of social calls that weekend."[112] Although his wife went upstairs early, Palmer stayed in the library reading, and finally, around 11 o'clock, he made ready for bed. As he climbed the stairs, he heard the sounds of a car stopping at the curb of their house, the car door opening, and the footsteps of someone approaching their front stoop. Outside, a man "rushed toward the Palmer's front steps, but tripped in the garden a few feet from the house. He fell, and the suitcase hit the ground."[113] Palmer told the newspaper reporters later, "I heard a crash downstairs as if something had been thrown against the front door. It was followed immediately by an explosion."[114]

The man was a Galleanist carrying a package containing an estimated 25 pounds of dynamite and shrapnel. He tripped on the stone steps, most likely from his excitement, and dropped the package that triggered the explosion. The Galleanist blew up with the bomb. The explosion did extensive damage to the door and shattered windows, including those across the street. The occupants of that house, Assistant Secretary Franklin D. Roosevelt, his wife, and son, were, needless to say, rattled, but unharmed. "I had just placed my automobile in the garage when the explosion took place," the future president told reporters.[115] Their front windows were blown into the house from the concussion of the bomb, and they could hear their cook yelling, "The world has come to an end."[116] The garage was located a few blocks away from the home. Roosevelt, two years shy of contracting polio, ran down the street, pulling up short at the damage to his own home. After ensuring that his family was safe, he rushed across the street to the Palmer residence, where he found Palmer and his wife also shaken but unharmed. Palmer told the reporters, "It blew in the front of the house. The door against which it was thrown leads into the library in which we had been sitting, and the part of the house blown in was in front of the library."[117] Although they found little of the bomber, they did discover a pamphlet entitled *Plain Words*, part of which read:

> There will have to be bloodshed; we will not dodge; there will have to be murder; we will kill you . . . there will have to be

destruction; we will destroy. . . . We are ready to do anything
and everything to suppress the capitalist class.[118]

It was signed "The Anarchist Fighters."[119]
While none of the intended targets was harmed, one of the
bombs killed a night watchman.[120] The reaction to the bombings
quickly became a two-way street between Palmer and the public. For Palmer, "the bombing of his own home in June, 1919,"
explains historian Murray, "acted as a catalytic agent."[121] Palmer
later explained it in this way:

> I was shouted at from every editorial sanctum in America
> from sea to sea; I was preached upon from every pulpit; I was
> urged—I could feel it dinned into my ears—throughout the
> country to do something and do it now; and do it quick, and
> do it in a way that would bring results.[122]

The Federal Bureau of Investigation notes from its own
history, "The nation demanded a response to the bombings,"
and added, "the Attorney General was ready to oblige."[123]
Palmer did so two days later by creating a special "Red-hunting
team."[124] After taking swift action, Ackerman explains, his
actions were "applauded by top officials in government, media,
business, academia, and religion, almost across the board."[125]
Murray explains, "as labor unrest increased and the nation was
treated to such abnormal events as general strikes, riots, and the
planting of bombs, the assumption that the country was under
serious attack by the Reds found a wide acceptance."[126]
The City of Boston was not exempt from such bombings.
The North End Salutation Street police station was targeted
on December 18, 1916, when a dynamite bomb exploded and
"shattered every window on one side of the building, blew
out the window sashes, and split the window casings."[127] It
was believed, writes Puleo, that "the police station bomb was
planted in reprisal against Boston police for the arrests of several
anarchists after a violent antimilitary preparedness riot in North
Square in early December."[128] It was the Galleanists.
After the war, Boston police noted that the North End, with
its large population of Italian and Sicilian immigrants, was fast

becoming not only the source of anarchist operations in the city but also in America.[129] Boston police officers were reporting the discovery of numerous placards, all threatening violence.[130] The placards read:

> Go-Ahead. The senile fossils ruling the United States see red! Smelling their destruction, they had decided to check the storm by passing the deportation law affecting all foreign radicals. We, the American anarchists do not protest, for it is futile to waste any energy on feeble-minded creatures led by His Majesty Phonograph Wilson. Do not think that only foreigners are anarchists, we are a great number right here at home. Deportation will not stop the storm from reaching these shores. The storm is within and very soon will leap and crash and annihilate you in blood and fire. You have shown no pity to us! We will do likewise. And deport us! We will dynamite you! Either deport us or free all! The American Anarchists.[131]

Historian White tells how Boston's business interests were "motivated by the fear of Bolshevism in a year of fear."[132] While that may be very true, the Boston police took the time to warn Boston's business owners of the threat from those very real bombs.[133]

On June 2, 1919, the same day Attorney General Palmer's house in Washington, DC, was bombed, Boston became the focus of two of the coordinated attacks. "The 'Red Terror' reached Boston late last night and early this morning," reported the *Boston Globe*.

> High-explosive bombs damaged the home of Judge Albert F. Hayden of the Roxbury District Court at 11 Wayne St. and Representative Leland Powers of Beaumont av, Newtonville. No one was injured at either house, the Hayden family being away from home and the Powers family being on the second floor of their dwelling.[134]

The Hayden bombing caused the most damage of the two. A neighbor inside the home next door felt the blast and called the fire department, while Hayden's son, who was returning home, witnessed the explosion from 200 feet away. The newspaper reported that, "The piazza of the Hayden house was wrecked, the plastering ripped from the walls of many of the rooms and the furnishings thrown about."[135] When asked for his response to the anarchists bombing his home, the judge nearly shouted,

> It was not to intimidate me, but to intimidate the whole community. We have got to defeat Bolshevists; we have got to deport them. They should not be allowed in this country. They should all be deported at once. I do not believe they know what they want. It is force, force, force. That's all they want.[136]

Like the judge's rhetoric, both men had taken strong stands against the anarchists and Bolshevists who were attacking their way of life in America, including Boston. Representative Powers had been targeted for his support of the Anti-Anarchy Bill passed by Congress in late 1918, while Judge Hayden had been targeted because he had been the presiding judge of the rioters from the recent May Day Riots—these riots were just one more issue that was preventing Boston's return to normalcy after the Great War.[137]

Although there were many riots throughout 1919, the most numerous and serious of the riots occurred in the summer and grew out of the tenuous relationship between black and white Americans. As criminal justice historian Samuel Walker explains, "The 1919 riots were the climax of several years of steadily worsening race relations in both the North and the South."[138] There had indeed been earlier race riots in America, such as the 1917 East St. Louis riots, caused by Black workers being lured to that city to serve as strikebreakers. These riots ended in the deaths of dozens of Black people and thousands being driven from the city.[139] In a similar fashion, during World War I Black people from the South had been lured to northern cities with the promise of industrial jobs. But as soldiers returned from overseas and the mostly white soldiers returned to civilian life, they hoped to fill jobs that many Black people now held. The tension built throughout the first half of that year, then spilled over during the summer. Because there were so many riots in the summer of 1919, they are now referred to as the "Race Riots of 1919," or, as James Weldon Johnson of the National Association for the Advancement of Colored People (NAACP) called them, "Red Summer."[140] The month of July 1919 proved to be the peak of the race riots, for by then there had been at least three serious riots. One occurred in Charleston, South Carolina, in May, initiated by US sailors, while another in Bisbee, Arizona, in early July targeted members of the 10th US Cavalry, the Black military servicemen known as the Buffalo Soldiers.[141] Other riots included one in April in Jenkins County, Georgia, another in Longview, Texas, in early July, and one in Garfield Park, Indianapolis, in mid-July.[142] Two of the most extensive riots occurred in late July—the Washington, DC Race Riot, which lasted for five days, and the Chicago Race Riot, which began on July 27 and lasted a week. Walker calls the latter, "the worst instance of urban racial violence to that time."[143] It was triggered by a Black youth crossing an imaginary line in a Lake Michigan swimming area from the "Black side" to the "white side." A fight ensued from this transgression, and after the youth was killed, the police refused to arrest anyone for the murder and violence broke out. The week of rioting left 38 people dead and over 500 injured, and "more than a thousand African American homeless because of arson."[144]

The riots in Boston followed a somewhat similar pattern, although they were less focused on racial tensions between Black and white Bostonians and more centered on the differences in racial identity. One early riot, the Patriotic Riot, occurred on July 1, 1917. Bostonians' support for World War I, like most Americans, had been growing after the war started, but there were some in Boston, as Tager explains, who opposed US intervention. "Irish and German Americans, isolated groups of progressive reformers, and socialists of various persuasions" were all against American involvement in the war.[145] After America did enter the war, these groups often came under attack, so when the socialists held a peaceful parade on the Boston Common on July 1, 1917, they became the focus of Bostonian war supporters' animus. "First an angry crowd, led by servicemen in uniform, assaulted the paraders," which was soon followed by "the police, supposedly protecting the paraders, launch[ing] an all-out attack upon them."[146] The so-called "Patriotic Riot" involved well over 20,000 people and continued for four hours of fighting before it began to break up.[147] Ironically, it was, in the end, US servicemen who "forcibly dispersed them."[148]

On May 1, 1919, at the annual workers' May Day celebration, the scene was nearly repeated. Although May Day had been an ancient pagan celebration of spring, it had become chosen as International Workers' Day by socialists and communists in commemoration of the deadly Chicago Haymarket Affair, the famous clash between workers and police in Chicago's Haymarket Square. In the case of Boston's May Day celebration in 1919, "The Lettish Socialist Workmen's Society of Roxbury organized a 'Red Flag' parade for May 1, with the support, not only of Latvian immigrants, but of Lithuanians, Russians, and some Irish."[149] As the parade began, the police tried to stop its progress for they had not filed the proper permits.[150] Greatly outnumbered, numerous police officers were injured, including patrolman Adolph Butterman, who had been shot, and Captain Hugh Lee, who, after assisting the wounded patrolman, suffered a heart attack and died.[151] Upon hearing or seeing this, the masses, many of them ex-servicemen who had served in the Great War, began spilling into the streets to do what the police could not.[152] The riot only lasted an hour before order was restored, once again by US servicemen.[153]

The Great War impacted the Boston Police Department in many ways, both directly and indirectly. In the prewar years, it had much to do with the ethnic clashes over America's involvement in the war and a changing economy due to war contracts. Once America declared war, it came directly from both the loss of patrolmen due to enlistments and the added burdens of dealing with wartime Boston. "The war has placed a great additional burden upon the police of Boston," wrote Police Commissioner O'Meara in his last report right before his death on December 14, 1918.[154] "To November 30 they had performed more than 20,000 tours of duty for exclusively war purposes without taking into account the innumerable daily activities created or increased by war conditions."[155] It was the impact of the war's aftermath, however, that influenced the department in so many untold ways from the changes in the purchase power of a patrolman's salary to having to deal with a pandemic, racial and ethnic clashes, bombings, and riots.

While the social and economic landscape of Boston had changed significantly in the wake of the war, so too had Boston's politics. On February 4, 1918, a new mayor, Andrew James Peters, had been installed, and it was he who guided Boston through the changes and fallout from World War I. After serving in office for only 10 months, his police commissioner, Stephen O'Meara, died and needed to be replaced. His choice for the new police commissioner was former Boston mayor Edwin Upton Curtis. Both men were members of Boston's Brahmins, and both men were interested in reasserting old-school elitist power in Boston's governance. However, where they differed was in the ways each hoped to achieve this, ultimately bringing about not only the Boston Police Strike, but their struggles for power against each other during that fateful strike.

Boston Mayor Andrew James Peters.
Photo courtesy of the Library of Congress.

Boston Police Commissioner Edwin Upton Curtis.
Photo courtesy of the Library of Congress.

5

Boston's Leadership

The year 1919 ushered in a renewed sense of hope for the future among all Bostonians, and leading them into this New Year were a set of recently established leaders—a new mayor and a new police commissioner. Democrat Andrew James Peters won the mayoral election and took the oath of office on February 4, 1918. At the end of that year, with the death of police commissioner Stephen O'Meara, Governor Samuel Walker McCall, who himself was soon to be replaced, appointed Republican Edwin Upton Curtis the new police commissioner on New Year's Eve. "These two," historian Lyons definitively states, "played the most important roles in the events leading up to, and during, the strike."[1] At the local level, this was certainly the case, for they were both integrally connected to the cause of the strike, they were Boston's leaders during the strike, and both paid a heavy price as a result of the strike.

Historian Robert Sobel writes, "Peters and Curtis came from the same background, but otherwise were quite different."[2] Both men had family lines attached to the Boston Brahmin and both were raised as heirs to that aristocracy, but in its simplest form, Peters had aligned himself with the Democratic Party, while Curtis was decidedly a staunch Republican. Although Curtis now ran the police department, Peters, as Francis Russell explains, "belonged to the same political party as the policemen."[3] This highlights the subtext of not only the ideological differences between the two men, but also their ethnic-nationalism and religion as well. This developed out of the fact that Protestant Yankee Republicans, namely Governor McCall and Commissioner Curtis, were seeking to control the Irish Catholic Democratic rank and file of the police department to whom Peters was sympathetic. Their personalities also played an important role, for as Russell explains, "By nature Peters was a more conciliatory type than the Commissioner," while William Allen White describes Curtis as "a large, serious man . . . with a reserve [that] embodied the spirit of traditional inherited wealth, traditional inherited Republicanism."[4]

Because these two men played such a significant role in the cause of the strike, as well as its managing (and mismanaging), it is important to understand each man's background and what led each to make the decisions they made, both before and during the strike. Since Mayor Andrew James Peters was elected to office prior to the appointment of Police Commissioner Edwin Upton Curtis, this chapter first turns to him.

Andrew James Peters was born on April 3, 1872, in West Roxbury, to his parents Andrew James Peters and Mary Richards Whitney. He entered the world in the late stages of Reconstruction in a city that was benefiting from both wealth and prosperity, but for which the city would pay a horrific price. Boston experienced a period of serious growth in the years following the Civil War, but its infrastructure could not keep pace. That November, Boston experienced its largest fire in history; an estimated 65 acres were consumed inside the heart of the city as the result of the conflagration.[5] The water mains had failed to keep up with growth, and the fire department's inability to get water to the fires intensified the disaster.

Peters was raised in a white, rambling old home in the Jamaica Plain, a home that no longer stands at 310 South Street, and it remained Peters's home for the remainder of his life. The residence was situated almost within the beautiful grounds of the Arnold Arboretum, 250 acres of land that has been a preserve since the year Peters was born.[6] Located at the south end of the preserve and standing 240 feet tall is Peter's Hill, so named for Andrew Peters after his tenure as mayor was finished. It is a fitting monument to Peters, for from its slight height, the skyline of the city he so dearly loved may be viewed.

His family and the family name were assuredly among those of the Boston Brahmin, for the first Andrew Peters had arrived in Massachusetts in 1657.[7] Their limited wealth, however, kept them mostly on the fringes of high society in the late 19th and early 20th centuries, and so too did the family's politics, for they were Democrats in a sea of Yankee Republicans. Still, Peters attended some of the finest schools offered to the upper classes of Boston society. He first attended Hopkinson School in Boston before traveling to the prestigious and bucolic St. Paul's School in Concord, New Hampshire. Upon graduation, he then—in good Boston Brahmin fashion—attended Harvard University, where he graduated in 1895.[8] The speaker for commencement on Memorial Day, May 30, 1895, was the notable learned Oliver Wendell Holmes Jr., who was an associate justice on the Massachusetts Supreme Judicial Court at the time and later became its chief justice before taking his seat on the US Supreme Court.

No doubt wanting to emulate the learned judge (who had been born and raised in Boston and attended Harvard and then the Harvard Law School after the Civil War), Peters followed in his footsteps by attending the law school where he graduated in 1898. The year prior, he took the bar examination and was admitted, positioning himself to begin the practice of law in Boston immediately upon graduation. Writing later as mayor for a Harvard College class of 1895 anniversary report, Peters explained what he did after achieving this milestone: "My first years after the Law School were passed in the practice of law in Boston, during which time I saw constantly many of our Class, and I was associated in a firm with Alexander Whiteside."[9]

It did not take long before Peters developed the desire for political office and seized the first opportunity for elected office that came his way. "In 1902," he wrote, "a chance for public work came to me as a member of the Massachusetts State Legislature, and in 1904 and 1905 in the State Senate."[10] Elected to the Massachusetts State Senate on the Democratic platform, he served two one-year terms in 1904 and 1905. "This experience," Peters continued, "opened an opportunity for Congress, and for four terms I represented one of the Boston districts."[11] He ran for the Massachusetts 11th Congressional District position in the US House of Representatives, which he won in the fall of 1906. He was seated in the 60th Congress on March 4, 1907, and served into the 63rd Congress before resigning from office on August 15, 1914.

Peters's temperament toward political office began to show some distaste as evidenced in his reflections of his tenure in the House of Representatives. "Service in Congress," Peters wrote to his fellow Harvard classmates on their 25th anniversary, "depends in a considerable measure on the committee on which a man finds himself, and on the chance of being brought into close touch with some of the larger legislative problems before that body."[12] While he did note that he was "fortunate in being a member of the Committee on Ways and Means," the most highly coveted committee in the House, he also added that "the cumbersomeness of legislative machinery requires such a waste of time of individuals that one gets very impatient at the delays involved."[13] Peters enjoyed the trappings of being a member of Congress. What he did not seem to enjoy was the business and proceedings of Congress. This became ever more evident during his tenure as mayor.

Upon entering Congress, he began dating a young lady named Martha Phillips on his return visits home to Boston, and in 1910 they married. Martha was, as historian Jonathan Goodman explains, "a member of one of Boston's oldest and richest families," a family and name that most assuredly belonged to the Boston Brahmin.[14] In fact, while the Peters family lived on the edges of Boston's upper society, Peters's marriage to Martha placed him fully within its fold, thus allowing him, for the first time, to be part of the elite Social Register.

Martha's parents were John Charles Phillips, a businessman and descendant of the first mayor of Boston, John Phillips, for whom he was named, and Anna Tucker. John and Anna were married in London on October 23, 1874. The family was very wealthy, and growing up in the family home, the children were all well educated, each going on to lead successful lives. The son and next John Charles Phillips became a noted zoologist, ornithologist, and conservationist. William Phillips served as an ambassador and US assistant secretary of state. Daughter Anna Tucker Phillips married Raynal Bolling, a lawyer who later joined the war effort in World War I and became the first high-ranking officer killed in combat. And Martha married a sitting congressman who became the mayor of Boston; together, she and Andrew would have six children, all of them boys, though three of them would die shortly after entering adulthood.

"In 1914, in the eighth year of my service," Peters recounted, "I resigned from Congress to become assistant secretary of the treasury, where I served for two years and a half, and after my resignation I returned to Boston."[15] Peters had left the House of Representatives for an appointment in the Wilson administration as an assistant secretary of the Treasury in charge of customs under then secretary William Gibbs McAdoo.[16] One anonymous supporter wrote of Peters as the "best man" for the position, because

Andrew J. Peters had for years been one of the big assets the Democratic party has had in Massachusetts. He represents the none too plentiful type of the American Democrat, clean-cut in appearance, eloquent in speech, pleasing in manner, and possessed of great ability. He has been a credit to his district, to the state and to his party.[17]

This individual considered him to be supportive of the party and a congenial person. Peters explained of his tenure in Washington, DC, "I found my later work as assistant secretary of the treasury much more attractive," that is, much more attractive than the business of Congress.[18]

One other reason he may have found his tenure with the US Treasury more attractive is because of the illicit affair Peters began at that time. Although unknown until much later, it was during this time period when he developed an attraction to young Starr Faithfull, born Marian Starr Wyman. She was the daughter of Peters's wife's cousin, Helen MacGreror Pierce of Andover, Massachusetts, and investment banker Frank Wyman II. Their daughter Marian, nicknamed "Bamby," was born on January 27, 1906, and first met Peters when she was 11 years old in 1917. That was also when he allegedly began sexually abusing her. The affair only came out when the scandal was revealed after her mysterious death by drowning on June 6, 1931.[19]

The affair developed out of Peters's close association with Bamby's family. Her father had been an investment banker, and the family had been once counted among the Boston Brahmin—that was, until he lost his fortunes through a series of bad investments. The family was left destitute, and Frank and Helen's marriage began to fall apart. The Peters were among the many families who assisted the Wymans during their times of financial trouble, and their assistance allowed for Bamby to receive a private school education. Helen Wyman, who had become estranged from her husband, often visited her cousin Martha and, fairly soon, began spending summers with them, living in the Peters's house. An alleged "father-daughter" relationship developed between Peters and Bamby, and he often took her on daily excursions. By the time she was 11, these excursions moved farther afield and necessitated overnight stays in hotels, and that was when the sexual abuse began. Peters held leverage over her not just because he was an adult who had control over a child, but also because he was the financier and host of the girl's family. The sexual abuse was not revealed by Starr until well after the Boston Police Strike, when she finally admitted it to her mother in 1926, but it still, in all likelihood, tainted Peters's behaviors.

In 1917 a faction of the Democratic Party desired to put forth a candidate to run against the current Boston mayor, James Michael Curley. Curley was a throwback to the late 19th-century days of the Democratic political machine; he believed in free spending to gain power and thought he could do so by running a corrupt government. Jack Beatty, the leading biographer of Curley, described him as "a disaster mitigated only by moments of farce."[20] In light of Curley's corruption, Boston's Good Government Association was also looking for someone who could run as a reform candidate in support of "good government." Curley often derided the members of this association, calling them "Goo-Goos";[21] he believed they were nothing more than naive do-gooders who were ignorant of the ways of government and blindly opposed to his machine control of Boston. Yet,

Curley was wholly corrupt in his tenure as mayor, and it was that corruption the association was seeking to end.

Their candidate of choice was the more congenial Andrew James Peters. The battle that Peters waged against Curley proved to be not just a race for the mayoral position, but for who had the right to lead the people of Boston. It pitted two Democrats against each other—the old-school, traditional Boston Brahmin Peters against the more irascible and lower-middle-class Irish Curley. Peters did have the backing of not only many in his own party but also a minority of Republicans. Curley, however, had the backing of the Irish Americans, and that proved to be a much larger and significant voting bloc, one almost guaranteeing his reelection.

It seems that Peters, up against such great odds, should have lost the election for mayor. What undid Curley, however, was his pervasive corruption, which is what had motivated the Good Government Association to run Peters for the position in the first place. Two Republicans, Martin Lomasney and John F. Fitzgerald (who generally went by the nickname "Honey Fitz" and who in May 1917 became the grandfather of future president John F. Kennedy), decided to run against Curley. They did not expect to win, but they knew full well it would split the vote, thus denying Curley another term in office. Peters acknowledged his election was more "a protest against the results of the personal and political influence which had too long been dominant at City Hall which tended to build up a personal and political machine."[22] Rather than being for Peters, the voters were against Curley.

Still, in the end, it proved to be a successful campaign for Peters, and on February 4, 1918, he became the 42nd mayor of Boston. In his inaugural speech delivered in historic Faneuil Hall, he spoke loftily of the issues facing the city when he highlighted,

> The gigantic task which we are called upon to perform is one which requires the mobilization of all our resources, material and morale. We cannot all of us fight for democracy on the plains of France. We can all help win the battle for democracy by our loyalty and sacrifice at home.[23]

He did mention the police department in the speech, but only as the topic was related to city expenditures and purchasing. With regard to his tenure as mayor, Peters told his fellow Harvard graduates, "Public service came to me without any particular intention on my part to seek it, or without any special qualifications for it, and while it is exacting in its demands, it has given me some interesting years."[24] This was certainly a self-deprecating statement that downplayed his involvement, but there is an element of truth in his words. As a mayor, Peters was well liked, mostly for his friendly manner; as Coolidge biographer Claude Fuess wrote, "Mr. Peters' record was unblemished, and he was respected even by his political opponents for his reasonable and temperate mind."[25]

Not everyone thought highly of his tenure, despite liking the man for his easy personality. Curley, not surprisingly, was one of Peters's greatest critics and noted later in his memoirs how Peters was a "Brookline squire endowed with three apostolic names" and described his tenure as mayor as a "do-nothing regime."[26] It was not that Peters did nothing, it was just that he did nothing in regard to his official office, for he acted as if he were nothing more than a figurehead of government, free to continue his elitist, upper-class social life. He did keep himself quite busy, but not with his mayoral duties. Rather, he spent most of his time frequenting the half dozen Boston clubs to which he belonged and where he whiled away much of the workday. Historian Goodman also adds,

> He was often away from the city for weeks on end: touring incognito, or horse-riding on the farm at Dover, west of Boston, that his wife had inherited, or, in the summers, cruising in his schooner-yacht from North Haven Island, off the coast of Maine, where he had bought a holiday-home.[27]

These trips were in addition to his many trysts with young Starr Wyman, who, by 1919, had turned 13.

"Somehow," historian Francis Russell wrote, "he was able to shut both his mind and his eyes to the corruption of his administration."[28] While his time in office was nowhere near as corrupt as the Curley administration, which orchestrated the corruption from the highest office in the city, Boston city governance under Peters remained corrupt because there proved to be little oversight or control coming from the mayor's office. "The problem was he hadn't much of an idea of how to be an effective mayor," historian Sobel explains, for Peters was the "type who sympathized with the 'lower orders,' and wanted more than anything else to ameliorate their conditions, but not if this required him to socialize with them."[29] His tenure as mayor proved to be a weak one, which explains why Jack Tager writes, "Andrew Peters would turn out to be the last Yankee Democratic mayor of Boston."[30]

In the meantime, Peters continued to preside over the more ceremonial trappings of office such as when the Great War ended on November 11, 1918, and he led the celebration alongside Cardinal O'Connell at Symphony Hall.[31] Like so many others, Peters had great hopes for a better 1919. In his Mayor's New Year's Greeting to Boston, he wrote,

> This is indeed a happy New Year for us all and one which should bring deep satisfaction to every American. . . . To the people of Boston who have stood together so loyally in the past year I send every good wish for a bright and happy New Year.[32]

The year, however, despite his many wishes, proved traumatic for both the people of Boston and himself.

The life of police commissioner Edwin Upton Curtis proved to be very different from that of the mayor. According to a biography of Curtis in *Munsey's Magazine*, "he was born with the proverbial golden spoon, and his taste for public life inherited."[33] Lyons wrote more pointedly, "He personified the Boston Brahmin in politics,"[34] and historian William Allen White wrote far more colorfully when he described Curtis as "one of those solemn, self-sufficient Bostonian heroes who apparently are waiting in the flesh to walk up the steps to a pedestal and be cast into immortal bronze."[35]

Curtis was born on March 26, 1861, in Roxbury, Massachusetts. His parents were George and Martha Ann Curtis, seventh-
generation Bostonians who were well entrenched among the
Boston Brahmin. The *Munsey's Magazine* biography of Curtis
explained, "He comes from an old Boston family, the Curtis
genealogy running back through seven generations to 1630.
All these generations lived within a mile of the homestead in
Roxbury where Mr. Curtis was born."[36] The Curtis estate was
well known among Bostonians at the time, for it had become a
landmark of the community.

Across those seven generations, the Curtis family had been
involved in politics, and George Curtis, his father, served first as
an alderman in Roxbury and then, after the town was annexed
by the city, as an alderman for the city of Boston.[37] It is from his
mother Martha, born an Upton (another of the Boston Brahmin
families), that Curtis derived his middle name.

The times in which Curtis was born were quite different
from the more prosperous times of Peters. Eleven years older,
Curtis was born just three weeks after the inauguration of President Abraham Lincoln and three weeks prior to the Battle of Fort
Sumter. Boston was awash in rallies to support the Union cause;
soon they would be awash in blood.

Growing up, Curtis went by the nickname "Ned," and he
remained so to his close family and friends throughout his life.
After the Civil War he attended the Roxbury Grammar and
Latin School for six years before transferring to the picturesque
Little Blue Family School for Boys in Farmington, Maine. *Munsey's* made note that while there, "he was a champion baseball
player."[38]

Upon graduation, Curtis attended Bowdoin College, a
prestigious private college founded in 1794 and located in
Brunswick, Maine. At the time Curtis attended college, Medal
of Honor recipient and Brigadier General Joshua Chamberlain
served as college president. The *Munsey's* article noted that "At
Bowdoin College he belonged to the boat crew,"[39] and he graduated in 1882.

"From Bowdoin," continues the biography, "he went to
Ex-Governor Gaston's law office in Boston, studied for the bar,

and joined an old school and college friend, William G. Reed, in starting the firm of Curtis & Reed."[40] William Gaston had served as the 21st mayor of Boston from 1871 to 1873 and then as the 29th governor of Massachusetts from 1875 to 1876, after which he returned to the practice of law. At the time that Curtis worked for Gaston, the method by which a person became a lawyer was through the "reading of law," a form of apprenticeship under a practicing attorney. After two years with the Gaston and Whitney law firm, he was admitted to the Suffolk Bar. Curtis then opened his own law practice, Curtis & Reed, with his college friend.

Like Peters, Curtis immediately became interested in politics. "He plunged almost at once into active politics," *Munsey's* explains, "becoming secretary of the Republican city committee, then—at the age of twenty eight—clerk of the municipality, and finally winning a remarkable victory in the battle for the mayoralty."[41] Curtis had not really been interested in the practice of law, for as a close friend of his later wrote, "The things that interested him were things that interested Boston, and in the service of the city he did not spare himself."[42]

Curtis first became involved in the Boston Republican Committee, taking on every responsibility that came his way. In a short time, having built a solid reputation, he ran for the position of secretary and won. From there, he ran for the position of Boston city clerk, for which, after winning, he served a two-year term. He chose not to run for a second term and returned to his law practice. He did this mainly because he was already eyeing the office of mayor, for which he then ran in 1894. It proved to be a bitter fight between the Republican Party and the Democratic political machine, well entrenched at the time, but in the end, Curtis won the day. Covering the election on December 11 that year, the newspapers reported,

> Edwin U. Curtis, Republican candidate for Mayor of Boston, was elected today by a plurality of 2,500. The campaign which thus closes has been one of the most bitter in recent years and personalities have entered into it to an unusual extent. The Republicans have made their fight against the Democratic

machine, which for three years has been intrenched in city hall. The charges of inefficiency and open corruption recently made by the nonpartisan municipal league gave a text for the Republican speakers.[43]

Upon taking the oath of office as the 34th mayor of Boston, Edwin Upton Curtis became the youngest man ever to have been elected to that position. He was 33 years of age, and this was the reason the Curtis biography had appeared in *Munsey's Magazine* in 1896. The article told of his long ties to Boston, noting that he and his father still lived in the family estate. The magazine described him as "only thirty five years old, very tall, and of athletic build."[44]

At the time when Curtis ran for election, the tenure of mayor was still one year, but that was changed to a two-year term for the election of 1896. Curtis naturally chose to run for a second term in office, but he found that his family name among the Boston Brahmin was not going to carry as much weight in his reelection campaign. Martin Lomasney, a staunch Democratic politician who was known as the "political boss" of Boston's West End, was looking for a means of defeating Curtis and returning the mayoral power to the Democrats.[45] He found it, explains historian Reppetto, when he "cleverly persuaded Josiah Quincy, descendant of two Yankee mayors, to run on the Democratic ticket, and Curtis was defeated."[46] This proved to be Curtis's first defeat in an election.

For his one term in office, Curtis chose to focus on reform. When asked what that meant, he is said to have replied, "Reform is Puritanism."[47] As a Boston Brahmin and counting himself among the Yankee Republicans, he saw it as his mission to undo the ministrations of the Democratic political machine and to remove the Irish Catholics from power and, in true Puritan fashion, remove any links with Catholicism. Again, it proved to be a struggle not just over ideology but ethno-nationalism and religion.

One government agency Curtis focused on for such treatment during his tenure was the Boston Police Department. In recognition of its growing ranks of Irish Catholics, Curtis sought to control the organization and sever those ties. The department at that time was highly decentralized with nearly 100 personnel reporting directly to the police commissioner. By centralizing the department, he could make it not only more effective and efficient but easier to control. While he did manage to centralize the police, his limited one year in office afforded him little time to make any lasting impressions on the department.

After losing the mayoral office to Josiah Quincy, Massachusetts Republican governor Frederic T. Greenhalge appointed Curtis as a member of the Metropolitan Park Committee, mainly out of recognition for his service to the Republican Party. It was, in many ways, a dead-end position, for there he was unlikely to gain the visibility necessary for higher, or really any, elected office. Still, he threw himself into the work with his usual disciplinary gusto, and a friend later remarked that while in that office, he did contribute to building "up the park police into a body which still has the impress of his discipline and organizing skill."[48]

Now in a less demanding position, Curtis had more time for a social life. He married Margaret Waterman in 1897 and together they had two children. She came from another of the esteemed Boston families, a family of undertakers.

Curtis remained active in the Republican Party and, as a tireless workhorse, took on all of the duties and responsibilities asked of him. As a result of his dedication, he was recognized by President Theodore Roosevelt's administration and received an appointment as assistant US treasurer in Boston. After Roosevelt's departure from office and the elevation of his chosen successor, William Howard Taft, to the presidency, Curtis was offered a new position—in 1909 he resigned the treasurer's position to become the Collector of Customs for the Port of Boston and Charlestown, a position he held for the next nine years. "His rule at the Custom House," it was noted in *New England Magazine*, was "characterized by strict adherence to the laws, by absolute impartiality in their application, and by business-methods of administration."[49]

With the new appointment, Curtis knew that any chance of reigniting his political aspirations was gone. It proved to be a comfortable, well-paying position, and his life settled into a bureaucratic routine. In 1914 his alma mater, Bowdoin College, bestowed an honorific degree on him in recognition of his public service. He was awarded an LLD, a doctor of law degree.

After nine years with the Custom House, fate had one more career change in store for Curtis. On December 14, 1918, police commissioner Stephen O'Meara passed away. "In spite of his desire to remain in harness," wrote the *Boston Globe*, "it is known that he has not been in the best of health for some time."[50] Although Peters was the mayor and a Democrat, the appointment authority for O'Meara's replacement went to the Massachusetts governor, who at the time was Samuel W. McCall, a Republican. McCall offered Curtis the appointment.

Curtis had already been the mayor of Boston and was sitting comfortably in a good-paying, noncontroversial position, leaving one to wonder his motivations for accepting such a position. Historian Francis Russell explains those motivations as tracing back to the same issues that had motivated Curtis during his tenure as mayor. "His class had governed Boston since the Revolution," Russell explains.

> Now it was being steam-rollered by the second-generation Irish. Curtis despised this new emerging group with its alien religion and its eye for political plunder. . . . That was why in the period of Boston's decline he accepted the office of Police Commissioner from Republican Governor McCall.[51]

Nominated for the position, Curtis was confirmed by the Executive Council on the day before Christmas and was set to take the oath of office on December 30.[52] As it turned out, the governor became ill, and the oath-taking was postponed. On the following day, December 31, 1918, the *Boston Globe* reported, "The oath of office was administered by Governor McCall at 11 o'clock in the Governor's home, Myopia Hill, Winchester, where the Chief Executive has been ill with Influenza."[53] Curtis was now the police commissioner of the Boston Police Department. He was 58.

Although long considered an ideal public servant, he has been described as "stubborn on matters of principle and invincibly courageous."[54] The matters of principle, of course, were those of the Yankee Republican Puritans of the Boston Brahmin elite. And so, as historian White observes, "Curtis brought a baggage load of Yankee elitism and disdain for the Irish."[55] And while he was indeed the police commissioner by appointment, armed with all the authority of the office, as White also points out, "He wanted O'Meara's authority, but he could command none of O'Meara's respect."[56]

Before Curtis even took his oath of office, however, police officer pay was already an issue. In anticipation of the new police commissioner being seated, the *Boston Globe* reported on December 26 that the "Boston policemen are out for a $200 annual increase in their salaries, instead of the $100 increase they formerly sought, and which Mayor Peters promised to try to provide for them."[57] The Boston Social Club met with the mayor in his office for an hour and a half in an attempt to get him to grant the raise, but he demurred.

In reaction to the mayor's stance and knowing that a new police commissioner was about to be seated, members of the Boston Social Club called a meeting of its members on the evening of December 30. "Seven hundred of the 1,200 odd members of the Boston Social Club, the organization of Boston patrolmen, packed Longfellow Hall, Dudley Street, Roxbury," the *Boston Globe* reported the next day, "to listen to more than two hours' discussion of salary demands. And the 700, to a man, voted not to accept less than an increase of $200 a year each."[58] The situation was heating up, and all eyes were now on the new police commissioner.

After he was sworn into office, Curtis made a definitive statement regarding the pay raise. "No increase can be given the Police Department except by the concurrent action of the Mayor and the Police Commissioner. We shall probably consult on the subject at an early date."[59] He then tried to calm the issue by adding that in the meantime, "Everyone should talk and act with moderation in regard to the matter. Knowing the members of the department by reputation, I believe that they will gracefully accept our final decision."[60] This did make sense, for he had just entered office and had yet to sit down with Peters to discuss the issue. However, the description of Curtis being "stubborn on matters of principle" became evident when he poured fuel on the fire by tersely adding, "If, however, any member of the force is so dissatisfied that he cannot continue to discharge his duties faithfully, honestly and cheerfully, he can resign."[61] Needless to say, that statement was not well received by the rank and file.

One of Curtis's other first actions in office was to pen an address to his officers that was reprinted in the newspapers and was designed to be issued as a "plain talk" speech. It was as much a set of instructions for his police officers as it was for citizens, for he told the police to be "gentlemen at all times," while telling the public they should obey the police officer when issuing an order, enforcing the laws, or making an arrest. Ironically (in hindsight), he also advised the police officers about their attitudes toward strikers, saying,

> If, unfortunately, you are called upon to suppress disorder where strikes prevail, you should remember that you are there for one purpose, and one purpose only, namely to preserve the public peace. You should neither sympathize with the employer nor with the employee, but preserve order at any cost.[62]

Press statement and speech out of the way, Commissioner Curtis next issued his first general order to all police officers in the Boston PD. It was to be disbursed the following day at all roll calls, noted his assumption of command, and "advised of the continuation, until otherwise ordered, of the rules and regulations governing the department."[63] Curtis, not yet police commissioner for 24 hours, was already digging in his heels.

Historian William A. White described Curtis as a "large, serious man, addicted to long double breasted coats, and with a reserve which passed easily for dignity in the pre–Civil War era."[64] More pointedly, he expounded upon the core of Curtis's own philosophical being when he wrote that he "embodied the spirit of traditional inherited wealth, traditional inherited Republicanism, traditional inherited skepticism about the capacity of democracy for self-government and a profound faith in the propertied classes' ultimate right to rule."[65]

Curtis was certainly a Boston Brahmin, but Boston governance had moved away from the traditional, old-school means of power to a newer, more progressive means, largely held by the Irish. Curtis refused to either see this or acknowledge it, believing that his ways were the right ways and that he would ultimately prevail. Added to this, Lyons writes that, "His judgement of human behavior outside his own class seems to have been poor; and until the strike he clung steadfastly to the belief that most of the police would remain loyal."[66] Again, he would be proven wrong.

There was, however, one more added complexity when Edwin Upton Curtis assumed the police commissioner's post. Very few people knew at the time, and would only learn after the strike, that Curtis had a potentially deadly case of angina pectoris and had been advised not to take the position of police commissioner but, rather, to retire. He refused. "He was hardly in the place when he was stricken by the first of the attacks which at least brought the end," a friend later wrote. "Few knew at the time, for he did not complain, but set himself to carry out the plan he had in view to make the body under his control the model force which it has now become."[67] Curtis proved defiant to the end.

These two men at the city level of governance, Andrew James Peters and Edwin Upton Curtis, played the most significant role in the lead up to and during the Boston Police Strike, and they both paid a price for their involvement, each in his own manner. There was, however, one other man who would play the most important role in the Boston Police Strike, and who would come to gain from it substantially. That was the man who was soon to replace Governor Samuel W. McCall—his own lieutenant governor and the incoming governor for the State of Massachusetts: Calvin Coolidge.

Calvin Coolidge taking the oath of office as the 48th Governor of the Commonwealth of Massachusetts.
Photo courtesy of the Calvin Coolidge Presidential Library & Museum, Forbes Library.

6

Governor Calvin Coolidge

Francis Russell, who authored the first history of the Boston Police Strike, wrote an earlier article of the strike for *American Heritage* magazine, "The Strike That Made a President."[1] It was his belief, and rightly so, that the person who benefited the most from the Boston Police Strike of 1919 was none other than Governor Calvin Coolidge. This strike launched him onto the national stage of politics, ushered him into the office of the vice presidency, and, after President Harding's unexpected death, into the presidency itself. When considering Coolidge's entire life and his continual progression upward in political office, perhaps the presidency seems a foregone conclusion in hindsight, but Russell asserts his career progression would most likely have ended as governor if not for the strike. Since Calvin Coolidge played perhaps the most critical role in the Boston Police Strike, it is to his life this chapter now turns.

Calvin Coolidge was born in what is generally referred to as Plymouth, Vermont. "The town of Plymouth lies on the easterly slope of the Green Mountains," Coolidge wrote in his brief auto-biography, "about twenty miles west of the Connecticut River and somewhat south of the central part of Vermont."[2] One of his biographers, Amity Shlaes, explains, "Their new 'citty' was really a chain of hamlets: Plymouth Notch, Plymouth Union,

Plymouth Kingdom, and others with settlements that had been given less obvious names—Frog City, for example."[3] Coolidge was born in the hamlet of Plymouth Notch. J. W. Stickney, a friend of the Coolidge family, gave an idyllic description of the small hamlet:

> In Plymouth there are no large villages; the population is widely scattered among its hills; the churches are too small to make trouble with one another and too weak to have troubles among themselves—which gives the town a quietude unknown to places of strong churches with large memberships. The absence of railroads, and of a foreign population consequent upon railroad towns, is escaped, and no real cause exists here for trouble.[4]

"It was into this community that I was born on the 4th day of July, 1872," wrote Coolidge, being the only president born on that celebratory day, although Thomas Jefferson, John Adams, and James Monroe all died on Independence Day.[5] Celebrating the anniversary of America's birth was an important day in Plymouth Notch, for it was one "the village marked with festivals and an annual game: the men of Plymouth Notch stole an old cannon; the men of Plymouth Union stole it back."[6]

According to his birth certificate, he was born John Calvin Coolidge Jr., named for his father and grandfather, but the designation of junior was never used, and rarely ever was John used, to avoid confusing his name with his father's.[7] "While they intended to name me for my father," Coolidge explained in his autobiography, "they always called me Calvin, so the John became discarded."[8]

Coolidge's father, John Calvin Coolidge Sr., was born on March 31, 1845, in the same town. He served in the Vermont militia, advancing to the rank of colonel, and was active in Plymouth and Vermont politics, rising from a member of the Plymouth Selectboard (1869–1872) to the Vermont Senate (1910–1912). Throughout this time period, he ran the local country store, and Coolidge believed "he was successful."[9] In addition to running the store, Coolidge recalled, "My father was nearly all his life a Constable or a Deputy Sheriff, and sometimes both, with power to serve civil and criminal process, so that he arrested those charged with crime and brought them before the Justice for trial."[10] Still further, at times, he served as "Justice of the Peace and he always maintained a commission as a notary public.[11] As Shlaes notes, John Calvin Coolidge Sr. was "everything a man could be in a town."[12]

Coolidge's mother, Victoria Josephine Moor, was born on March 14, 1846. She had known John Coolidge as a neighbor and, after attending the Black River Academy for one year, they married and set up house. She tended the garden, cooked, sewed, helped with her husband's country store, and raised their two children, for in addition to Calvin, Abigail Gratia Coolidge was born almost three years later, on April 15, 1875.

Coolidge's mother suffered much of her life from what was then known as consumption, the greatly feared and dreaded disease of pulmonary tuberculosis. She kept a brave face throughout the illness, but as she neared her 39th birthday, she knew she was going to lose the battle against the disease. Coolidge, in his autobiography, recalled what she did next:

> When she knew that her end was near she called us children to her bedside, where we knelt down to receive her final parting blessing. In an hour she was gone. It was her thirty-ninth birthday. I was twelve years old. . . . Life was never to seem the same again.[13]

She died on March 14, 1885.

Unfortunately, another tragedy awaited the Coolidge family just five years later, almost to the day, when Abigail, who was 14 at the time, suddenly suffered from appendicitis, and after having been "ill scarcely a week," died on March 6, 1890.[14] Before Calvin Coolidge had entered adulthood, he had lost both his mother and his sister.

His father remarried on September 9, 1891, for after his wife and daughter had died, he found himself alone with only Calvin on his visits from school. The lady he married, Caroline Athelia Brown, had been one of Calvin's elementary school teachers.[15] Such is life in a small hamlet.

It is with this backdrop that Coolidge grew up quickly, reaching his full height of 5 feet, 9 inches, with a very slight build. His facial features were well chiseled, and he is described as having had "a narrow pointed nose, cleft chin, small deeply set blue eyes, and thin pursed lips."[16] He had been born with red hair, but as he aged it turned to a sandy color. He spoke with the speech pattern common to the New England area, a sort of nasal twang that was smattered with local colloquialisms and sayings, which were excised from his vocabulary as he rose in politics. He was nearly always a burst of energy and walked in short, quick steps.

Calvin was never the outgoing type and was described as "shy, undemonstrative, restrained, cautious, wholly self-reliant, and a man of few friends."[17] From the earliest age, it became clear that he was to follow in his father's footsteps by becoming an asset to his town, for as his biographer Shlaes writes, "the entire Coolidge clan focused on training this new son to take his place as a citizen in the Vermont community."[18]

In many ways, Coolidge's education began with his life in the country and his work on the farm, for as he later wrote, "Country life does not always have breadth, but it has depth. It is neither artificial nor superficial, but is kept close to the realities."[19] He was required to perform many chores around the house to help the family, and in so doing learned a variety of skills, including cabinetmaking and even quilting. His father was always proud of his accomplishments, including his success at one of the quintessential Vermont traditions, the gathering of maple sap. "Young Calvin," his father proudly boasted, "could get more sap out of a maple tree than the other boys around here."[20]

His more formal education began when he attended the local elementary schools in Plymouth from ages 5 to 13. Reflecting back on his earliest education, one of his teachers recalled, "He was not an inquisitive boy."[21] She explained that Coolidge "seldom asked for an explanation of anything we had in hand," because "he seemed to understand every question that came up in class. He always seemed to be thinking of something."[22] Coolidge remained introspective throughout his life, although that did not mean he was withdrawn; in his own manner, he was always highly engaged.

Like his mother, Coolidge was sent to the Black River Academy to further his education and prepare for college. Located in Ludlow, Vermont, the academy had been chartered in 1835. A popular anecdote is recounted of Coolidge Senior taking his son to the new school. They had traveled there in the family buggy, and Calvin's father, ever the efficient person, decided to take a calf along to sell in Boston after he dropped off his son. They spoke little along the way, neither being the talkative type, but when they arrived at their destination, his father looked at his son and told him, "Well, good-bye Cal. You may some day, if you work hard, get to Boston. But this calf's going to beat you there."[23]

Coolidge did not have a successful first year at the academy, in part because the level of work was far more difficult than his previous schooling, but mostly his lack of accomplishment was due to being homesick.[24] Whenever he was lonely, which was often, he would walk the four miles to spend time with his aunt and uncle who lived in nearby Proctorsville. He spent a good amount of time there, which helped improve his spirits. He also worked some Saturdays in a nearby town that had a small toy factory, earning money for his expenses, while at the same time gaining some early experience in American industrialization.

Coolidge, as was his nature, did not participate in many of the activities in which the other children were involved. One childhood acquaintance remembered how "he didn't play ball or skate nor did he hunt, swim or fish, or go in for any sports, except that he walked every day."[25] In addition, because "Calvin's favorite avocation was reading," he spent much of his time in the local library, and, as his friend also recalled, he spent so much time there that he read "every book in it."[26]

One story that is recalled from his time at the academy is indicative of how much he kept to himself. In his biography of Coolidge, *A Puritan in Babylon*, William Allen White explained that a group of the boys he lived with pulled a prank by tying a rope around the leg of a stove in the upper-floor classroom and dragging it down the stairs. The leaders were caught, but the professors were looking to see who else was involved. They inquired of Coolidge, who was sleeping in his bed at the time, if he had heard the noise. He replied that he had. When asked, "Why didn't you do something, give the alarm?" he replied, "It wa'n't my stove!"[27]

He graduated from the academy in the spring of 1890, in a class of "five boys and four girls."[28] He then took the entrance exams for entrance into Amherst College and, unexpectedly, failed them. Coolidge was then enrolled in a college preparatory program at St. Johnsbury Academy, founded in 1842 and located in the town it was named for. The school was one of the leading preparatory schools, located within 90 miles of Plymouth, where Amherst was located, and was a common feeder program into the college. He spent just a little more than two months there when the headmaster certified him for admission into college.[29]

That fall he began his baccalaureate studies. However, as Amity Shlaes explains in her biography of Coolidge, "No freshman in the history of Amherst College seemed less likely to succeed than John Calvin Coolidge, class of 1895."[30] In addition to failing his first attempt at admission, when he did finally arrive at the college, he had a cold that turned into bronchitis, and the new student missed his first battery of tests. He struggled with the academics at Amherst, highlighting the fact he had clearly not been adequately prepared for college.

Coolidge's course load would easily overwhelm any college student of today, but then again, that was the very reason it had produced so many successful graduates. Ralph Waldo Emerson spoke highly of the college, once stating "the infant college is an infant Hercules" and that "never was so much striving, outstretching, and advancing in a literary cause as is exhibited here," for the students "write, speak, and study in a sort of fury, which, I think, promises a harvest of attainments."[31] The college set high standards and expected its students to live up to them.

Perhaps reflective of his academic difficulties, one of the first things Coolidge recalls in his autobiography about this part of his life was, "Not the least in the educational values of Amherst was its beautiful physical surroundings."[32] Despite the need for more studying, he still went for many long walks in the countryside. The subject that plagued him the most was physics—he only managed a D in the class—but he also had difficulties with the languages. And although he excelled at math, it has been noted that his "favorite instructor was philosophy professor Charles E. Garman, who greatly influenced Coolidge's social values and encouraged his interest in public service."[33]

Already interested in politics because of his father, Coolidge closely followed the upcoming 1892 presidential election and, after throwing his support behind Harrison, he joined the Republican Club on campus. "Coolidge was never a joiner," explains Sobel, one of Coolidge's many biographers, "Even though it would have been useful politically and professionally, as an adult, but he never became a Mason, an Elk, a Red Man, and Odd Fellow, or a member of any other fraternal organization."[34] Still, he put all of this aside and became part of Amherst's Republican Club and, as Shlaes explains, "Politics inspired Coolidge to begin to speak publicly."[35]

It was not so much his involvement in the Republican Club as it was his interest in politics that led him, with his quiet and introspective personality, to gravitate toward public speaking. And when that happened, something changed in him—he began to flourish. While no one expected much from him as he stood before the student body and spoke, one classmate recalled, "The class had the surprise of its life. He spoke cogently, fluently and with a good sense of humor and won his case hands down. It was as if a new and gifted man had joined the class."[36] Indeed, he so excelled at speaking that, in his junior year, he won the J. Wesley Ladd prize for best oration, and just prior to graduation, he earned the right to deliver one of the commencement addresses.[37]

Coolidge competed in his senior year to be one of the "Grove Orators," one of six who would deliver a class address.[38] He was selected to speak and was designated to give the humorous speech. Coolidge delivered in a monotone voice what—in today's parlance—would be called a roasting of both faculty and students. "While my effort was not without some success," he wrote in his autobiography, he did bring about peals of laughter from his audience; however, "I very soon learned that making fun of people in a public way was not a good method to secure friends, or likely to lead to much advancement, and I have scrupulously avoided it."[39]

Still further, for his senior essay, he wrote on "The Principles Fought for in the American Revolution," and it was entered into a national contest sponsored by the Sons of the American Revolution. He won first prize and received a $150 gold medal for his efforts.[40] On graduation day the introspective boy who struggled at first walked across the stage with cum laude honors, only missing admittance into Phi Beta Kappa "by a hair."[41]

While his fellow students remembered him fondly, it seems no one thought he would ever amount to much. One of the other class leaders, Jay Stocking, offered these insights into what he thought of Coolidge at the time:

> I was not one of those who expected Coolidge to have any spectacular career. I did not think he would become famous. The last place in the world I should have expected him to succeed was politics. He lacked small talk, and he was never known, I suspect, to slap a man on the back. He rarely laughed. He was anything but a mixer. The few who got in personal contact with him had to go the whole way.[42]

After graduation, Coolidge moved to Northampton, Massachusetts, where he "read law" in the law office of Hammond & Field (John C. Hammond and Henry P. Field), both of whom were also Amherst alumni. In addition to teaching him the law and its practice, they gave Coolidge insights into politics, for shortly after he joined the law firm, Hammond was elected local district attorney and Field became the mayor of the city.

Someone once asked Field why he had given Coolidge the job in his law firm, to which he replied, "I liked to laugh and Calvin Coolidge was very funny."[43] It seems that this was highly reflective of Coolidge's more personal side. However, after seeing the professional side of Coolidge around the law office, it left Field to remark, "I guess we've added the Sphinx to our staff."[44]

After studying the law for two years, Coolidge took the bar exam on June 29, 1897, passed, and was admitted. He remained with Hammond & Field for the rest of the year, after which he began searching for a place to open his own law office. "I was looking about for a place to locate," he wrote in his autobiography, "but found none that seemed better than Northampton."[45] There was a new Masonic building under construction on Main Street and, when it was ready for occupancy, he wrote, "I opened an office there February 1, 1898. I had two rooms, where I was to continue to practice law for twenty-one years, until I became Governor of Massachusetts in 1919."[46] Coolidge had chosen to practice commercial law, for it was his belief that he would be doing his job if he could keep his clients and himself out of the courtroom; this suited his personality perfectly.

Right from the very beginning, as he settled into his practice, Coolidge took an interest in politics. At the time, Northampton was staunchly Republican, and he naturally gravitated to that political party.[47] He quickly became active in the party and its campaigns, and in 1897 he received his first political reward for his efforts: selection for a seat on the Republican City Committee for Ward 2. The following year he was sent to serve as a delegate at the Republican State Convention.[48]

In the fall of 1898, Coolidge ran for his first elected position, a seat on the common council, which he won in December. The following year he chose not to run for a second term; the position was costing him so much in time and money, he often found himself having to ask his father to help make ends meet. In addition, he was eyeing the position of city solicitor. His father was supportive of his political endeavors and always "complied and never complained."[49] When the solicitor position became available, Coolidge ran for the position, won, and served a one-year term. He then ran for reelection and served until March 1902.

As Northampton's city solicitor, Coolidge began building experience as a lawyer, and this helped him greatly with his finances, for unlike the common council position, it actually paid a salary. The other benefit as solicitor was the training he received for, as Coolidge noted, it "gave me a good grasp of municipal law that later brought some important cases to me."[50]

However, before returning to his own practice, a new opportunity arose when a member of the local courts died, and Coolidge was appointed to fill the vacancy. He became the clerk of court for Hampshire County, where he kept the civil and criminal records for the county courts. The position was another salaried one, earning him the unprecedented amount of $2,300 a year. But he felt that his exposure from having been city solicitor was bringing him more clients and realized he could make more money in his private practice. After a year he returned to his law office, since the city solicitor position did not allow him to continue practicing law.

Although he was back to earning money as a lawyer, Coolidge still wanted to keep his hands in the political game, so in 1904 he ran for a seat on the Northampton school board, running against an Irishman, John J. Kennedy. It very well may have been the most difficult campaign of his career since it seemed his opponent had all the advantages. Despite his opponent needling him on the issues of the day, Coolidge had learned to not insult or attack anyone. When the cocksure Kennedy told him, "Calvin, I think I've got you beaten," Coolidge diplomatically replied, "Either way, they'll get a good man."[51] In the end he lost by less than a hundred votes. It proved to be his only defeat at the ballot box. A neighbor willingly told him that the reason he had not voted for Coolidge was that it was a school board post and Coolidge had no children. Coolidge, with his usual subtle humor, did not miss a beat when he replied, "Might give me time."[52]

After Kennedy took office, Coolidge believed he was doing a good job, and taking the high road, he openly praised Kennedy. As his biographer Shlaes explains, this was an important realization for him, "that attack politics yielded poor results."[53] "The best way to win," he had come to believe, "was to stick to the issues and forgo any personal attacks or name-calling. Civility would be his rule from now on."[54] He decided he would give this philosophy a test run in his next campaign.

In the meantime Coolidge did live up to his request to "give me time," for it was during that year when he met Grace Anna Goodhue.[55] She had graduated from the University of Vermont in 1902 and went to work at the Clarke School for Hearing and Speech in Northampton. They met at a banquet honoring the 250th anniversary of the town that was put on by the Daughters of the American Revolution. They were soon dating, "streetcar rides, picnics, church socials, walks, and the like," writes biographer Sobel.[56] "They must have seemed an unlikely pair. Grace was quick to smile and laugh, while Coolidge was tight-lipped and not given to banter, sometimes cranky, and, in public at least, undemonstrative."[57]

In the spring of 1905, Coolidge appeared one day at the house of Grace's father. Surprised at finding him in his living room, Mr. Goodhue said, "Hello Calvin," and asked, "What are you doing in Burlington?" Got some business here?"[58] "No," came Coolidge's reply, "Came up to marry Grace." Her father looked at Calvin and asked, "Why, have you spoke to her yet?" to which Coolidge quickly replied, "No, I can wait a few days if it's any convenience to you." And with that, Coolidge asked Grace to marry him. They were engaged throughout that summer and into the fall, and on October 4, 1905, they were married in the same living room in Burlington, Vermont.

Calvin and Grace Coolidge soon had two sons, John, born on September 7, 1906, and Calvin Jr., born on April 13, 1908. John lived a long life, passing away in 2000, while Calvin Jr. died during Coolidge's campaign for president in 1924.

The campaign that gave Coolidge the opportunity to test his new rule of civility was for a seat in the Massachusetts House of Representatives, referred to as the General Court in that state. The campaign in the fall of 1906 coincided with the birth of his first child, and his new civility rule won the day—he captured the seat and took office on January 2, 1907. It was not, however, the pledge not to demean his opponent that won him election. It was simply that he had not only won the Republican votes but had managed to capture a fair amount of the Democratic vote as well. This would prove to be of great assistance to him in his future elections.

While serving in the General Court, Coolidge quickly found himself under the advantageous wing of Winthrop Murray

Crane, a senator and former Massachusetts governor. Crane had become widely known for successfully defusing a Teamsters strike while governor and was brought in by President Roosevelt to help defuse the Coal Strike of 1902. His mentoring relationship with Crane helped boost Coolidge's standing within the General Court.

In 1907, with Crane's support, Coolidge ran for a second legislative term and won, serving on the General Court until January 6, 1909. "When the session of 1908 ended," explains Shlaes, "Coolidge decided he would not run again that year, in part to spend time with the new baby and John [his other son], in part to scare up some cash."[59] Despite his success in politics and his somewhat modest success in his law practice, he was still dependent on remittances from his father. Coolidge Jr. was certainly no spendthrift, but he simply had too many expenses that were not covered by his political position. Although his law practice compensated him more than the political offices, as Shlaes noted, "Lawyering did not compensate for the fun of the political chase."[60]

At this time, however, the serving Northampton mayor, a Democrat, decided to step down, and Coolidge, naturally, decided to run for the position. The campaign took place in the summer and fall of 1909, and on Election Day he once again won over a number of Democrats to his side, thus winning the election. Coolidge obtained 1,597 votes to his Democratic opponent's 1,409 and became the 16th mayor of Northampton.[61] The local newspaper, the *Gazette*, praised Coolidge for securing the mayoral seat, stating, "Congratulations, cool Calvin!"[62] This was the first known use of what came to be Coolidge's sobriquet, "Cool Cal."

Upon winning the election for mayor, Coolidge became the consummate politician, for as he explained, "On the first Monday of January, 1910, I began a public career that was to continue until the first Monday of March, 1929, when it was to end by my own volition."[63] He remained in political office until he chose to step down after serving the remainder of Warren G. Harding's term in office and one of his own as president of the United States.

"The mayor's job suited him," writes biographer Shlaes, for "he found executive oversight less enervating than negotiation."[64] It seems he did prove successful as the city's mayor, for as political biographer DeGregorio explains, "During his two terms as mayor, Coolidge cut taxes and partially retired the city's debt while at the same time expanding the police and fire departments and upgrading sidewalks and streets."[65] Indeed, he reduced the city debt by $90,000, and it should be added that he managed to run "the city without issuing a single bond for borrowed money."[66]

As was becoming his custom, Coolidge ran again for election and won. Still, having served in the General Court, Coolidge believed it was time for him to return to Boston.[67] While there were no term limits on the mayor's position, tradition and his own ethics dictated he should only serve two terms in office, so in the fall of 1911, he ran for a seat in the Massachusetts Senate. "He campaigned all over Hampshire County, even in Amherst," writes Shlaes, explaining that it "meant another half year of weekdays in Boston," but that "To sit in the Senate was an elevation."[68]

Coolidge began his tenure on January 3, 1912. The Massachusetts Senate was composed of only 40 members, so it is not surprising that Coolidge was placed on numerous committees and became chair of two—the Committee on Legal Affairs and the Committee on Agriculture. In his first term, he remained active but largely behind the scenes. In his second term, as Coolidge simply states, "I began to be a force in the Massachusetts Legislature."[69]

His rise in stature was, in some ways, foisted upon him by national politics and Theodore Roosevelt's form of statecraft that effectively divided the Republican Party. Coolidge saw himself as a Progressive Republican, and that may very well have been the case. As his biographer Shlaes highlights, Coolidge "voted for women's suffrage, the state income tax, a minimum wage for female workers, and salary increases for teachers, thereby preempting territory before Democrats or other new candidates might get to it."[70] Still, he had inclinations tracing back to his roots that made him more of a Populist Republican, for he adhered closer to his agrarian-farmer roots and freedom from the tyranny of government and big business. As it was, certain events were beginning to cause him to make decisions that would run up against his Progressive ways.

The Lawrence Textile strike began on January 1, 1912, when workers at the American Woolen Company in Lawrence, Massachusetts, announced they were walking off the job. This strike predated the Boston Police Strike by seven years. The woolen company workers were protesting a new Progressive law that created a wage reduction for workers at that factory. The law was aligned with a new radical union, the International Workers of the World, known simply as the Wobblies. As a result of this ruling, the workers kept their word—they walked out.[71] Of the more than 32,000 workers in the company's mills, 14,000 employees walked out of the Lawrence facility, and other workers began to unite around their cause.[72]

The Senate decided to form a special committee to attempt negotiating an end to the strike, and Coolidge's political mentor, Winthrop Murray Crane, placed Coolidge as the chairman, which Shales explains was "an honor and an opportunity" that allowed Coolidge to "retrace Murray Crane's footsteps as a labor go-between."[73] While Coolidge accepted the challenge, it would not prove easy, for what made the strike so unique was the fact it was being led by women and, in time, it came to be known as the "Bread and Roses Strike" because all the women said they wanted "was decent conditions and higher wages so that they might live—bread and roses."[74]

The first problem Coolidge faced was the lack of a counterpart with whom to negotiate, so he began talking and cajoling workers to form their own committee so his special committee could sit down at the table with them. "Somehow, by March," writes Shlaes, "Coolidge reported that he had sealed a strike deal."[75] He had navigated the popular sentiment, the petty politics, the violent acts, and the cynical workers to iron out a deal that met the demand for a wage increase in trade if the workers would return to their industrial sewing machines.[76] Despite his success, however, he was greatly disturbed by what he saw coming from the union leaders. In a letter to his stepmother, he explained to her, "The leaders there are socialists and anarchists, and they do not want anybody to work for wages. The trouble is not about the amount of wages; it is a small attempt to destroy all authority, whether of any church or government."[77]

In light of his success with the strike and the support of Crane, Coolidge easily won a second term as state senator, and he made himself an important asset to both the workings of the Senate and those of the Republican Party. As had become Coolidge's practice, he had intended to step down after a second term in office, but the president of the Senate was planning to run for lieutenant governor, so Coolidge decided to stay one more year in the hope of serving as the Senate president. After securing the third term, he began lining up votes in the Senate to become its president. It was then he learned that the incumbent president was not leaving to become lieutenant governor, and he was in a quandary over what to do. Coolidge decided to stay in the race for president of the Senate and, once again, the fact he managed to pick up both Democratic and Progressive votes, as well as those from a divided Republican Party, placed him at the head of the Massachusetts Senate.

"The office of President of the Senate is one of great dignity and power," Coolidge wrote in his autobiography. "All the committees of the Senate are appointed by him. He has the chief place in directing legislation when the Governor is of the opposite party" (which he was, since Governor Walsh was a Democrat).[78] His rapid elevation to this important position had everyone talking about how far Coolidge would possibly go, but they also "saw too what Coolidge himself did not yet see: that he was becoming more conservative."[79] While he may not have noted it at the time, he did recognize it later in his autobiography, writing, "In taking the chair as President of the Senate I therefore made a short address, which I had carefully prepared, appealing to the conservative spirit of the people."[80]

What should have been a time of victory celebration, however, turned to tragedy when Coolidge's son, Calvin Jr., contracted pneumonia and was taken to the hospital.[81] At first, the circumstances looked bleak, but he soon began to recover and was brought home just in time for Christmas. Sadly, however,

Calvin Jr. died in 1924 at the age of 16 from blood poisoning brought about by sepsis from a blister he had developed while playing tennis.

Once he took office as the president of the Senate on January 7, 1914, Coolidge found himself dealing more with party business rather than with that of the state.[82] This came about because the Republicans had split after President Roosevelt ran under the Progressive Party banner, thus causing Republicans to have to choose supporting either Taft or Roosevelt. After Taft won reelection, those who had supported Roosevelt found themselves outside the party. Fellow Republicans had found it difficult to accept them for their handing the presidency to Democrat Woodrow Wilson, so Coolidge spent much of his time trying to bring the Progressive Republicans back into the fold. In light of his movement between these two arms of the Republican Party, he may well have been the best man for the job.

"When I went home at the end of the 1915 session," Coolidge writes in his autobiography, "it was with the intention of remaining in private life and giving all my attention to the law."[83] However, his name had come up as a possible candidate for the lieutenant governor's position. Republican Samuel W. McCall had attempted to run for governor against Democratic incumbent David I. Walsh in 1914, but he lost. There was a Progressive Party candidate on the ballot who took votes from McCall and split the vote; this led to McCall's defeat. The Republicans nominated McCall again in 1915, and this time he won. To help balance the Republican ticket, Coolidge was put forth as the lieutenant governor candidate.

After accepting the nod, Coolidge began campaigning in the primary against Guy Ham, a Boston lawyer and Progressive Republican who fashioned himself after Theodore Roosevelt.[84] This was the first time Coolidge had to campaign statewide, but he found it relatively easy due to the proliferation and refinement of the automobile, although he had never bothered to purchase his own.[85] "Coolidge's own tactic was simple, and he stuck to it," explains Shlaes, "backing up McCall as he backed up the party."[86] All of Coolidge's energy went into explaining to the electorate why McCall should be reelected, while there was little attention given to him personally. In the end he won the primary—McCall defeated his opponent in the state election by about 6,000 votes, and Coolidge garnered more than 52,000 votes over his Democratic opponent.[87] "I have no doubt that my being on the ticket elevated Mr. McCall," he wrote his father in a letter.[88] The Republicans took the governor's office as well as the Massachusetts House and Senate, leading the *Daily Hampshire Gazette* to comment, like his father, that "Calvin Coolidge is the great vote-getter, and will be governor in time."[89]

"The office of Lieutenant-Governor of Massachusetts differs from that of most states," explained Coolidge, for "he does not preside over the Senate. The constitution of our Commonwealth is older than the Federal Constitution and so followed the old colonial system."[90] In that position Coolidge managed his business well; both he and McCall ran for reelection in 1916, both winning by an even greater margin. Coolidge again dominated in the votes for, as biographer Sobel writes, "Not only did he outpoll McCall, but he received more votes than any other statewide candidate."[91] McCall and Coolidge repeated this feat again in 1917.

Throughout his three terms as lieutenant governor, Coolidge was loyal to McCall, almost to a fault. To every constituent who thanked him for some service or another, he always advised that person that McCall deserved the thanks, since he was simply the governor's "temporary agent."[92] Despite this, as Coolidge later wrote, "It was no secret that I desired to be Governor," adding that "Under the custom of promotion in Massachusetts a man who did not expect to advance would scarcely be willing to be Lieutenant-Governor. But I did nothing in the way of organizing my friends to secure the nomination."[93] Regardless, when McCall decided not to run again, Coolidge seized the opportunity and campaigned in the fall of 1918 against Democratic businessman Richard H. Long.

Coolidge ran on McCall's record and did not engage in petty politics, as he had long ago vowed to do. However, Long was more than willing to criticize McCall's record and his lieutenant governor. There is little doubt this hurt Coolidge, for in all his recent elections he was garnering the most votes and winning by a wide margin. This time, it was a close election, being the smallest margin of any statewide campaign at that time.[94] He had a plurality of only 17,000 votes.

Still, he won the election on November 5, and his timing proved fortuitous because on November 11, the armistice ended the Great War. Governor Calvin Coolidge took office as the 48th governor of Massachusetts on January 2, 1919. However, despite his own victory and that of the nation, the times proved tumultuous because of those very same victories. "While the war was done," Coolidge explained, "its problems were to confront the state and nation for many years. I was to meet them as Governor and President."[95] He wrote this in 1929, adding that "They will remain with us for two generations. Such is the curse of war."[96] He was correct.

Throughout the war Massachusetts had spent liberally, but this proved the first thing that needed to change. "Reversing the spending would be difficult," wrote Shlaes, for "the war was being taken as a progressive victory. The old way of life was changing. Some of the useful old knowledge was being lost."[97] Coolidge spent much of his first months in office making appointments to the many posts he needed to fill, mostly made to those loyal to the Republican Party, although he avoided making appointments to past friends, perhaps with the hope of forging new allies. He was ever the practical, efficient, and taciturn politician.

There was, however, another side to Calvin Coolidge—one that was not often seen. Author Francis Russell's father used to tell him that Coolidge was "the laziest man who was ever Governor of Massachusetts" and how "he'd sit in his office smoking a cigar. In the afternoon he used to take naps."[98] This appears to be true, for he had a penchant for Cuban cigars and because of health reasons, he often slept nine hours at night and took a two-hour nap every afternoon.[99] It was well known that he kept his silence, which many considered a demonstration of his ignorance. Yet, it seems he held the belief that it was far better to listen than to talk, which was highlighted in a profile of Coolidge as governor in the magazine *Current Opinion* that recounted this anecdote:

The Governor has a homegoing habit of adjourning to Northampton when his presence is not required in Boston, and on alighting from the train generally walks to his modest residence. Above the fireplace in the parlor is a little framed legend which may or may not have a bearing on his character. It reads:

> A wise old owl lived in an oak,
> The more he saw the less he spoke,
> The less he spoke the more he heard,
> Why can't we be like that old bird?[100]

Coolidge also held the belief that doing nothing was often better than doing something because the latter, he believed, usually created more problems. As historian Lyons explained, "One of the tenets upon which his political philosophy rested was to keep out of a controversy until the properly designated subordinate had failed to cope with the problem."[101] This is highlighted in what President Coolidge once told Herbert Hoover when he was the secretary of commerce: "Mr. Hoover, if you see ten troubles coming down the road, you can be sure that nine will run into the ditch before they reach you and you have to battle with only one of them."[102] Many, however, confused his lack of speech and his presumed laziness as an inability to action, but as Lyons also explained, when Coolidge was "forced to act he did so vigorously and without hesitation."[103]

When Calvin Coolidge was elevated to the position of governor at the beginning of 1919, there was no possible way for him to have known what awaited him in the fall of that year. In addition to making appointments and reorganizing the administration with an eye toward fiscal savings, Coolidge found himself immersed in a multitude of issues (mostly resulting from the war) including the fear of Bolshevism, the revival of the Ku Klux Klan, the Red Scare, the threat of riots, and the growing tensions between workers and businesses. All of these challenges were being played out in the form of the rapid growth of unions and the use of the labor strike. The Police Strike, although the most significant, was only one among many.

Samuel Gompers, founder and president of the American Federation of Labor.
Photo courtesy of the Library of Congress.

7

The Call for Unionization

The call for police unionization in America slowly developed from the founding of the American Federation of Labor (AFL) in 1886 until the AFL voted to allow police unions in the summer of 1919. Equally slow was the development of a police union within the Boston Police Department. Although Police Commissioner O'Meara had allowed the formation of the Boston Social Club in 1906, it was expressly *not* to be used for the purposes of collective bargaining.[1] Still, it had become a means by which the Boston patrolmen could share their grievances with the administration, so when the AFL allowed police officers to join their union, the policemen of the Boston Police Department had a ready-made organization by which to do so. It was the confluence of these events in the summer of 1919 that led the Boston patrolmen to consider affiliating with the AFL.

During the Colonial Era, Americans had followed the English practice of using trade guilds as a means for protecting workers. These guilds dated back as far as the Roman Empire but were not mainstays of Western civilization until the High Middle Ages; they remained the sole means of protecting workers until the Industrial Revolution.[2] As the size and number of American industries grew in the late 19th century, businesses were in greater need of labor, which was supplied by the ever-increasing numbers of immigrants coming to America from the Old World. As trade unions became common in Europe, immigrant workers in the United States looked for the same form of protective organizations. However, they did not find American businesses open to the concept and began organizing in order to represent worker interests and to advocate for change; some of the more extreme organized to demand change through force, threats, intimidation, and violence.[3] The man who came to the forefront and created a formal type of organization was a cigar maker by the name of Samuel Gompers.

Born in London, England, on January 27, 1850, the son of Solomon Gumpertz, a cigar maker, young Samuel was destined to follow in his father's footsteps.[4] Despite showing signs of being an astute student, he left school at the age of 10 to begin his apprenticeship as a cigar maker. "When I left school I stood third to the highest in my class," recalled Gompers in his autobiography, and his teacher "told father that it was wrong to rob me of an education, particularly as I showed ability."[5] It seems, however, there was little his father could do since the family was too poor and needed Samuel to work to help make ends meet. Still, even that did not prove to be enough, and the family did what so many other impoverished families did in the late 19th century: They moved to America.

Solomon Gumpertz arrived in New York in 1863 when Samuel was 13 years old and found contract work rolling cigars at home. Samuel helped his father, and in his spare time, the boy formed a debate club with some friends to help develop his public speaking skills; he thirsted for more education. The following year Samuel joined the Cigar Makers Local Union No. 15 and began a cigar-making career in his own right, one independent of his father, by securing work outside of home in a cigar shop.

"Any kind of an old loft served as a cigar shop," Gompers recalled, noting that wherever it happened to be located, the workers "were always dusty from the tobacco stems and powdered leaves."[6] "Each workman supplied his own cutting board of lignum vitae and knife blade," he continued, describing how "the craftsmanship of the cigarmaker was shown in his ability to utilize wrappers to the best advantage to shave off the unusable to a hairbreadth, to roll so as to cover holes in the leaf and to use both hands so as to make a perfectly shaped and rolled product."[7] To produce a good enough income, the work was tedious and the hours were long, but to while away time, they talked and often selected one worker to read from a book, sharing a portion of their cigars with him so he, too, could earn his keep. "The fellowship that grew between congenial shop mates," Gompers fondly recalled, "was something that lasted a lifetime."[8]

Some of Gompers's coworkers in the cigar shops were women, so it is not surprising that he met his wife, Sophia Julian, in one of these shops. They were married in 1867; he was 17 and she was 16. Samuel continued to work, and Sophia began raising the children. Gompers proved quite skilled in his trade, and in 1874 he joined a "high-class shop where only the most skilled workmen were employed"—David Hirsch & Company.[9] In addition to higher wages, what proved most important to Gompers and his future was the fact that it was the only union shop in New York City.[10]

As a result of Gompers's cigar-making skills, his erudition, and the bonds he built through his congenial personality, his fellow union members elected him president of Cigar Makers' International Union Local 144 after Gompers had only been in David Hirsch & Company's employ for a year. Two years later, however, the financial crisis of 1877 nearly left the union in total ruin. Gompers, along with his friend Adolph Strasser, capitalized on the tragedy by building a new cigar makers' union, thus giving him more political pull with the workers and a greater voice with the cigar-making industry. For the next eight years, he worked not only to rebuild a union, but to advance workers' wages and work conditions.

The most significant event in American labor relations also proved to be the most significant moment in the life of Samuel Gompers. That event occurred some 800 miles away from New York City in Chicago, Illinois, on May 4, 1886, and has come to be known as the Haymarket Affair.[11] On May 1 the traditional May Day celebration for workers in Chicago included the central feature of the annual parade. What made that year different was the fact that some 30,000 to 40,000 workers in the Windy City had gone on strike. The workers were primarily advocating for the eight-hour workday. One company, the McCormick Harvesting Machine Company, employed strikebreakers, and those on strike harassed the so-called "scabs" who tried to enter the factory to replace them. On May 3, at the end of the workday, when the strikebreakers left the factory, the confrontation turned violent, and the police officers present fired into the crowd in an attempt to restore order. It was reported that when the violence ended, two had been killed in the clash, while four were killed by the police officers' shootings.[12]

On the evening of May 4, workers gathered in Haymarket Square and began making speeches in support of their cause and to protest the killings. It was estimated that nearly 3,000 workers gathered, and by all accounts it was a peaceful protest. At least this was the case until someone threw a bomb into the crowd. The workers claimed it was the police, and the police claimed it was the workers. The officers began marching toward the speakers platform as the police inspector shouted, "I command you in the name of the law . . . to disperse."[13] It was then the bomb fell into the path of the police. One officer died instantly, and another six received mortal wounds. The police opened fire, killing several and wounding dozens more. The workers who could do so fled from the carnage.

The Haymarket Affair proved to be a significant event in police history, because the bomb resulted in the single greatest number of officers killed in the line of duty in one event at the time. In addition, it was also the most significant event in America's labor history so far. "The Haymarket Affair marked a juncture in our history," writes historian Green, "when many Americans came to fear radicals and reformers as dangerous subversives and to view trade unionists as irresponsible troublemakers."[14] Gompers called the affair a "catastrophe," since it effectively "halted our eight-hour program," but he also understood the anti-labor sentiment and knew that the best way to move forward was to unite the various unions and divest itself of both the violence and the political extremism. It was at this time when Gompers decided to organize the AFL, and from that point forward, as historian David Kennedy wrote of Gompers, "He spent his career promoting 'pure and simple' trade unionism, strictly divorced from ideology."[15]

Although Gompers was elected the second vice president of the Cigar Makers' International Union that year, most of his energy went into creating his new national federation of the numerous trade unions. What Gompers wanted for this organization was not only to advocate for better pay, working hours, and work conditions, but as AFL historian Lewis Lorwin explains, "He also wanted the AFL to be perceived as a respectable organization."[16] That was what he tried to communicate at the first conference, which was held only eight months after the Haymarket Affair, on December 8, 1886, in Columbus, Ohio. Many of the local and national unions sent delegates, and it became clear to all that Gompers's federation was now up and running.

Over the next decade the AFL grew only gradually, but by the turn of the century, it was beginning to see rapid growth.[17] In 1897 there were 250,000 members in the AFL, but with sudden industrial growth as America entered the 20th century, its membership exceeded 2 million by 1904.[18] Historian Gage explains that much of this growth came out of America's Progressive movement. "Faced with a growing disjuncture between rich and poor, between workers with the Money Trust, thousands of reformers, loosely joined in the new progressive movement, had begun to reject the 'standpattism' of the nineteenth century in favor of child labor laws, antitrust regulation, and the eight-hour day."[19]

Once the Great War began overseas and the American economy started to change, Gompers realized he needed to assert even more power, so he began pushing hard for additional reforms. However, when America entered the war, Gompers faced a dilemma. If he asserted more power at a time when America needed everyone to pull together, the AFL would be looked upon poorly. He reasoned it would be better, under the circumstances, to work for change within the system rather than working outside of it, and because Gompers also considered himself to be deeply patriotic, he decided to call an emergency meeting on March 12, 1917.[20] There, he explained his reasoning for cooperation with government and businesses and called for the passage of a resolution committing the AFL to supporting the war effort if or when a war resolution was passed. It was unanimously endorsed.

"In return for its cooperation," explains historian David Kennedy, "Gompers reasoned, the trade-union movement could ask for stronger government guarantees of the right to organize and bargain collectively, and for the preservation of union standards of pay and working conditions."[21] He proved to be correct. Labor historian John S. Smith explains that as a result of Gompers's efforts, President Woodrow Wilson became supportive of organized labor like "no other President before him."[22] The AFL ceased to push more organizing campaigns during the war, and thus they were praised for setting "aside their roles of organizers and strike leaders to become conciliators and mediators."[23] By the end of the war, AFL membership had exceeded the 3 million mark, many workers were seeing their wages rise, and the "the long-sought eight-hour day was at last becoming the national standard."[24]

"At the close of the war," historian Richard Lyons correctly describes, "the power and prestige of the American labor movement, and particularly of the A.F. of L., had reached a new high." However, as historian Robert Murray adds, "as the war drew to a close and the cost of living increased markedly, organized labor went on the offensive."[25] With the war over, it did not take long for labor unions and the AFL to assert more power, for the cost of living was rising fast in the postwar boom; this rapidly diminished the value of workers' wages. The unions immediately began going into collective bargaining and renegotiating war contracts; when they failed to obtain what they were after, they went on strike. The year 1919 proved to be a year of labor strikes.

On the West Coast, some 25,000 Seattle, Washington, workers joined 35,000 shipyard workers in February 1919 to go on strike to demand better wages.[26] On the East Coast, New York City dwellers experienced numerous strikes, such as when 35,000 dressmakers walked out from behind their sewing machines.

Another strike involved the National Association of Ladies' Hatters, and yet another was the Actors' Equity Association strike that effectively shut down Broadway. And it was the same throughout the country. Historian Lyons reports there were a "total of 3,360 strikes called in 1919 [that] involved 4,160,348 men."[27] He also reports that this ultimately led to an increase in the labor union rolls, for they "increased by 922,600 recruits during the year."[28]

It was the same in Boston. Numerous strikes occurred that year, but two of the most significant for the workers of Boston and events that had some bearing on the Boston Police Strike were the telephone operators' strike and the strike of the Carmen's Union by the men who operated Boston's elevated rail trains, known popularly as the "L."

The telephone operators' strike came in April 1919. On the 12th, the president of the Operators' Department of the International Brotherhood of Electrical Workers, Miss Julia O'Connor, announced the strike in a statement to the newspapers. "At 7 a.m. on Tuesday, April 15, 1919, a strike will be called," she declared. "This strike will affect the entire jurisdiction of this union, namely every exchange of the Boston Metropolitan District. No member of the union will report for duty on that date."[29] On the day the strike was to begin, the headline of the *Boston Globe* declared in all capital letters, "Business Men Fail to Avert Tieup: Telephone Strike to Begin Today."[30] As Miss O'Connor explained to the reporters, "It is impossible to call off the strike. It is impracticable to postpone it."[31]

The issue arose from the war contract that had ended on January 1, 1919. O'Connor, naturally, had tried to negotiate a new contract with the postmaster general Albert Burleson. Oddly enough, during the Great War the telephone company had been placed under the postmaster's jurisdiction, so the telephone operators' union she represented had to negotiate with him. Frustratingly, she could not even get him to talk to her, and so by April 15, 1919, with no new contract in hand, the operators walked out.

O'Connor was certainly unique for the time period, for she was one of only a handful of women who served as president of a labor union. This was because the telephone operators' union consisted mainly of women, and every one of them supported her in the call and vote to strike.[32] More than 12,000 of the workers employed by the New England Telephone and Telegraph Company (that stretched far beyond the city limits of Boston) walked off their jobs that day. They were demanding higher wages, stronger collective-bargaining rights since the war had ended, and a 48-hour workweek.[33]

As one can imagine, the strike was highly disruptive—telephone lines across New England went dead, and the lives of citizens trying to phone for personal reasons were disrupted as were businesses for purposes of commerce and the government for its administrative duties, including the coordination of the strike negotiations. Most people, businesses, and agencies resorted to the use of runners who relayed messages and delivered goods to those who needed them. This also included the police department, which was harassed by news reporters wanting to know the impact of the loss of phones on policing. Exasperated by the battery of questions, the spokesmen responded, "We are all right as long as things remain normal, but if there is another molasses tank affair or some such calamity, good night!"[34] While the police call boxes were on their own system, the ability to make contact with other agencies (such as calling for physicians or medical examiners) was greatly diminished, thus necessitating the use of runners.

The policemen of Boston found themselves in an awkward position with regard to this strike. Labor historian Herbert Gutman noted that police officers were often sympathetic with the plight of striking workers yet found themselves in an adversarial role against laborers during a strike.[35] Police historian Joseph King also pointed out a practical reason for their stance when he wrote, "Many of these women were the wives, daughters, or sweethearts of Boston's Finest."[36] There were others who sympathized with the operators as well, including military soldiers. Postmaster Burleson considered the easiest way out of the strike was to replace the operators with soldiers. That particular idea backfired, however, because, as Shlaes states, "The soldiers found it unchivalrous to face off with the telephone ladies."[37] In light of this, Burleson had little choice but to sit at the table with O'Connor and negotiate a new contract.

There were other incidents of violence during the strike, much of which revolved around the strikers and their sympathizers, such as the threat of scabs—those who crossed the picket line to take the strikers' jobs. By April 21, however, it was all over; the *Boston Globe* headline declared, "Employees Get Raise, Strike Ended, Operators to Resume Work Today."[38] The newspaper was pleased to report that the workers would be back on the job at 7 a.m. that morning, having seen their wages increase from $16 a week to $19 a week. Although they had originally asked for $22, as O'Connor admitted, it was the best settlement ever won by a telephone union.[39]

Gompers, who tended to choose his battles carefully, had not been overly supportive of the telephone operators' strike, but there is no doubt he saw it as a major victory for the labor unions. Governor Coolidge, on the other hand, became involved and went so far as to plead with President Wilson to intervene; the governor also considered having the postmaster of Massachusetts take over the telephone company.[40] In the end he, too, was pleased the strike was over, for he stated in a speech the day services resumed, "It will be a great relief to the public to know that they are no longer to be deprived of telephone service."[41] He also added a line of consideration that he carried with him going into the Boston Police Strike:

> There is another principle involved which has received very little attention and that is the obligation that exists on those who enter the public service to continue to furnish such service even at some personal inconvenience. This obligation reaches from the highest officer or Government official to the humblest employee. The public has rights which cannot be disregarded.[42]

The other strike that had some bearing on the Boston police came three months later in July, and that was the Carmen's Union operators strike. The union represented the 7,000 workers of the Boston Elevated Railway who ran both the "L" and the Boston streetcars.[43] The men of the L decided to emulate the ladies in the telephone exchange and attempted to renegotiate their wartime contract, which had expired on May 1. They, too, wanted higher wages and shorter workweeks.[44] When the president of the union, Matthew J. Higgins, issued the strike order, it stated:

> The members of this association have been informed through the newspapers of what progress has been made since Monday night's meeting. In view of the great efforts made to secure an award from Chairman Taft and Manly of the National War Labor Board, the committee cannot predict what will happen. Every member must be prepared to carry out the vote of Monday night's meeting unless notified to the contrary. Consult your barn captain and executive board member at your respective stations at 4 o'clock Thursday morning.[45]

Former president Taft was called upon to be the arbitrator of the strike, but he had difficulties bringing all of the parties to the table. By the time he managed to do so, it was too late. The headline for the *Boston Globe* on July 17 announced in all capital letters, "Elevated Strike Is On."[46]

Once again, it is easy to imagine what happened when something the people of Boston had come to rely upon, in this case public transportation, was taken away from them. As the *Boston Globe* reported that first day,

> The complete paralysis of the street car service in Boston and its suburbs which depend upon the lines of the Boston Elevated Railway for transportation caused an unparalleled situation yesterday afternoon when the hour arrived for the workers of the city to return to their homes. Literally not a wheel was turning on the entire Elevated system and those who had growled at the 10-cent fare a few short hours before would gladly have given double that amount for the chance to ride home in the usual manner.[47]

Employees such as telephone operators and police officers could not get to work, people without cars could not go shopping for needed supplies, and just about anyone who had come to rely on this form of transportation could not move freely about.

The Boston & Albany Railroad announced it would send more cars into Boston, but this proved to be too little, too late. Those who had automobiles chose to drive to work that day, which caused the city to become so overwhelmed by the amount of traffic that there were traffic jams throughout the city. This problem was then compounded by the fact that the traffic officers were pulled off that duty to guard the trolley company property from retributive destruction.[48] And although the police did not have as many close personal connections to the operators, they were still sympathetic because what the L and streetcar operators were demanding was the same thing the police officers wanted.

Once again, Governor Coolidge stepped in to attempt to find a solution that would appease both sides. As had occurred with Taft's attempts, the union at first refused the selection of arbitrators, but by Saturday, they accepted Henry D. Endicott, who was generally loved by all (a founder of a shoe company and a multimillionaire who was active in many roles of public service). They negotiated a contract that included what the union wanted. Their wages were increased from 7 to 12 cents an hour, and they were granted the eight-hour workday.[49] The *Boston Globe* gladly headlined, "Strike Settled—Cars Now Running," adding the note: "Men Awarded Increase in Wages."[50]

Boston police officers no doubt had mixed views of this victory. On one hand, it certainly had to gall them that the operators were now making "fifty cents a day more than the police."[51] In addition, the operators of the L not only showed them a strike produces results, so too had the telephone operators. This last strike came in July, and the fact that the AFL had just voted to charter police unions had to have crossed the minds of every police officer in the Boston Social Club—perhaps unionization was what was needed for them too, so they could obtain the higher wages and better hours they were seeking. And if collective bargaining failed, the Boston police could go on strike just like those other workers.

Despite its notoriety, the Boston Police Strike was not the first strike by police officers in the United States.[52] The first strike was by the Ithaca Police Department in Ithaca, New York, who went on strike on April 3, 1889.[53] A mayoral election had created a change in the political party in charge of the city, and the new Democratic mayor decided to cut police officer salaries from $12 a week to $9 a week. In protest, the officers went on strike; they demanded a pay raise, not a pay cut. As the local paper the *Evening World* reported, "Ithaca's police have presented the somewhat singular spectacle of laying down their clubs and shields and demanding $14 a week instead of $9."[54]

The mayor's response was to fire all of the officers. This escalated the conflict, for as the *Camden Daily Telegram* reported, "The excitement caused by the police strike here still continues."[55] "On Sunday," (April 9), the story continues, "the city was without protection and several small riots occurred. In the afternoon Mayor Bardeen put on a police suit and kept guard until the next morning."[56] The mayor also dug in his heels by hiring new recruits—all good Democrats—and then rescinded the pay cut, returning it back to the $12 a week salary.[57] Although animosity still existed among the officers who had been fired, the local sheriff appointed all of the members of the old force to work for his office.[58]

The other known police strike took place in 1918, when the officers of the Cincinnati Police Department went on strike. At that time the Cincinnati police were paid $1,250 annually, having received a $100 raise in early 1918.[59] Yet due to increasing inflation, not only had the officers lost any benefit from the raise, they were now woefully worse off due to inflation and the loss of their buying power. Out of protest, they considered forming a union.

At first, they began holding secret meetings, but when the chief's office found out about this, the four officers leading the effort were suspended for conduct unbecoming. One of the officers, John Hill, eventually took the leadership role and formed a committee to negotiate. "The policemen ask a wage increase," The *Atlanta Constitution* reported, "which would give them $1,500 annually instead of their present salary of $1,250."[60] The reason for that particular figure was in light of inflation; this amount would allow them the buying power that the January raise had meant to provide them. When the police chief refused to even provide an answer to their request, the officers went on strike at 3 p.m. on September 14, 1918. Mayor Galvan's response was immediate, "I believe in labor unions and have always been friendly to union labor. But a labor union in the Police Department is incompatible with the discipline and work of the department."[61]

The strike actually proved to be an amiable one. Members of the Home Guard were sent to serve as police officers in the city. Historian R. Herron explains what happened next: "Striking patrolmen in civilian dress accompanied the Guardsmen for the first few hours to show them their duties."[62] "Home guards as patrolmen," the *Atlanta Constitution* reported the next day, "and Boy Scouts as traffic policemen took the place of Cincinnati's police here today, except for about 100 members of the force who failed to answer the strike order."[63] Because there were three groups working patrol and traffic, the newspaper noted, "No disorder was reported."[64]

A grievance committee met with the mayor and safety director who refused not only the raise, but any leniency for the four suspended officers.[65] Ultimately, three of the officers were dismissed, and the suspension of the other was upheld. Still, in trying to be at least somewhat amiable, the mayor stated that if they decided to do away with all of the union nonsense, all of the officers could go back to work, and they would be allowed to create an association similar to the Boston Social Club. That evening,

> Cincinnati's police strike came to an end . . . when the 417 striking patrolmen, in session at Central Turner Hall, voted unanimously to return to their posts. . . . The men voted unanimously to abandon their union and to form a welfare association composed exclusively of patrolmen and not affiliated with any other organization.[66]

Police Chief Copeland addressed many of the officers the next day, saying, "I'm very glad to see you back. Right here let's forget all past unpleasantness and get down to real police business again."[67] In his amiable way he added, "I may have been wrong, and you may have been at fault. Nevertheless I believe you will see it was overhasty action which caused the break. Every patrolman who returns to his post will be restored to his former standing."[68]

The Ithaca Police Strike actually resulted in the hiring of all new police officers, while the Cincinnati Police Department Strike ended with nothing gained but their old jobs back. Despite the difference in time and size, the Boston Police Department was much closer to the Cincinnati Police Department, but their strike resembled the Ithaca strike more in some ways. In neither case, however, were the officers able to create a union with the power of collective bargaining

While there had been many so-called police unions in existence prior to the one created by the Boston police officers, most of these did not have the power of collective bargaining and were, in fact, little more than police social clubs. The first police department that attempted to organize a union by affiliating with the AFL was the Cleveland, Ohio, police department. In 1897 they made application to the AFL, but at their next convention, the AFL voted to issue the following policy in regard to police unionization: "It is not within the province of the trade union movement to specially organize policemen, no more than to organize militiamen, as both . . . are too often controlled by forces inimical to the labor movement."[69]

As the labor movement grew during the war, there were many additional requests by police departments that sought to join the AFL, and while they considered it at their 1918 convention, the AFL did not deem it advisable at that time either.[70] Had the AFL kept to that policy, they would not have affiliated with the Boston Police Department, but in June 1919, at their members' behest, the AFL changed its policy. A resolution was again put forth to accept police unions—Resolution No. 75—and this time it passed. The resolution stated the following:

Whereas, there are a number of cities, organizations of police or peace officers who are under one form of civil service rule or another and whose sympathies are with the principles of the American Federation of Labor, as well as its policies; and Whereas, In many cities, city employees under civil service rule are being admitted through Federal Unions to the American Federation of Labor; therefore, be it Resolved, That all police or peace officers be admitted to membership to Federal Unions the same as other city or county employees under civil service laws in compliance with the constitution of the American Federation of Labor.[71]

After the passage of the resolution, many police officers already in existing groups moved fast and "by September 1919," writes Joseph Slater, "the AFL had received 65 requests from police organizations and had chartered 37 locals."[72] This led Gompers to remark that since becoming president in 1886, "he had never seen as many applications in as short a time from any other trade."[73]

That did not mean, however, that the police departments or city leadership necessarily approved. The *Boston Herald*, assessing the status of police unionization across the country to put the Boston situation in perspective, reported they were not well received. For example, in Jersey City the mayor demanded the police chief "suspend and prefer charges against the promoters of the plan," while in Portland, Oregon, the mayor "fought unionization, claiming that it would cause divided loyalty in labor disputes."[74] This attitude would prove to be the same in Boston.

Police Commissioner O'Meara responded to the 1918 resolution for the police to be affiliated with the AFL when he issued General Order Number 129, on June 28, 1918. It began,

It is probable that the printed rumors to the effect that members of the police department are discussing the advisability of organizing a union to be affiliated with the American Federation of Labor represent no substantial sentiment existing among them.[75]

He continued by explaining that a police department was meant to impartially enforce the laws, but if incurring "obligations to an outside organization" they would be abandoning their impartiality. Although he supported these "outside organizations" that assisted employees in the private sector, he believed it inappropriate in the public sector. He then concluded by writing that if a vote to affiliate ever did happen, "I trust that it will be answered with an emphatic refusal by the members of the force who have an intelligent regard for their own self-respect, the credit of the department and the obligations to the whole public which they undertook with their oath of office."[76]

O'Meara laid out his beliefs, and they were followed, but the police were not afforded the opportunity to affiliate with the AFL that year. And when the opportunity finally came available, O'Meara was no longer chief. Much happened in the first six months of 1919 when Edwin Upton Curtis was the new chief, and in January, when the Boston Social Club met with Curtis, he refused to deal with the representing officers. He decided, like the Cincinnati Police Department, to create his own committee to handle employee grievances—the Grievance Committee. In organizing this committee, Curtis did allow the patrolmen to elect their own representatives, and the election took place at the end of January. It did not take long before suspicions arose that it had not been an honest election.[77] Unable to investigate themselves, the Boston Social Club hired a private investigator who "disclosed that the grievance officer from the Brighton station house, Stillman B. F. Hall, had not really received the majority of the votes cast, and that this sort of skullduggery had occurred in other station houses as well."[78] Frederick Koss explains that, "such a situation was indeed possible, since the division captains counted the ballots secretly in the privacy of their offices."[79]

An additional problem arose, for it was not clear who Curtis had appointed as his own representatives to the committee, suggesting he did not want anyone to know this information. Curtis was also evasive about calling for meetings of the Grievance Committee. While they were supposed to meet monthly, Curtis simply made no effort to convene the group, so when members were asked when they would meet, officers received answers such as "I don't know" and "Search me."[80]

Some officers tried going directly to the police commissioner, but that, too, proved ineffective. The members of the Boston Social Club became so frustrated after a month of these shenanigans that they decided to go over the commissioner's head and hold a meeting with Mayor Peters. He was more congenial than Curtis and agreed to meet with them at the end of February. When they met, the mayor listened to their grievances and their demand for a $200 across-the-board pay raise for all officers. Mayor Peters countered with "a 7% increase for three-fourths of the men."[81] Although their demands were not honored immediately, the Boston Social Club had now entered into collective bargaining with the mayor. It was a start.

Mayor Peters wanted the issue resolved and brought Commissioner Curtis in on the issue. They crafted a compromise plan of "an across-the-board increase of 10% which would amount to a $140.00-a-year raise."[82] The Boston Social Club considered this but chose to reject it and hold out for their original demand. The issue continued to fester, but in April the state legislature voted to lift the tax limit of the city; this allowed for the additional revenue needed. The city could now afford to meet the police officers' demands, and on May 10, 1919, the mayor announced, "the city would raise the pay of both the police and firemen by $200 a year."[83] The Boston Social Club had finally achieved a victory for the police officers of the Boston Police Department.

Although the officers were elated at first, the reality of their lives was quickly soured. The raise had been their first in six years and had achieved what they wanted. The increase amounted to a "14% to 20% salary raise," but as Koss explains, it hardly proved "an adequate pay adjustment in the face of the fact that the cost of living since 1913 had risen 79%."[84] In just the two years since they had begun making the request, inflation had soared 17.43 percent in 1917, 17.97 percent in 1918, and by the end of 1919, it would see an additional increase of 14.57 percent. Moreover, in comparison with what the telephone operators had just achieved in April, it was woefully inadequate. The

138 / Chapter 7

operators had also achieved a reduction in their hours, while the police had never been able to get that on the table. And still more difficult were the deplorable living conditions that one officer described as,

> so deplorable and the vermin so numerous . . . that the leather was eaten off the helmets of the men. Bedbugs and roaches were so numerous it was nothing unusual when changing one's clothes to go home to find he had carried considerable of these vermin with him into his house to the distress of his wife and children.[85]

In the end, they realized they had not obtained much beyond an inadequate pay raise that had been absorbed by inflation before they ever received it. Yet, they had won one victory, which is why, as Koss explained, "the salary increase, rather than quieting the men, may possibly have encouraged them to undertake, in spite of the Commissioner's disapproval, even bolder action."[86]

That bolder action came when the AFL reversed its policy at their June 1919 convention in Atlantic City. Police Commissioner Curtis knew that resolution would likely empower the Boston Social Club. To try to stave off any movement in that direction, like his predecessor, Curtis decided to issue a General Order. Politically, however, he wanted to make sure he had the backing of the governor, so he took his proposal to Henry Long, Governor Coolidge's secretary.[87] Since Coolidge was away on vacation, Curtis wanted Long to carry the message to the governor asking him if he had his support in this matter. Long made the phone call and explained the circumstances, whereupon Coolidge instructed Long "to tell the Commissioner to go ahead in the performance of his duty."[88]

Curtis issued his General Order on July 29, 1919, almost echoing O'Meara when he opened, "I note that a movement among the members of the Boston police force to affiliate with the American Federation of Labor is actively on foot."[89] He then invoked O'Meara's General Order in the hopes of swaying those who were fond of the man and echoed many of his same sentiments, even quoting him. He then closed with his own statement:

> As Police Commissioner for the City of Boston I feel it my duty to say to the police force that I disapprove of the movement on foot; that in my opinion it is not for the best interests of the men themselves; and that beyond question it is not for the best interest of the general public, which this department is required to serve.[90]

This statement proved to have no effect. The members of the Boston Social Club made their formal application for affiliation with the AFL on August 10, 1919.[91] Events moved incredibly fast, and although people considered what all this meant, no one was willing or able to slow it down and consider the ultimate ramifications. Many worried about what police unionization meant when they were called upon to enforce the laws against other AFL chartered unions, while some wondered whether police unions were even legal. More importantly, many considered the ramifications of a police strike. The AFL formally believed that for the public sector, when collective bargaining failed, legislation was the last recourse. The use of a strike by public sector employees, however, was left rather ambiguous.[92] So many worried about what would happen when a city was left unprotected. The Boston Police Strike, tragically, resolved all their worries. The next day, on August 11, 1919, the Boston Social Club's application to charter with the American Federation of Labor was granted.[93]

Boston Police officers after voting to go on strike.
Photo courtesy of the Calving Coolidge Presidential Library & Museum, Forbes Library.

8

The Road to Hell . . .

August 1919 opened with the police going on strike, but it was not the members of the Boston Police Department who were striking. Rather, it was members of the first police department ever created—the London Metropolitan Police. At the time, there were 20,000 police officers working the streets of London, England, but they, too, had their grievances. The British Parliament had recently passed the Police Act of 1919, which was set to go into effect on August 1. The act did authorize the London police to unionize, but their union could not be affiliated with any other labor union or collective union organization, and they were not allowed to go on strike.[1]

Despite all efforts on the part of the National Union of Police and Prison Officers to keep the Police Act from going into effect, as the date approached, it became evident it would soon become law. In response, they called for an emergency meeting on the evening of July 31 and called for a strike vote. Those who attended voted overwhelmingly to go on strike the following morning. Ironically, the London police were going on strike to fight a bill that said they could not go on strike.

In the end only 1,500 Metropolitan police officers walked off the job—a small percentage of the entire force of 20,000.[2] The Liverpool City Police, however, also joined the strike, and they brought an equal number of officers with them. However,

141

since that department only numbered 1,900, it encompassed a far larger percentage of the total number of officers in Liverpool.[3] They were soon joined by an additional 100 officers from two other police agencies, one in Birkenhead and the other in Birmingham.[4]

By the time the Boston police were affiliating their union with the AFL, the London Metropolitan Police were seeing their strike fail miserably.[5] Since too few officers joined in the strike, their endeavors quickly faltered, and their National Union folded. As for the Liverpool police, every officer who went on strike was subsequently fired.[6]

Stateside in America, dozens of police organizations were seeking to form their own unions, either by converting their benevolent organizations or creating them out of whole cloth. All of them were motivated by the AFL's newfound willingness to charter police members. The police officers of New York City had been planning their own union all summer long but were suddenly energized by the possibility of affiliating with the AFL. Their union came into existence on August 7, at which point they immediately presented their own grievances and made demands for a pay increase.[7]

Both the strike in London and the formation of new police unions throughout the United States must certainly have helped motivate the patrolmen of Boston and reaffirm that they were doing the right thing. Armed now with the backing of the AFL and, by extension, the support of its other affiliated members, they were ready to reassert their efforts to air their grievances with not only Mayor Peters and Commissioner Curtis, but with anyone who would listen. All of their hopes and dreams, however, came crashing down when Curtis issued General Order Number 110 on the same day they received AFL membership, August 11. Commissioner Curtis's order stated:

> It is, or should be, apparent to any thinking person that the Police Department of this or any other city cannot fulfill its duty to the entire public if its members are subject to the direction of an organization existing outside the department.[8]

Before prefacing the rule Curtis was about to promulgate, he explained that an officer is a public official charged with the authority to enforce the laws. The commissioner claimed that the rule did not interfere with "a policeman's interests and activities as a man and a citizen," but that it does "forbid him and the department from coming under the direction and dictation of any organization which represents but one element or class of the community."[9] He then added Section 19 to Rule 35 of the Boston Police Department's policies:

> No member of this force shall join or belong to any organization, club or body composed of present or present and past members of the force which is affiliated with or a part of any organization, club or body outside the department.[10]

He did add the exception for veteran organizations from the Civil War, Spanish-American War, and World War I, but they had to be veteran posts formed *within* the department. By the order, they were not authorized to affiliate with any community veteran post, including those in the neighborhoods in which they lived.

The newspapers reported on the ban against union affiliation the following morning, calling it "the strongest of several issued by the commissioner recently dealing with this subject."[11] Because the police union had no elected leadership yet, the patrolmen had no one authorized to speak on their behalf regarding the order. However, individual members spoke out, and most of the policemen, reported the *Boston Globe*, "expressed their indignation" at the manner in which Commissioner Curtis was "dictating to the policemen as to what post of the Legion the ex-service men of the department must become members."[12] Indeed, even one of Curtis's own commanders, Alfred J. L. Force, commented to the *Globe*, "It was with considerable surprise that I read in the press of Boston that Police Commissioner Curtis has forbidden the members of his department to join any other post of the Legion other than that within his department."[13] With regard to the ban on unionization, as Curtis later wrote, "No attention was paid to the rule; it was deliberately disregarded. The men met, organized and elected officers August 15."[14]

It took all of that week to organize the meeting of the Boston policemen, but they met on Friday at the headquarters of the Boston Street Carmen's Union, holding two sessions, one in the afternoon and the other, after a break for dinner, in the evening. An estimated 1,400 patrolmen were in attendance, many of whom claimed that those currently working the streets of Boston would have been there had duty not called.[15] The men listened to speeches made by many of their fellow members, representatives of other local unions, and the AFL. James T. Moriarty, one of the Boston city council members sympathetic to their cause, addressed the men. "If the Boston Police Department was under the control of the Boston City Government instead of being a weapon for the use of State politicians," Moriarty told them, "the present troubles due to trying to organize would never develop."[16] When it was all said and done, the men in attendance swore the oath that officially made them members of the AFL and made nominations for the officers who would lead their union.

The Boston newspapers described the behavior of the men at both sessions as "enthusiastic," and pointed out that "the word 'strike' was not mentioned at either the afternoon meeting or the night meeting."[17] However, papers outside Boston such as the *New-York Tribune* recognized the realities this might portend when they wrote, "Boston to-night faces the probability of a police strike."[18] Commissioner Curtis also saw the same potential threat, and in order to keep an eye on the union's developments, it was said that he had placed "spotters" on the street of the meeting location and had the names of every police officer entering the building recorded.[19] That afternoon he had also received the "rushed order" that he had placed the day before for "one thousand suspension and discharge forms."[20] The form read, "To _____, Boston Police Officer. By authority conferred on me by the Police Commissioner, you are hereby suspended until further order of said Commissioner."[21] They were to be signed by Michael H. Crowley, the Superintendent of the Boston Police.

Because the Boston policemen were now being unionized and affiliated with the AFL, the Boston Central Labor Union called a meeting for Sunday afternoon, August 17, to consider their support for the new police union.[22] The Central Labor Union represented the 80,000 union workers of Boston, so their backing was important to the new fledgling police union. Not only did this umbrella organization of Boston's union support the police "by a unanimous vote," they "pledged themselves to support the members of the Boston Policemen's Union."[23] In addition to showing the police their solidarity, they also formed a committee of 17 delegates who represented the different trades across the city and pledged to help the police organize and elect their leadership.[24]

The following morning, Governor Calvin Coolidge returned to the governor's office in Boston. As Coolidge recalled in his autobiography, "In August I went to Vermont. On my return I found that difficulties in the Police Department of Boston were growing serious and made a statement to the reporters at the State House."[25] The pronouncement came on Tuesday, August 19, after Coolidge had been informed of the issue the day before. "Mr. Curtis is the Police Commissioner invested by law with the duty of conducting the office," Coolidge succinctly stated. "I have no intention of removing him, and as long as he is commissioner I am going to support him."[26] Although it was within the governor's power to remove Curtis from his position, Coolidge saw no reason to take such action. However, he went much further than he needed to when he stated his full support "as long as he is commissioner."

Meanwhile, Curtis was taking administrative action in order to prepare for all possibilities, no doubt bolstered by the governor's statement. He had met Monday morning with 30 police sergeants to plan out all eventualities with them, and later, in the afternoon, he met with his captains from the various Boston police stations. On Tuesday Curtis issued General Order 119, which canceled all leave for all command-level staff and detectives, and he had the superintendent's office begin notifying all retired officers about the potential for their recall to active duty.[27] The commissioner also met with the special committee of the Boston City Council to discuss the situation.[28] As Curtis busied himself with his planning, not far away at Fay Hall, on the corner of Dover and Fay Streets above J. J. Foley's bar, the members of the new police union themselves were planning to vote for their leadership.

Around noon on Tuesday, August 19, the members of the new Boston Policemen's Union began optimistically gathering to cast their ballots for their leadership—the people who would lead them to better pay, better hours, and better working conditions. "The election was very spirited," reported the *Daily Globe*, "as every office was contested and more than 20 candidates were on the ballot."[29] They were guided in the process by Frank H. McCarthy, the New England organizer for the AFL, and tellers were appointed to receive and count the ballots. The polls closed at 9:30 p.m., giving all the officers, regardless of shift, a chance to vote. Over 1,000 votes were cast. The tellers then began counting, making sure each vote was certified and properly tabulated, then rechecked for accuracy. It was after midnight before they had the final results.

To those who were still around to hear it (and most were there unless on duty), it was announced that John F. McInnes had been elected president and John P. Whitten vice president. In addition, Edmund Burke was elected treasurer, and Michael King and William P. Willis were chosen as the financial and recording secretaries, respectively. William Brown was elected guardian and John Maloney as guide, while the three trustees were James L. Butler, Thomas J. Driscoll, and Michael Joyce. These 10 men, along with nine delegates to the Boston Central Labor Union, were to be sworn in later that night, August 20.[30]

Before they even had the chance to be officially sworn in to their new leadership positions, they were ordered to report to police headquarters that very morning. Commissioner Curtis had his informants.

By 8 a.m. that morning, the summons was received by eight members of the union leadership, including McInnis and Whitten. Their orders were to report to police headquarters by 9:30 a.m. There, they were placed in a waiting room and were then called one by one into a meeting with both Commissioner Curtis and Superintendent Crowley. A stenographer was present during each of the interviews, and all were asked the same questions. They were asked to verify who they were, their affiliation with the department, and their activity in the union. They were then specifically asked, "Did you know that Rule 35 of the police manual has recently been amended?"[31] They, of course, all had to admit both their affiliation in the union and knowledge of Rule 35, which meant that they were knowingly in direct violation of departmental policy. It was no doubt a devastating experience for the eight men, especially since they had just been elected by their peers to represent them.

The last of the eight men left police headquarters around noon.

The meetings with the officers, of course, sparked a flurry of debates, opinions, and speculation on the situation. Attempting to make his position clear, especially after having met with a special committee of the Boston City Council the day before, Commissioner Curtis issued a statement to the press. The committee had focused most of its attention on whether the promulgation of Rule 35 was legal, so Curtis primarily responded to that line of inquiry. He told the reporters that what had been reported regarding his meeting with the city council members had been fair, but what he wanted to add was "to say that in the event, which he cannot believe possible, of a judicial decision holding that the rule in question is invalid or in excess of the commissioner's authority, he would, of course, act with immediate recognition of obedience to such decision."[32] Lacking such a court decision, however, anyone "denying the authority of the rule" would face disciplinary actions.[33] He then began moving forward with those actions, but first, having decided the situation was growing more serious, he ordered the suspension of vacations for all division commanders, lieutenants, and sergeants indefinitely.[34]

That night, August 20, the Boston Policemen's Union met again in Fay Hall, this time to ceremoniously install their leadership. The police commissioner's actions earlier that day made the start of the meeting a somewhat sober affair, although it did not take long for feelings of optimism to take hold once again. Speeches were made, the officers' oaths were sworn, and the hall broke out in wild applause. "The Boston Policemen's Union is now permanently organized," Frank H. McCarthy, the AFL representative proudly declared.

> A full board of officers elected and regular meeting times appointed. This union will be known as Boston Policemen's Union, No. 16, 807, A. F. of L. The purpose of this union is to render assistance, best carried on through legal lines, to promote the economic condition of the policemen and establish the principle of collective bargaining in all matters affecting the working conditions of the policemen.[35]

McCarthy added that the AFL would not "'in any manner interfere with the executive direction of the department," but he stressed they were always "available to assist them as they navigated through the process."[36] Representatives of the Boston Central Labor Union also promised their support of the new police union.

Now that Boston Policeman's Union No. 16,807 had their leadership installed, it was their role, with the assistance of the AFL and the other labor unions of Boston, to represent their membership, to speak on their behalf, and to negotiate with Mayor Peters and Commissioner Curtis to gain the benefits the Boston police had long sought. The high of the evening's celebration, however, would be followed once again with a new low come the following morning when the eight men, including both the newly installed president and vice president, learned they were being charged with violations of Rule 35. The next day's *Boston Daily Globe* headline said it all: "Expected Break Between Police and the Commissioner Today."[37]

The eight officers immediately set about retaining legal assistance, and James H. Vahey and John P. Feeney, two prominent Massachusetts lawyers, were hired to represent them.[38] Their first action was to file an injunction in the Superior Court in an attempt to stop the charges from going forward.[39] The hope was to have the issue brought before the Massachusetts Supreme Court for a quick and final resolution.[40]

Meanwhile, Police Commissioner Curtis issued a statement that provided details regarding the department's contingency procedures. In addition to initiating a callback notification of all retired officers, there were plans being set in motion to call upon other police agencies for assistance and to create an unpaid, volunteer police force. Curtis asked William H. Pierce, a retired superintendent of police for Boston, to organize and equip the force for service should it become necessary.[41] Without hesitation, Pierce agreed and set about creating an all-volunteer police force.

Upon hearing of the commissioner's statement, AFL's Frank McCarthy felt he needed to respond. "Men have been called to headquarters and asked questions," he told Boston reporters, "under the threat that if their answers were not satisfactory they would be punished."[42] Since there were lawyers handling the legal side of things, McCarthy's hope was to move public sentiment in favor of the Boston police by painting the commissioner's plans as entirely reactionary. To highlight this, McCarthy added that "a volunteer police force is being organized, all in the face of the fact that the word 'strike' has never been mentioned by an officer of the Policemen's Union or at one of the meetings."[43]

The people and various groups in Boston were, indeed, already beginning to divide their loyalties between the commissioner and the Policemen's Union. Moreover, a number of police chiefs from other agencies in the state (who were currently forming police unions themselves) issued a statement that if a strike was called, "they would not send members of their department to Boston."[44] The story across the nation, however, simply played upon fears of the worst-case scenario, carrying headlines such as "Boston Police May Soon Strike."[45] Newspapers as far away as the *San Francisco Chronicle* made claims that "In authorizing the formation of a volunteer police force for Boston, Officials and union police say the organization of 'vigilantes' is to be met only by a walkout before the new citizens' body can be completed."[46]

All eyes were now focused on Tuesday, August 26, the day the officers would be tried for misconduct.

The eight officers again reported to police headquarters for the formal hearing that morning.[47] "To the Police Commissioner for the City of Boston," Superintendent Crowley read aloud in the unexpected presence of the commissioner himself. All had thought he would delegate the hearing to Crowley, the eight men, their lawyers, and a stenographer.[48] "I hereby bring a complaint before you against patrolman Richard J. Austin of Division 1, for violation of Rule 35 of the rules and regulations of the Police Department, to wit: Charge 1—Violating section 19 of said rule."[49] After the reading of the first complaint, each of the other men waived their right to a reading of their own complaints, and the hearing began.

The commissioner and superintendent focused the trial on the officers' awareness of the rule and that by joining and being elected as leaders of the union, they were in violation of the rule. In addition, the concerns given in the General Order regarding the problem of divided loyalties between the union and the department were highlighted. The union attorney, James H. Vahey, spoke on behalf of the eight officers. "I regard the rule promulgated by the Police Commissioner to be the greatest invasion of a man's personal liberty," he detailed as his main argument later to the local newspapers, calling it "the most far-reaching attempt to restrict his freedom of action that I have ever known."[50] The hearing lasted for two and a half hours.

"Now, gentlemen," Commissioner Curtis began at the end of the hearing, "I will take the case under advisement and will render my decision as soon as is consistent with the careful study of all the evidence which has been put in here today."[51] Both the lawyers and the officers were stunned. Most everyone had believed the commissioner would fire the officers at the end of the hearing, so they were surprised when he did not do so.[52] "I am a busy man and have many other things to do," and then he succinctly stated, "I will not promise to do this very soon."[53] And with that, he walked out of the hearing.

As president of the Boston Policemen's Union, patrolman John F. McInnes made the organization's first official statement to the press after the meeting and after conferring with the union lawyers. "Much has been said about the present situation in the Boston Police Department by everybody but the members of the department who are connected with the Boston Police Union, which is the only organization within the department directly concerned," he began.[54] "This is the first public utterance . . . and is given to correct wrong impressions which have been created in the minds of many citizens."[55] To allay fears, McInnes pointed out, "There is absolutely nothing in 'obligation' to the American Federation of Labor which interferes with the duties of a police officer in the slightest degree." He drove home his point by stating, "It is simply an obligation to do the things which should appeal to every clean, Christian person as the right things to do of their own free will."[56] He then closed with the bold statement that the members of the union "intend to do their full duty as police officers in the future just as they have in the past and retain their full membership in the American Federation of Labor."[57]

As the seriousness of the issue increased, Mayor Peters also spoke to the press. "The issue between the Commissioner and the policemen is clear-cut," he began.[58] "It is the question of whether the policemen have a right to form a union and become affiliated with the A. F. of L."[59] In order to explore this question, Peters created a citizens committee to look at the issue, and he selected James J. Storrow to serve as chair. Storrow was a Boston lawyer and investment banker, who, like Peters, was well entrenched within the Boston Brahmin. He had helped to form General Motors and served briefly for two months as its third president. Although his attempt to become mayor in 1909 failed, he never lost his love for his city and worked on many public service projects for the betterment of the citizens of Boston. In 1925 he began serving as the second national president of the Boy Scouts of America, but he died the following year.

Although Storrow had been planning to go on vacation, he decided to stay in Boston and lead the committee; he immediately made the statement that, "Boston policemen should not join the American Federation of Labor" on the grounds they are "engaged in the administration of the law."[60] Still, the committee (consisting of 34 members of the community) met, and Storrow issued their report the next day. "I have given this question the best, the most impartial and the most sympathetic consideration I am capable of exercising," he prefaced his report, which was sympathetic to the officers. But in the end he concluded, "our police officers should not join the American Federation of Labor."[61]

The committee adopted a number of resolutions supporting the police and the AFL, and although they urged the men not to join, they met at length with the Boston Policemen's Union leadership and their lawyers, allowing them to detail their side of the story.[62] They also met routinely with the mayor and once with Commissioner Curtis.[63] Yet after five days of conferencing, "during which the police situation has been discussed from every angle" the *Daily Globe* reported, "there appears to be no solution of the difficulty in sight."[64]

Meanwhile, Curtis focused on his own preparations for all possible outcomes but chose not to announce any decision until after the other 11 officers in leadership roles in the Boston Policemen's Union were placed on trial; he announced their upcoming trials on Friday, August 29, 1919, in advance of the Labor Day weekend.[65]

At the same time the first hearings were held, William H. Pierce, the ex-superintendent of police, was busy enrolling men for volunteer police work. The advertisements began appearing in all the local newspapers:

> Able Bodied Men willing to give their services in case of necessity for part of day or night for protection of persons and property in the City of Boston. Apply to me at Room B, Third Floor, Chamber of Commerce Building, Boston, daily except Sundays. William H. Pierce, Supt. Of Police (Retired).[66]

The first to respond was Harvard physics professor Edwin Hall, who immediately reported for duty after reading of the call for volunteers in the newspaper while eating breakfast. Hall was already a noted physicist, having discovered a phenomenon in electromagnetism that is named for him—the "Hall effect."

Harvard University was still on summer break since classes did not begin until after the Labor Day weekend, so Dr. Hall put his full energies into volunteering as a police officer and wrote a letter to the *Boston Herald* praising Curtis for his stand, before lamenting the lack of young men responding. He felt they should have been lining up at the door. At the end of the letter, he added his own call for volunteers: "Come back from your vacations, young men: there is sport and diversion for you right here in Boston."[67]

Many of the students, at least those who had already returned to Boston, heeded the call. Two seniors reported for duty, as did many "former Harvard football players, baseball players and oarsmen."[68] In addition, members from the chamber of commerce and former servicemen presented themselves for service as volunteer police officers. Over the holiday weekend, they received drill instructions from Captain King at the Irvington Street Armory.[69]

On the day after Labor Day, the members of the Policemen's Union received their notice to report Thursday morning, September 4, for the disposition of their misconduct hearings. If the potential realities of the Boston Police going on strike were not present on the minds of Bostonians who had recently experienced the telephone operators' and the Carmen's Union strikes, it should have been obvious for those attempting to go to the theater after Labor Day. The Actors' Association had gone on strike and, thus, all the theaters in Boston were closed. These strikes filled the headlines, crowding out the news of a potential police strike.

Once again, the officers reported in the morning to police headquarters and were ushered into the hearing with Commissioner Curtis presiding. The meeting was opened, there were some prefatory remarks, and all the officers and their lawyers awaited the final decision when a knock came at the door. "While they were there, and before the decision had been announced," the police commissioner's annual report later explained, "a letter arrived from his honor the mayor."[70] Curtis opened the letter and read that in light of the activities of the mayor's citizens' committee, he was "impressed with the belief that a solution may be found honorable and satisfactory to the men, and consistent with the principles which must be observed in an orderly administration of the police force."[71] "The importance to the public of having this question settled satisfactorily," Mayor Peters explained, "impels me to ask you to postpone action for a few days, only until the developments of the pending conferences may be seen."[72]

Everyone, especially Curtis, was stunned by this turn of events. Curtis had found it curious that if a request for postponement was in anyone's best interest, it should have come from the two lawyers on behalf of the policemen. "Yet they were not in favor of the idea," he explained in his report, "believing there was little hope for a settlement.[73] It seems, Curtis noted, "they were indifferent, and refused to request the continuance themselves."[74] The mayor had issued the request in the hope that perhaps over the weekend, some resolution could be found. Although almost everyone at this point did not think it possible, Curtis felt he had little choice but to comply and agreed to wait before issuing his final decision. When Curtis asked the lawyers if they concurred with the postponement, they "reluctantly agreed to say that they did not object to the continuance."[75] He then set the new meeting for Monday morning, September 8.

The Policemen's Union held a meeting that afternoon and late into Friday night to discuss the situation.[76] They learned that officers were being questioned by their commanding officers about their involvement in the union and if they were cognizant of Rule 35.[77] One unidentified member of the union told the newspapers over the weekend that, "If one man in the department is discharged on Monday, not a union policeman will report for duty Tuesday morning."[78] The Policemen's Union president McInnis advised the reporters that whoever it was, he did not speak for the union. About the only definitive action they could take, however, was to set a meeting for the afternoon of September 8, after they had heard the commissioner's final decision.

The mayor's committee met in conference all day Saturday, but by 10 p.m. that night, all Storrow could say was that he was "not optimistic" but that he "still had hope."[79] They met again Sunday afternoon, at which point they issued a report to Mayor Peters. Once again, it concluded, "The Boston Policemen's Union should not affiliate or be connected with any labor organization."[80]

Rumors were flying about Mayor Peters himself, for many believed he was planning to "buy off" the police officers by giving them a raise.[81] He did no such thing; instead, he spent his time in meetings trying to find a solution to the problem, but none came readily. When the final report from Storrow's committee was received, it concluded the police should not affiliate with the unions. However, it essentially implied the expectation that rather than taking any immediate action, the issue would undergo arbitration with the possibility of finding a satisfactory resolution. The mayor, hoping that Curtis might be open to the report's recommendation, drafted a letter to him. "Sir: I beg to enclose herewith the report of the Committee of Citizens appointed by me to consider the police situation."

> The report commends itself to me as a wise method of dealing with the subject, and I recommend it to your favorable consideration. If acceptable to you and the men, it affords a speedy and, it seemed to me, satisfactory settlement of the whole question.[82]

Peters sent the letter and a copy of the report to Curtis, but then he did something to apply more pressure on the commissioner. The mayor sent the letter and the report to the newspapers. At 10 p.m. Sunday night, he issued the following statement: "The public has a right to be advised of the police situation—a matter which is of deep concern to every inhabitant of Greater Boston. I am, therefore, giving to the press the following statement and letter."[83] Peters was hoping that perhaps the pressure from both the media and the public might give Curtis reason to reconsider issuing his decision.

Curtis replied, acknowledging receipt, and explained, "The commissioner can discover nothing in the communication transmitted by Your Honor and relating to action by him which appears to him to be either consistent with his prescribed legal duties or calculated to aid him in their performance."[84] He informed the mayor he would stay the course.

Mayor Peters had been rebuked.

Early on the morning of September 8, Commissioner Curtis reported to his office, where he met with Herbert Packer (the former Massachusetts attorney general) for some legal advice. Then, at 9:25 a.m., after all the officers and the union's attorneys had assembled awaiting his decision, Curtis began detailing his findings. "I deem it appropriate to state at some length some of the reasons and to present some of the lines of judicial authority which have led me to the decision which I am to announce."[85] He stated that although the policemen wanted to be considered "employees" of the department, he explained that they were, in fact, "public officers," in accord with state law. He also believed that the department had the right to address conditions of employment, which he did, in light of the change during their summer meeting in the AFL's policies allowing for police union affiliation. He also explained that officers take an oath to "faithfully and impartially" discharge their duties, and that they are required to follow the rules and policies of the department. Because they had failed to do their duty, he believed he had a duty to do his. He then issued his final judgment: "Upon due procedure and hearing in accordance with the requirements of the law and in the discharge of the judicial authority and duty thus imposed upon me, I find the following," at which point he listed 16 charges against the officers:

> Guilty of the charges preferred against each one of them, and in accordance with rule 40 of the rules and regulation I shall embody my findings and judgement in a general order, which shall be read at the several station houses in accordance with the rule, beginning with the rollcall tonight.[86]

His speech lasted 45 minutes.

The men were found guilty, but they would have to wait until the evening roll call to learn of the penalty imposed upon them for their misconduct. Most assumed they would be fired.

After the commissioner's announcement, Curtis met with the mayor. Afterward, reporters asked the mayor about the meeting, and Peters replied, "It is too delicate a situation even to discuss plans for policing the city in the event of a strike."[87] Curtis was more succinct when he was caught a few minutes later and answered, "I can't say anything now."[88]

Mayor Peters began turning his hopes of forestalling a possible strike toward the statehouse. Sending a copy of the Storrow Report to the governor, he added a note that read, "I have been and am still trying to get in touch with you on the telephone this afternoon, as I should like to go over the matter with you personally."[89] Coolidge had only returned to Boston in the late afternoon, having been away for the weekend in Northampton and delivering a speech that morning in Pittsfield before the state convention of the AFL. As Coolidge recalled in his autobiography, "When the policemen's union persisted in its course I was urged by a committee appointed by the Mayor to interfere and attempt to make Commissioner Curtis settle the dispute by arbitration."[90]

"The Governor appoints the Commissioner and probably could remove him, but he had no more jurisdiction over his acts than he has over the Judges of the Courts," Coolidge noted, before adding, "I did not see how it was possible to arbitrate the question of the authority of the law, or of the necessity of obedience to the rules of the Department and the orders of the Commissioner."[91] Deciding that he had no right to intervene, Coolidge chose to let the situation play out without his interference, something that was well in keeping with his past policy of not overreacting, because it was his stance that most problems tended to work themselves out.

All anyone could do at this point was to wait for the 5:45 p.m. roll call to learn of the disposition of the 19 members of the Boston Police Department who had affiliated with the AFL, served as the leadership of the new Boston Policemen's Union, and had been found guilty of violating Rule 35, as amended, of the department's policies.

The world watched and waited.

The crowds gather in Scollay Square during the Boston Police Strike.

Photo courtesy of the Calving Coolidge Presidential Library & Museum, Forbes Library.

9

In the Absence of Police

September 9, 1919

The balloting on the strike vote began at 10 p.m. on September 8 and did not end until the morning of September 9. After certifying the ballots, the Policemen's Union released a statement to the press at 10 a.m. The final tally of those in the union and voting was 1,134 to go on strike, two opposed, and one ballot left blank. It was officially announced that at 5:45 p.m., the Boston police officers were going on strike.[1]

The morning newspapers had already been printed when the announcement was made, so either the publishers had to put out a late edition or hold the information for the evening papers. By the time the announcement appeared on newsstands, however, it merely confirmed what people already knew: The police were going on strike. "Police Voted to Strike Tonight: Walkout at 5:45 P.M. Rollcall," the *Boston Post* announced, while the *Boston Evening Globe* headlined, "Nearly Unanimous Strike Vote by Boston Patrolmen" and "Harvard Organizing Force for Police Duty in Boston."[2]

Questions the reporters tried to answer mainly focused on just how many of the officers would walk off the job, and how many would remain on duty. If 1,134, officers voted to strike out of a total of 1,544 patrolmen in the department, that left only a little over 400 to police the streets of Boston.[3] Still, it was possible that some of the men intending to go on strike had not voted, leaving even fewer policemen in the count. Assuming the department's leadership (none of whom joined the union) remained on duty, only an additional 229 men were available for patrol, mostly consisting of sergeants and lieutenants.[4]

The newspapers also tried to determine the status of additional police officers who might be available for patrol duty. There were discussions about the number of state police officers working in Boston proper and the surrounding area, as well as how many might be available for patrol during the strike. Locally, there was the Metropolitan Park Police who, it was made known, had 100 officers ready for duty. Other local police departments in the surrounding area appeared much more hesitant to get involved, and some said they would not allow their officers to serve as strikebreakers. Others believed they needed to keep their officers at home in case any of the problems arising in the city proper spread to their jurisdictions.

The majority of the attention was focused on the volunteers. "While the order of suspension of the union policemen was being promulgated last night," it was reported, "about 100 volunteer policemen were assembled in secret in the Chamber of Commerce Building and told by Supt William H. Pierce to be ready for instant service as police officers of Boston."[5] It was also noted that some 350 men had been sworn in as "special policemen," and that they were "given their special badges and license to carry a loaded revolver."[6] Nearly all of these men worked for a bank such as the National Shawmut Bank or for large businesses like F. W. Woolworth Company.[7]

Because the information on these volunteers was not very forthcoming, most of the newspapers' attention rested on the more visible and accessible Harvard University volunteers. "In accordance with its tradition of public service the university desires in a time of crisis to help in any way that it can to maintain order," began the public statement of Harvard president Lawrence Lowell that morning in his plea to his students to volunteer as patrolmen.[8] He urged "all students who can do so to prepare themselves for such service."[9] According to the university's newspaper archives, "more than 250 students volunteered as strikebreakers, and along with an additional 150 faculty members and alumni, the Harvard student body, for a few days at least, became the new face of the Boston Police Department."[10] In fact, it would seem that the only person on campus opposed to the students serving as strikebreakers was Harold J. Laski, a lecturer on government who was pro-union, "warmly supported the cause of the police," and was severely criticized for voicing his opposition to faculty and students volunteering. As historian Richard Lyons explained, "He was lonely in his stand."[11]

Perhaps the most visible of the Harvard volunteers were the members of the Harvard Crimson football team; the *Evening Globe* reported, "The entire football squad of 125 students are scheduled to do police work."[12] Although he later denied ever saying it, head coach Robert Fisher was reported to have remarked, "To hell with football if the men are needed."[13] In the end though, the police duty must have been good for the team. They went on to win the 1920 Rose Bowl against Oregon.

In addition to active students, former students of Harvard also answered President Lowell's call for service, including the highly regarded Harvard Crimson football alumnus Huntington R. "Tack" Hardwick.[14] While playing for Harvard, the team had gone undefeated, and in 1954 he was inducted into the College Football Hall of Fame. Other well-known alumni included Morrill Wiggin, who had been a member of the crew team and volunteered for police duty.

Most of the Harvard University students and alumni who volunteered to serve came from families with names associated with the Boston Brahmin.[15] This meant that when they served as volunteer patrolmen, they would be placed in a position of authority over the people of the community, most of whom were from the lower, immigrant classes. For this reason, the Harvard volunteers soon found themselves the target of working-class animosity.

Meanwhile, as the volunteers gathered, the mayor and his committee conferred with Governor Calvin Coolidge to see what he could do to help prevent the strike. After their meeting Mayor Peters released a statement saying the governor "has taken under advisement what action, if any, he can take."[16] What the press wanted to know the most was whether Coolidge was going to heed the growing call for Commissioner Curtis's removal. At noon Coolidge answered this by stating, "I know of no reason for the removal of the commissioner, and if he were removed, of course, I would have no authority to reinstate the men."[17]

By early afternoon Coolidge responded in a letter to the mayor and the citizens' committee, detailing point by point his belief that he had no authority to interfere. When it came to who had authority over the Boston Police Department, Coolidge explained, "It seems plain that the duty of issuing orders and enforcing their observance lies with the commissioner of police and with that no one has any authority to interfere."[18] In regard to the striking officers' demands for improved conditions of employment, he told Peters, "The law requires that they be initiated by the Mayor and City Council, subject to the approval of the commissioner."[19] In the end Coolidge succinctly told the mayor, "There is no authority in the office of Governor for interference in the making of orders by the Police Commissioner."[20]

This was largely true, for the governor only had the ability to appoint the head of the Boston Police Department. By virtue of that power, he could also remove him from that office, but as a lawyer and politician, Coolidge knew he would have to show cause. When he signed off on his letter, Coolidge added the line, "I am unable to discover any action that I can take."[21] Specifically what he meant was that at that point in time, there was no legal course of action available to him, at least as Coolidge saw the situation.

Mayor Peters decided that if the governor would not remove the police commissioner or take charge of the situation himself, the least he could do would be to call out the state guard in advance of the walkout. At 3 p.m. that afternoon, less than three hours before the strike was to commence, Coolidge met at the mayor's request with him and Police Commissioner Curtis.[22] The discussion centered on calling out the state guard.

After the meeting, in speaking before the gathered reporters, Coolidge tried to simplify and clarify his stance. "The Mayor is responsible for the city," he explained.

> The Governor appoints the Police Commissioner, but after appointment he is the Police Commissioner of Boston. The Mayor maintains order by the police of Boston, and if for any reason they became inadequate, he has authority to call out any unit of the military which is in Boston, and also call on the citizens.[23]

Coolidge had denied Peters's request for him, as governor, to call out the state guard, but he told Peters it was within his power as mayor to also call upon the state guard without having to go through the governor.

Although Massachusetts state law did give authority to both the governor and the mayor to call out the state guard, there was a catch. The law stated the guard could be deployed but that it had to be "in case of a tumult, riot, mob or a body of persons acting together by force to violate or resist the laws of the commonwealth."[24] Until the police walkout and even in the hours immediately following, there simply was no indication that any of these conditions existed at the time. So, while calling up the state guard may have been the prudent thing to do, it would not have been, technically speaking, the legal thing to do.[25]

Mayor Peters expressed his disappointment with the outcome of the meeting, but he did take up part of the governor's suggestion when he issued an appeal to the citizens of Boston. "In the present situation," he wrote,

> I call upon the citizens to do their part to assist the authorities in maintaining order. The security of the city depends upon the good intentions of its people, and I am confident that the law-abiding, orderly citizens of Boston will insist that order is maintained and will support the constituted authorities.[26]

Not one of the men in that last meeting before 5:45 p.m. (Commissioner Curtis, Mayor Peters, or Governor Coolidge) made the call for the deployment of the state guard. This proved to be a source of contention then and has remained so ever since. According to historian William White, "Commissioner Curtis still was sure an hour before the walkout that the strike would not occur."[27] If the strike actually did occur, Curtis did not believe that all of the patrolmen who voted to go on strike would actually do so. His best estimates, based on the intelligence he had been gathering for weeks, was that only about 600 would violate their duty. The rest would stay. Because of those who remained, combined with his command element, the Metropolitan Park Police, and the police volunteers, Curtis believed he had enough policemen to maintain control of the city, and that calling the state guard at that point in time would be overreacting. It would also show, he no doubt thought, that he believed the Boston Policemen's Union was bluffing. So, as White observed, Curtis "was determined to wait until actual trouble started before calling out the troops."[28] Still, many, like Coolidge's biographer Claude Fuess, believed that "a less obstinate man might have saved money and bloodshed" by calling out the state guard.[29]

As for Mayor Peters, although Governor Coolidge informed him he could call up the state guard himself, he chose not to do so. After being reelected later that fall, at his February 1920 inaugural address, Peters explained:

> I consulted with the Police Commissioner. Mr. Curtis said that he had the situation well in hand, had made adequate provisions for any emergency and assured me that there was no occasion for alarm. I asked him whether it would not be wise to have the state guard mobilized in order that sufficient forces might be on hand in case of an emergency. Police Commissioner Curtis stated in no uncertain terms that he did not wish their aid at that time.[30]

Mayor Peters, it seems, felt he had little option but to trust the police commissioner.

Coolidge argued that the issue, at that moment in time, was not a state issue, but a City of Boston matter. He also did not believe he had the right, by law, to call up the state guard since there had been no indication that there was an omnipresent threat of "tumult, riot, or mob."[31] Later, in his autobiography, however, Coolidge wrote, "I have always felt that I should have called out the state guard as soon as the police left their posts," suggesting that once the strike began, regardless of any evidence of a riot, he should have taken action. He then explained the reasons he did not do so when he wrote:

> The Commissioner did not feel this was necessary. The Mayor, who was a man of high character, and a personal friend, but of the opposite party, had conferred with me. He had the same authority as the Governor to call out all the Guard in the City of Boston. It would be very unusual for a Governor to act except on the request of the local authorities.[32]

While the latter statements are consistent with Coolidge's long-held beliefs, the fact he lamented not calling out the state guard immediately after the strike went into effect is curious. It simply does not comport with Coolidge's personality to react to a situation before a problem arises. "Never go out to meet trouble," he once explained. "If you will just sit still, nine cases out of ten someone will intercept it before it reaches you."[33] Unfortunately, the strike proved to be one of those one out of 10 exceptions to this particular rule of his.

In the end the three men went about their business and eventually made their way home. The commissioner, feeling ill and exhausted from the day's events, went to his home early in the evening, leaving instructions that he was not to be disturbed.[34] Coolidge dined at the Union Club with members of the Citizens Committee and Attorney General Henry A. Wyman, and then returned to the Adams House.[35] He later wrote in his autobiography that "I remained in Boston and kept carefully informed of conditions," because, as he noted, "I knew I might be called on to act at any time."[36] However, by 10 p.m., being tired from the day's events, he too "went to bed and told his secretary not to disturb him until the morning."[37] The only one who remained vigilant was Mayor Peters. He did go home to his Brookline house but, as Lyons wrote, he remained awake, "receiving calls throughout the night keeping him abreast of events."[38]

At 5:45 p.m., when the strike began, a scene was playing out in the many police station houses all across the city of Boston.

Outside the station houses, crowds were continuing to gather despite the light drizzle that continued to fall—there had been intermittent showers throughout the day. Inside, the officers presented themselves at the evening roll call, prepared to go on strike.

The first officer believed to have announced the strike was patrolman George E. Ferreira at Station House 1 on Hanover Street. A handsome, tall, and heavy 28-year-old, he was born of an Irish mother and a Portuguese father.[39] Ferreira had joined the Boston Police Department in the fall of 1917, three months after he had married. The reason he became the first officer fired was because right after roll call had commenced, he stepped up to the front of the room, stood before the captain, saluted, and proudly announced, "Sir, the Boston police are on strike."[40] "Here, wait a minute," came Captain Matthew J. Dailey's reply at this break in protocol.[41] "Ferreira, you are suspended, go outside."[42] As such, he was the first patrolman to leave the station house.

At most of the station houses, however, the officers followed along with protocol. At Station House 7, located on Maverick Square in East Boston, the roll call was read, and the men responded with either "here" or "present." After the roll call was completed, patrolman Cunningham raised his hand and requested to speak. He was 31 years old at the time and had been first appointed a police officer on March 18, 1918. Married with one daughter, he was described as being "tall with a medium build, gray eyes and dark hair."[43] He had been elected by his peers to serve as their spokesman, and once recognized by Captain James Hickey, the station house commander, Cunningham announced that the men were not going on duty. Hickey simply replied, "You men are level-headed and know what you are doing."[44] Patrolman John Thornton, 29 years of age and appointed in July 1917, then stood up and said, "Captain, speaking on behalf of the rest of the men, I want to thank you for your unfailing courtesy in this case."[45] Someone shouted, "Three cheers for Captain Hickey!" and they gave the somewhat surprised, but saddened, commander of the station house three hearty cheers. The men then left roll call, gathered their personal belongings, and left the station.

At Station House 14, in Brighton, the scene was also repeated before Captain Forest F. Hall. Roll call was read, the strike was announced, a few kind words were spoken, and the men began gathering their things. As the patrolmen walked out of the station house in their civilian clothes, burdened with partial uniforms and equipment, Captain Hall, saddened by what he was witnessing, watched them go. As the last man left the station house, he commented to his sergeants, "Well, this is something that I never would have believed could happen in the Police Department."[46]

Despite the surrealness of the situation, with almost an entire police force walking off the job and going on strike, it was fast becoming a reality. This was made most evident by the physical realities of the policemen turning in their revolvers, badges, belts, clubs, and helmet numbers, while taking various parts of the uniforms they had been required to purchase, such as the helmet itself, and any personal property they kept in their lockers at the station.[47] Once they had emptied the station houses, a process that in some cases took as long as an hour and a half, the reality became even more absolute to the command staff. The usual buzz of activity was for the most part absent, and an eerie silence took over inside the station houses.[48] The captains of the station houses, however, had the added realization that they had to mark the status of nearly every name on the roll call sheet "absent without leave."[49]

Outside the station house, there was not much in the way of silence—in fact, just the opposite. When the officers had reported for roll call, the people who were gathering outside to watch only numbered about 100 at any given station house. Yet, while they were in roll call and gathering their things, the people kept arriving. By the time the officers were leaving the stations, in most cases, less than an hour later the numbers had reached into the thousands in some locations.

History professor Samuel Rezneck, who had graduated from Harvard College in the spring of 1919, was preparing that day to travel to England. Although he had been out running errands in preparation, he became witness to the scene outside of the station houses. "The policemen struck today at 6:00 in the afternoon," he recalled in his journal that evening. "It was a peculiar sight to see many of them going home half dressed in civilian garb, with their uniforms and helmets under their arm."[50] As a trained professor of history, he had become used to taking the long view of such events, and what he witnessed left him to remark,

> Tomorrow we shall see what a city without police protection and traffic guidance looks like. The significance of this strike is greater than that of any other recent one. It attests to the instability of the present order. It requires only the collapse of the military power to have it crumble in the dust. Then what?[51]

Most of the people who had gathered were about to find out what a city without police protection would be like, but few were likely concerned about tomorrow. Most were caught up in the here and now of the spectacle they were witnessing. In some cases, such as in front of Station House 4, it was reported that "More than 3,000 persons jammed La Grange [Street] in the rain."[52] Over in East Boston, another 3,000 or more people had gathered in Maverick Square before Station House 7.[53]

In some cases there was a rather festive mood shared by onlookers outside the station houses. The people were laughing and joking, acting as if everyone had gathered for one big celebration as they had for the parades when the soldiers came home from the Great War. At Station 14 in Brighton, the patrolmen exiting the station houses were received with warm greetings, good wishes, and cheers.[54] Joining in the celebratory mood were many of the officers, who shook hands and thanked the people for their kind words. Officers William Gibbons, Thomas Donahue, and Daniel Murphy, all recent appointees to the force and aged 30, 32, and 33 respectively, walked out laughing and smiling, which was captured by one of the many cameramen out to record this unique event.[55]

In a few cases simply no one bothered to show, such as in West Roxbury in front of Station House 17. In most locations, however, there was no festive celebration, for the police were met by angry mobs. For instance, when the patrolmen exited Station House 13 in Jamaica Plain, a noisy demonstration erupted with shouting, taunts, and jeers, and the men were, at first, blocked by the crowd from leaving. The bystanders begrudgingly opened a path for the policemen, who were then forced to walk through the gauntlet "made by the vituperative and hostile mob."[56] Many of the youths who had gathered carried sacks of fruit that were thrown at the passing officers, while others carried rocks. "Come on out and steal apples," someone shouted, "No more cops!"[57] And because the officers were no longer in their police uniforms, people gladly informed them, "You'll have to pay your fare home tonight!"[58]

It was the same at Station 19 in Mattapan, where officers received the rough treatment of taunts, jeers, and the occasional object thrown at them.[59] It was Station 10 in Roxbury Crossing, however, where the patrolmen probably received the worst treatment of all.[60] A large crowd of over 1,200 had gathered there and jeered them loudly as they exited "carrying their uniforms, rubber boots and coat hangers."[61] "This place is unfair to organized labor," one person was heard shouting.[62] "Station house for sale," came the shout of one kid, "A second-hand clothing shop will open here."[63] The rest booed and hurled curse words at the police officers.

The evening became even more difficult, however, because it had been raining all day and the streets were not all paved. One small boy who was described as "perform[ing] a bit of private research, gathered up a handful of mud from the street and hurled it at a policeman's face."[64] He, of course, ran off into the crowd. "The policeman," reported one witness, "glumly wiped away the mud and continued homeward without a word."[65] That experiment opened up other boys, men, and some women to follow suit. As the officers passed through the gauntlet made by an angry mob, they too were splattered with mud. Seeing this from the station house door, Sergeant Patrick Bryne tried dispersing the crowd to get them to cease their unruly behavior. Not only did he fail to move the crowd, but he too ended up with a face full of mud. In response, the crowd tried to tear down the station house awning, forcing Sergeant Byrne to retreat inside, where he called for reinforcements. Even so, it took nearly an hour for them to clear the throng.[66]

These minor acts of violence were occurring in isolated incidents around the city and were, in all actuality, revenge against the police in many cases. At the City Hall Avenue Station in Downtown, one patrolman exiting the front entrance was loaded down with "a pair of rubber boots, an extra uniform, a heavy overcoat, and various other articles."[67] The crowds there were thick, but a large burly Irish truck driver began elbowing his way through the people, shouting for them to get out of his way. They complied. When he broke out into the passage made by the parting sea of humanity to let the patrolmen pass, he confronted the officer loaded down with gear. "Gave me a traffic ticket the other day, would you?" he shouted in his face, before striking the officer on the chin.[68] The patrolman, knocked to the ground, lost hold of his equipment while the crowd wildly cheered the actions of the Irishman. The policeman, wisely, did nothing.[69]

By 7:30 p.m. the striking patrolmen had all left their respective station houses, either going home or making their way directly to Fay Hall.[70] Just how many officers had gone on strike has always been a source of some confusion. It was reported at the time that at 5:45 p.m. "only 30 of the 420 first-half men reported for duty."[71] All told, it was reported that only about 100 uniformed men remained on duty, although that included 19 captains and 38 lieutenants, the rest being sergeants and those officers who were close to retirement and did not want to jeopardize their pensions.[72] In the end, however, as Coolidge wrote in his autobiography, "about three-quarters of the force left the Department" and that "this number was much larger than had been expected."[73]

In the days and weeks leading up to the strike, Commissioner Curtis had tried to determine the number of officers who would go on strike. His captains, command staff, and many informants had been feeding him information, but it proved to be inaccurate. He later wrote,

> Most diligent inquiries had been made throughout the department by the superior officers who, through personal contact

with the men at the stations, many of whom they had known for years, were in the best position to size up the situation.[74]

Curtis added,

Yet this most careful canvass did not produce any definite information either in respect to the number of members of the union, or whether a strike had been determined upon, or, if so, when it would probably take place, or how many of the men, if any, would desert.[75]

His best guess was that of his men, "700 or 800 patrolmen would refuse to desert."[76] However, as it turned out, approximately 400, not 700 or 800, policemen remained on duty. The final official tally was that "1,117 patrolmen out of 1,544 in the department abandoned their office as police," explained Curtis in his annual report, adding, "or, as it is more commonly termed, 'struck.'"[77] And it quickly became clear that those 427 patrolmen could not do the work the 1,544 had done prior to 5:45 p.m. on September 9, 1919.[78]

After the station houses had all been emptied of their striking officers, the crowds remained behind. There was no reason for them to stay there, but they did so in a sort of restive anticipation of what was next to come.[79] Almost immediately after the excitement of the patrolmen leaving the stations had ended, and with no other excitement pressing at the moment in most of the crowds throughout the city, impromptu craps games broke out, a "favorite piece of bravado being to shoot the dice out in front of a police station."[80] According to the *Boston Herald*, the craps games broke out "to celebrate the new era of freedom" and that they "attracted hundreds of people."[81] The *Boston Globe* wrote that so many craps games were being played across the city that "it looked momentarily as though 'craps' and not baseball was our National sport."[82] One craps game on the sidewalk in front of the Park Street Church featured a self-appointed announcer who kept those in the crowd who could not see the dice informed of the game's progress, including the monetary value of the pot, which often grew to several hundred dollars. The winners were cheered, and when a large pot was won, they were lifted on the shoulders of others and carried about for praise and adulation. Some of the men who won large pots of money probably later rued this particular adulation, for when they walked away with their winnings, they were subsequently robbed by other members of the crowd.[83]

In addition to the many craps games, there were other incidents of minor crimes such as many false alarms for fires pulled during the early evening hours, as well as many false calls to the police. One such call was for "a man being beat up in Howard [Street]."[84] The officer arriving on the scene found nothing. There was a report of a young boy of 11 who broke into a fruit stand behind the South Station, from which he took cigars and cigarettes.[85] He was caught by the remaining police on duty, while another mischief-maker tried breaking into a petticoat factory on Otis Street; he was caught before he managed to get inside the building.[86]

Over on Court Square, where another large crowd had gathered in front of Station House 2, there was a loud explosion. Someone had fired off a pistol or set off some fireworks, causing the crowd to scatter. Hearing the explosion, Captain Sullivan stepped outside and shouted, "You'll have to cut that out and get away from here. I'm captain of this station, and I'm not going to have that sort of stuff around here."[87] The crowd just jeered at the man and began to press the station house steps. The crowds were becoming ever more bold.

The patrolmen who had remained on duty and were walking a beat were beginning to sense this as well. Around 8 p.m. four officers had briefly walked patrol together near Court Square on Hanover Street. As they started to separate and go in different directions on patrol, they realized the crowd was watching them intently, as if they were waiting for them to be alone. Sensing the threat, the officers rejoined each other and placed their backs to a wall. The crowd moved on, but the policemen knew the tension was building.[88]

These were not, however, the officers the crowds were looking for. Most of them were hoping to catch the volunteer policemen, and especially the Harvard University volunteers out on patrol.[89] At least that night, the troublemakers were greatly disappointed, for neither group was deployed. Despite all of the training to prepare the volunteers for patrol duty should the patrolmen go on strike, they were not deployed the first night of the strike and, indeed, were not placed on patrol until 8 a.m. the following morning.[90] There were some volunteers who worked the first night, but most of them helped to run the station houses, while two served as drivers for the patrol wagons used for transporting arrestees.[91]

Other assistance was less than stellar, and fewer men were deployed than had been anticipated. Commissioner Curtis had requested health commissioner W. C. Woodward to deploy his nine patrolmen (those assigned for special duty in the Health Department), but they were not told to report until 7:45 the following morning.[92] The Metropolitan Park Police had promised 100 officers would be ready to assist should a strike vote be called, but less than half responded that evening because most did not want to serve as strikebreakers.[93] Most of the officers were dispatched in the early evening to try to maintain order among the rapidly growing crowds in South Boston.[94]

Governor Coolidge had held 30 or 40 state police officers ready to deploy, and they did go into service, but their primary function was to guard the State House, not the city of Boston.[95] He also had the Motor Corps of the state guard ready to deploy if necessary, but they were held at the armory until about 8 p.m. As Coolidge explained, "As everything was quiet the Motor Corps went home."[96] In fact, he later gave the reason for no state resources being deployed onto the streets of Boston as being "No disorder existed." "It would have been rather a violent assumption that it was threatened, but it could have been made," he asserted, and that "such action probably would have saved property but would have decided no issue."[97] Despite the enormous and growing crowds that had not dispersed as it grew dark and the evening hours passed, neither the governor nor the police commissioner appeared worried. In fact, they had both gone to sleep. And although the mayor was concerned, he was still safe at home in his guarded house.

Although the crowds remained on the streets well into the evening, and in many cases continued to grow, relatively speaking, there was little in the way of serious crime. However, "The rowdyism increased as the night advanced," reported the *Boston Globe* the next morning, "and by midnight it had reached serious proportions."[98] Ground zero for these "serious proportions" appears to have been Scollay Square.

The square was once a large open affair at the intersection of Cambridge and Court Streets in downtown Boston. It was affectionately named in 1838 for William Scollay, who had notably served as a militia officer during the American Revolution and had purchased a four-story merchant building on the square. It had gone through many changes over the years, from an early thriving location for commerce to a theater district, and, by 1919, to the red-light district. As Boston historian Jack Tager explained, it was "the downtown center of bars, burlesque houses, tattoo parlors and squalid rooming houses."[99] Because of those attractions and the size of the square, it became a focal point for people turning out to "watch" the police strike. By the time the police had left the station houses, the number of people in Scollay Square was estimated to be at 3,000, and by nine o'clock it had risen to 5,000.[100]

One eyewitness that evening was Charles Wood, who later wrote, "I stood on the upperside of Scollay Square at nine o'clock on the night of the 'Police Strike,'" which he described as being "mostly silent" with people "talking in low tones, like those you hear before funeral services begin."[101] "There was an air of expectancy without knowing what was expected," he continued. "There was no patrolman. No police power. None in sight. The people were 'on their own.'"[102] The people mostly milled about through the throngs of onlookers, stopping to watch many of the continual craps games. "For over three hours," Wood reported, "nothing happened."[103]

Then, just before midnight, the mass took on a life of its own and everything changed. "Without apparent leadership," Wood wrote, "several men started toward Washington Street" along Court Street, and "others followed, unhurried, still aimless."[104] Wood describes what changed:

Then came the sharp sound of two hard substances in sharp impact, followed a second later by a louder one and the thrilling crash of falling, splintering glass. A plate show window had been shattered. Instantly the window and its immediate vicinity were filled with struggling men, a mass of action, from which emerged from time to time bearers of shirts, neckties, collars, hats. In a few seconds the window was bare. Some with loot vanished. . . . Lootless ones were attacking the next window. . . . None appeared who failed to show a desire to take part in the looting.[105]

The bonds of civilization were loosed, and the masses had turned to barbarism. As is typical in any riot, only a few, criminally inclined people tend to take action, but the masses, generally common everyday people, become caught up in the frenzy that takes over the crowd, and barbarism reigns for a time. Charles Wood later philosophized about what he had witnessed when he explained:

The sense of distinction between right and wrong which had been emphasized by nearly three hundred years of discipline disappeared in three hours. I did not, until then, realize how frail we are, how thin the veneer of civilization, how easily we may be led into a situation capable of breaking down defenses which most of us indifferently accept as a matter of fact, because they are existing order.[106]

What became the existing order for the next several hours was stunning.

A sea of humanity began traveling down Court Street, smashing the storefront windows and looting the window displays. At first the crowds were reluctant to be caught in the stores by some unknown enforcers of the law and merely grabbed these items, but that fear quickly abated because no one was there to stop them, and the crowd grew ever bolder.

The sound had echoed back into Scollay Square, and the smashing of plate-glass windows became endemic. Unable to move down Court Street because the street was clogged with so many people trying to do the same thing, much of the crowd started moving north on Cambridge Street. A photography studio was smashed on the north end of Scollay Square, and the same phenomenon occurred among this moving mass of people as well.[107] Smash the windows, loot the window display, and move to the next store up the street.

The thousands of people moving up Cambridge turned on Hanover Street and began making their way on that street, smashing and grabbing. The thousands moving along Court Street turned onto Washington Street. Each time someone in the crowd threw a rock and broke the plate-glass windows, it created a frenzy in front of that store. As the crowds began working both sides of the street simultaneously, each stop to raid a store created a jam of people behind them, who, frustrated that they could not get in on the action, splintered off down other streets.

One crowd of about 300, who appeared to be at the front of the Washington Street masses, had started at Milk Street. It consisted of mostly boys and men with "a sprinkling of young women" and "a few sailors and soldiers."[108] They hit the windows of Adams, a local tailor shop, at 357 Washington Street first. Once the window was smashed, "There was a scramble and the window was quickly cleaned of its goods."[109] The group methodically moved up the street, hitting Aronson's shoe store at 365 Washington Street, Peter the Rabbit (a hat store located next door at 367 Washington Street), and then the United Cigar Stores Company at 369 Washington Street. What followed next was the smashing of the window at the Boston Tailoring Company at 371 Washington Street, and finally, Posner's, located at the intersection of Avery and Washington Streets.[110] Nearby, between West and Avery Streets on Washington Street proper stood the Adams House, where Governor Coolidge was fast asleep.[111]

One lone patrolman near Winter Street tried being civil and appealed to the crowd to disperse and go home. It was reported, "They laughed at him."[112] The crowd seemed to be in a truly festive mood, for they even laughed when two sailors in unform across from Macullar, Parker, and Company's store held a gun on a man and robbed him of everything in his possession—most of the items had been obtained while looting the stores. It was reported that 500 people looked upon the robbery and laughed.[113]

Many of the people participating in, if not instigating, the smashing and looting were sailors. Many of them were armed with sticks, bricks, and other missiles, and were among the ones smashing the store windows. Perhaps they were empowered by the hundreds of people who looked on with glee and followed them from store to store. Not long after midnight, "Word was sent to the Charlestown Navy Yard that the leaders in several of the mobs of rioters were sailors in the uniform of the United States Navy."[114] By one o'clock in the morning, they had dispatched a group to go after the rioting sailors.[115]

Another crowd broke off and turned down Union Street, and like all the rest, it seemed there was nothing to stop them. In this case, however, there actually was. The crowd first hit the Lewis Shoe Store, which proved popular with the looters, primarily because new shoes were a luxury item that most of the rioters could not afford. They then hit a clothing store, another popular storefront from which to smash and grab, as well as a cigar shop. They next raided the Dock Square Fruit Company stand storefront and then smashed the window of the Wholesale Provision Company from which spilled forth oranges, rolling around their feet on the sidewalk. It was at this store that 70-year-old night watchman James J. Burns burst from the store wielding a .38-caliber revolver in his hand. "Get back there," he yelled at the crowd, "or I'll send you before your God."[116] The crowd, momentarily afraid, backed off, but then became amused at the old man holding a gun. Some were then brazen enough to test him by making movements toward him, but Burns was quick to turn the gun toward anyone threatening him. For the next 20 minutes, the crowd taunted the night watchmen, but finally, growing bored and impatient, they moved on. The Wholesale Provision Company was the only store on that block not completely looted that night.

The mob pressed on, moving wherever there were storefront locations, smashing further along North Street, before making its way toward Sudbury Street, where it emptied out Coleman & Keating's Store, looting all of its bottled goods. It then flowed around toward Court Street. Into the early hours of Wednesday, September 10, the crowd was, as the *Boston Globe* noted, "still marking its progress by the smashing of glass."[117]

As the masses moved along Court Street, it had now been smashing and looting for nearly two hours. It was at this time that 10 of the Metropolitan Park Police were dispatched with Sergeant Flaherty to try to control the crowd. Despite the incredible odds, the sergeant gave a valiant effort; with pistol in hand, he charged forward and met the crowd coming up the street. He was assisted, in part, by someone in the crowd firing off several gunshots that sent the people scurrying for cover. Realizing nothing had happened from those shots, the crowd re-formed and continued moving forward, and the 10 Metropolitan Park Police officers, with a "vigorous use of their clubs," somehow "managed to disperse the people."[118]

In South Boston it was much the same, but the trouble had not begun there with smashed windows; instead, some of the men and boys pulled the trolley cars off their wires and smashed the cars' windows.[119] It did not take them long, however, to start emulating the Scollay Square crowds by smashing and looting storefronts. The rest of the Metropolitan Park Police, 30 in number, were dispatched to try to stop the damage to the trolley cars. When they arrived the crowd was estimated to have grown to about 5,000, and they were moving along Broadway Street. Again, despite the overwhelming odds, the park police, along with some of the Boston patrolmen who remained on duty, met the mob with their clubs. The mob barbarically responded "with a barrage of stones and sticks and bottles and eggs."[120]

Special Officer Sheehan was driving his car through the crowds moving through South Boston, trying to make his way to the City Point Station House to report for duty. He saw a man, later identified as George Marks, throwing a rock through the window of a shoe store along Broadway. "Jumping from the machine," it was reported the next day, "Sheehan chased the man."[121] After the pursuit turned down several streets, Sheehan fired one shot in the air while running, and Marks, scared by the sound, stopped. Sheehan then brought his suspect back to his automobile and handcuffed him to one of the uprights on top of the car before taking him to headquarters, where Sheehan was hailed for his actions.[122]

Another crowd moving through Roxbury, southwest of the South Boston neighborhood, had been active since before midnight. The mob was not as large, numbering only around 600, but it proved just as destructive. Mostly consisting of young men and boys, described as "hoodlums from 14 to 20 years," they moved along Dorchester Avenue toward Andrew Square, smashing plate-glass windows and looting every store along the way.[123] In addition to the theft, however, this group proved to be more violent.

Walter Essley, a peddler in Highland Park, was walking along Tremont Street when he was attacked by a group of boys who threw stones and bricks at him. One of the bricks struck him in the head, and he had to be taken to the hospital.[124] Another group of boys found an empty, unlocked cab they set on fire and rolled into Roxbury Crossing in front of Police Station 10.[125] The officers manning the station sounded the alarm, and the fire was eventually put out. Thomas Innes, a streetcar conductor, was passing through a large crowd when he heard a gunshot and found he had been struck by the bullet. He was taken to the City Hospital for treatment.[126]

One boy, who later confessed to having been involved in the Roxbury mob, said, "But you should have seen the crowd that night," clearly caught up in what had happened after the police went on strike.[127] "I was in a crowd of about 600," he said before admitting, "We broke in and looted several stores."[128] "You should have seen them hand out the drawers and the cloth," he continued, "giving it out or selling it all along the sidewalk."[129] Most of the other crowds had consisted of young men and boys, and he confirmed his crowd was no different when he noted, "I bet you there wasn't a kid older than 25 years."[130] Finally, in describing the reason for the rioting, he explained, "They were in it for the fun. Half of them had bags with them to carry the stuff away in."[131]

It was the same all over Boston—the crowds had taken over the city. In Andrews Square, windows were smashed, and the stores were cleaned out.[132] On the West End, at Mechanic's

Hall, a sports venue, there was a boxing match underway, and the crowd rushed the building, flooding in through side doors, back doors, and smashed windows. It was estimated that "600 got in free."[133] Even in the quiet neighborhood of East Boston, with only two sergeants on duty there, there were a number of clothing and shoe stores looted, including the one owned by Jack Goldenburg, who later discovered the looters had done the following:

> [They] had pulled out every drawer in the place, ripped the fixings from the walls and done all in their power to wreck the place. Neckties, shirts, and underwear . . . were scattered from the rear of the store out onto the muddy sidewalks and streets.[134]

And even out in the northwest neighborhood of Brighton, there were numerous store windows smashed and shops looted along Main Street.[135]

There were many incidents of robbery throughout the city, such as the holdup on Ashmont Street of a Dorchester grocer, when the robber took the grocer's wallet at gunpoint, jumped into a waiting car, and drove off.[136] But most of the activity that night and well into the morning consisted of looting, like in the downtown area, where it was reported, "Men walked along the street with shirts or neckties, shoes, jewelry and haberdashery, openly trading shirts for shoes or jewelry or either."[137] "Shoe stores were the favorite target," it was noted often in the newspapers, because "of rioters from poor backgrounds."[138] When interviewed by the reporters, one such "witness" explained, "Somebody would say, 'Let's go!' Laughing and joking," and then "they would surge along to the next shoe store; somebody would lean against the show window, or give it a kick, and a scramble to reach in for shoes would follow."[139] After the looters obtained their goods, they would then sit "down calmly on the curbstone to try on their new acquisitions."[140] And if their new shoes didn't fit, it apparently did not matter, for they knew "they could be traded for something else a few minutes later."[141]

Other than the stores that were guarded, the only stores that were safe from looting were bookstores. One mob was moving down the street looking for the right merchandise to steal, usually clothing and shoe stores, and the leader of the gang would shout, "Come on! Let's go in here, fellers! Come on!"[142] Once finished, they started to cross the street to the next store when the leader stopped. Realizing it was a bookstore, one owned by Francis J. Gagnon, he shouted out, "Them's books. Naw! What in hell can we do with them things?"[143] As it turns out, his dislike for books might have saved his life. Gagnon and his employees were waiting inside the bookstore, armed.

The crowds were somewhat satiated by 1 a.m., and they had, by that time, stopped increasing in numbers. They were also not afforded the cover of darkness in the late morning hours, because Superintendent Crowley had requested the Edison Electric Illuminating Company to keep the streetlights burning until daylight.[144] They were usually turned off by 1:30 a.m. and not relit until the next night.

By 3:30 in the morning, much of the crowd had gone home, but there were still some straggling groups out looting either what had been picked over or finding the stores that had been untouched down some of the less traveled side streets.[145] A call came into Station House 16 in Back Bay about that time reporting that a mob was ransacking Sawyer's Drug Store on Huntington Avenue, and Sergeants Campbell and Waugh responded.[146] There, they found 10 young men in the store rifling through the merchandise. When they spotted the patrolmen, they ran, separating into three groups. Sergeant Campbell chased one group, firing into the air to try to get them to stop, with no success. Sergeant Waugh chased another of the groups, and he focused on the one man he could see carrying a number of boxes under his arms. He pursued the man, yelled for him to stop, and when he failed to do so, he fired a shot. The bullet hit John Scully, age 20, in the back of the head near his ear, and he crumpled to the ground, his boxes belonging to a local haberdashery store spilling everywhere. He was rushed to the City Hospital, and his condition was listed as critical. The doctors were fairly certain he would not live the rest of the night.

That proved to be the last serious incident of the night, and the city of Boston crept toward dawn.

As the sun came up on Boston, everyone began assessing the damage from overnight. "For the first time in the memory of man," reported one local paper, "Boston was given over to lawlessness."[147] All of the papers duly reported on how the city had fared overnight.

The business establishments had many storefront windows smashed, and there was an extensive loss of property. Since most of the looting had been of clothing and shoes or alcohol and cigars, these stores were hardest hit. Because no goods were available on State Street in the banking district, and because they had guards on duty, they had remained safe. Four of the United Cigar Stores across Boston were hit for a loss of $5,000 (the loss of nearly $80,000 in modern dollars), while Edward D. Kakas & Sons had lost $7,000 worth of furs (equivalent to $110,000 in today's dollars).[148] "Two hundred thousand dollars will not cover the property damage and thefts committed in Boston last night," declared superintendent of police Michael H. Crowley that morning, "but we hope for no such serious repetition of lawlessness as prevailed during the night."[149] It was the first mention of a possible repeat night of rioting.

The courts were crowded that morning with those the limited police force had been able to arrest for their crimes. It was reported "there were 129 arrests at 11 of the 19 stations."[150] Most of these were for breaking and entering and larceny, although it was reported that more than 20 automobiles had been stolen overnight.[151]

The hospitals had assisted numerous people who had been injured by flying glass, but no one had been seriously hurt other than Scully, who was still somehow managing to linger. Perhaps the second-worst injury from overnight was that of Joseph Huggs, a 47-year-old African American who had not been involved in the looting. He found himself in a heated argument about the strike with someone who became so angry with him he pulled out a knife. Huggs "was stabbed on the head and in the face."[152] His assailant escaped.

It seems the only entity that had managed to gain rather than lose overnight was the Policemen's Union. President McInnes reported that they had managed to increase their membership by 50 additional patrolmen since the walkout.[153] Buoyed by this increase, they were determined to press on with the strike.

Soldiers from the Massachusetts State Guard break up a craps game taking place in front of Brewer Fountain, near the corner of Park and Tremont Streets.

Photo courtesy of the Boston Public Library, Leslie Jones Collection.

10

The Boston Riots

September 10, 1919

"True to their word, the policemen struck last night," recorded future historian Samuel Rezneck in his journal the next morning.[1] He had not yet left for England and so bore witness to the aftermath of what he called the "rowdyism of a populace let loose from all restraints."[2] "The results of the night made a wonderful sight this morning," he continued. "Stores by the score in all parts of the city had been broken into and wrecked, and presented a deplorable appearance in the morning with their shattered windows and disordered goods."[3]

The local newspapers also recorded the previous night's destruction. The *Boston Herald* called it "A Night of Disgrace" in their headline, and they laid out the allegation that "Somebody blundered! Boston should not have been left defenseless last night in the face of the rioting in Liverpool and other cities. . . . It was a sickening scene and no hand was available to arrest the unlawfulness."[4] Although the national newspapers noted the destruction caused by the police strike, they took less of a focus on the local impact and, instead, fixed their attention on the social implications. The *Wall Street Journal* headlined with "Lenin and Trotsky on the Way," for they saw the strike and destruction as no less than the beginning of an American Bolshevik revolution.[5]

185

Despite all of the varied reports in the newspapers, most people—at least those who had not participated in the mob riots—were asking, as the *Boston Herald* did, why the city had been left defenseless, especially in light of London's previous example and the full knowledge that the strike was forthcoming. It was perhaps one lone unnamed "police official," however, who summed it up best when he told a reporter for the *Boston Globe*:

> Something will have to be done and done immediately. This condition of affairs cannot last another day. Last night's depredations were bad, but if the mob spirit is allowed to run riot there is no telling where the trouble will end. . . . Why not call out the State Guard?[6]

His concern was that the rioting would likely continue and, lacking a full police force, there would be nothing to stop it. He knew it was time to call out the state guard. Fortunately, those in power finally began thinking the same thing.

The first person, it seems, who had made this call was not the mayor but rather his secretary, E. V. B. Parke. As he monitored the situation overnight from the mayor's office, while the mayor stayed home, Parke felt the situation demanded troops. So, at 2:30 a.m. Wednesday morning, he drove to Jamaica Plain to the mayor's house to tell him so.[7] They then began working on a statement to be released to the press immediately. The statement read:

> The occurrences of last evening, as reported to me by the newspapers, demonstrate the need of concerted action on the part of the better element of the community for the preservation of law and order. The better element, which is in the large majority, will not tolerate this type of vandalism, and the better element must make itself felt. The Police Commissioner is the one by law charged with the enforcement of the law. I shall make every effort to get in touch with him in reference to the situation.[8]

The mayor effectively placed the blame on Curtis, and after releasing the statement, the mayor sent the police commissioner a message signifying that because he was the one in charge, the commissioner needed to get the situation under control.

As Curtis was driven to police headquarters that morning, he witnessed much of the damage that had been caused by the mobs the previous night, and after receiving updates from his staff on just how bad the situation had become, Curtis had a change of opinion. He then wrote to the mayor in response to his letter, "I am of the opinion that tumult, riot or mob is threatened and that the usual police provisions are at present inadequate to preserve order and afford protection to persons and property."[9] Less than 24 hours prior, Curtis had told the mayor the state guard would be unnecessary, but now that realities of "tumult, riot, or mob" were present, he asked the mayor to make the call for additional forces. Mayor Peters acted immediately upon receipt of the police commissioner's message and sent his request for the activation of the 10th Regiment of the Massachusetts State Guard. He then issued another statement to the press:

I have hitherto relied upon the statement of the Police Commissioner that he had complete control of the situation. I am now in receipt of a communication from him in which, in substance, he says that riots are threatened, that the police provisions are inadequate to preserve order, and requests me to take the steps . . . to call upon such militia as are within the City of Boston to preserve order.[10]

Peters's statement again blamed Curtis for the disorder and demonstrated he was taking charge of the situation.

Governor Coolidge had arrived at his own office a little later than Curtis. He wrote in his autobiography, "On reaching my office in the morning it was reported to me that the Mayor was calling out the state guard of Boston to report about five o'clock that afternoon. He also requested me to furnish more troops."[11] Coolidge, having been advised of the situation, wrote back to the mayor,

> In accordance with the understanding between the Police Commissioner and yourself, he has transmitted to me a copy of his request to you for additional forces to maintain law and order. I am awaiting any request you desire to make. . . . You are at liberty to call on whatever you desire.[12]

Peters immediately fired back a one-sentence letter making his "formal request for additional troops."[13] Upon receipt of the letter, the governor directed the 4th Brigade, "less the bands of the several organizations and the Machine Gun Company of the 14th Regiment of the State Guard," to report to the mayor for duty.[14] As Coolidge stated in his autobiography, "I supplemented his action by calling substantially the entire State Guard to report at once."[15] Coolidge, however, then issued a statement to the press at noon in which he effectively blamed Mayor Peters for the rioting the night before, suggesting he had in his power the ability to call up the state guard earlier but chose not to do so.[16]

Mayor Peters was busy with the activation of the state guard and was slow to respond to the governor's statement, but by early afternoon, he issued his own defense. "I have been so engrossed this morning in arranging the steps necessary to restore and maintain order in the city," Peters began, "that I have only now had the opportunity to consider the statement issued a few hours ago by Gov Coolidge, in which he tries to place on me the responsibility for the distressing disturbances which occurred last night."[17] The mayor then pointed out that he had been told numerous times, "the only person who has authority to police the city is the Police Commissioner," and that after consulting with him, "Mr. Curtis said that he had the situation well in hand."[18] He emphasized that after asking Curtis if he needed assistance from the state guard, the "Police Commissioner stated in no uncertain terms that he did not wish their aid at the time."[19] Mayor Peters, once again, placed the blame on Police Commissioner Curtis. However, he was not finished, for he also defended himself against the governor's attack by adding,

Furthermore, in a recent communication from the Governor, he states so plainly that no one has any authority to interfere with the Police Commissioner. . . . I had no alternative but to give the Police Commissioner a chance to demonstrate that he had adequately provided for the situation.[20]

The mayor thus placed the ultimate blame on both the police commissioner *and* the governor.

Curtis had remained relatively quiet throughout this exchange. Amity Shlaes explains in her biography of Calvin Coolidge that "Curtis sat deluged with applications by security firms and other private groups to carry guns."[21] The commissioner essentially focused his energies on his administrative duties, rather than on policy solutions for the problem. He was quite busy handling all of these requests that had to pass across his desk, for all told, "1,052 individuals had applied for gun permits in Boston and 390 people for licenses to serve as special policemen."[22]

Already incensed over the police commissioner's lack of preparation, the mayor had lost all confidence in the man, having not seen or heard from Curtis. The mayor then decided to deal with that issue immediately. He released a stunning proclamation:

It having been made to appear to me, Andrew J. Peters, Mayor of the city of Boston, that tumult, riot and violent disturbance of public order have occurred within the limits of the city of Boston, and the exigency in my judgement requiring such action, I hereby . . . assume control for the time being of the police of the said city of Boston, and call upon the Police Commissioner to execute all orders promulgated by me for the suppression of the such tumult and the restoration of such public order.[23]

Mayor Peters had both rebuked the police commissioner and placed himself in charge.

Realizing that he would effectively be in charge of the entire response, the mayor needed someone to handle the state guard mobilization. The mayor delegated responsibility to General

Samuel D. Parker and selected General Charles H. Cole to serve as his military adjutant to advise him on all things military.[24] Parker immediately took command of the situation, but he complicated the political dynamic by moving his headquarters from the South Amory to police headquarters in order to work closely with the remaining police force.[25] While this meant he would be working closely alongside Curtis and not the mayor, it most certainly had a demeaning effect on the police commissioner.

From the governor's standpoint, he, too, had been undermined, for the police commissioner was his appointee. He also had other fears, as he explained in his autobiography:

> It was soon reported to me that the Mayor, acting under a special law, had taken charge of the police force of the city, and by putting a Guard officer in command had virtually displaced the Commissioner, who came to me in great distress. If he was to be superseded I thought the men that he had discharged might be taken back and the cause lost. Certainly they and the rest of the policemen's union must have rejoiced at his discomfort.[26]

Coolidge was clearly more concerned about the "cause" than restoring order to the city—the cause in this case being the right for police officers to unionize. His fears, as he put it, were concerned with the prospect of Peters hiring the suspended officers back, thus undermining the rights of government to prevent police unionization.[27] In fact, one of the first questions Mayor Peters was asked by the press after the proclamation was released was if he would negotiate with the union. Peters answered, "I can say nothing on that point now. My immediate aim is the restoration of normal conditions."[28]

For Governor Coolidge, "This next choice was simple," explains Shlaes. "Coolidge could back up Peters, or he could back up Curtis."[29] Backing Peters was the easy choice, while "sticking with Curtis would be the most controversial move of his career."[30] Mayor Peters had quite effectively defended himself and placed the blame on the governor and the police commissioner. The fact that "Curtis clearly had not prepared for the extent of the strike or the onslaught in the city," meant, as

Shlaes details, "Coolidge could be blamed for that alone."[31] The decision, however, had to wait. Coolidge needed to consult with the state's lawyers, as well as do a little legal research of his own.

As for the police commissioner himself, the strategy Curtis took was to simply abide by the mayor's order. He sent a short message to the mayor stating, "Dear Sir—Your note of Sept 10, notifying me that you assume control for the time being of the city of Boston has been received. I respectfully await your action. Respectfully, Edwin U. Curtis."[32] The police commissioner would only do what he was told to do, knowing that it was likely the mayor who would find the task of restoring order overwhelming. Then, the blame would shift back to the mayor.

Throughout most of the day, all three of the leaders—the governor, the mayor, and the police commissioner—spent their energies on blaming each other for the situation the city of Boston found itself in. The same unnamed police official who had so sensibly seen the need to call out the state guard also wisely cut through all of the accusations when he told a reporter, "Someone must back down in this crisis. Pride should be pocketed, even at the loss of dignity."[33]

The striking policemen had gathered in large numbers at Fay Hall, where reporters were stationed to capture their activities regarding the strike. Throughout the morning, reported the *Boston Globe*, "Many enthusiastic speeches were made and the hall repeatedly rang with cheers for the speakers."[34] Sometimes the men broke out in song, singing renditions of "Hail, Hail, the Gang's All Here."[35] They also greeted news from the State AFL Convention, the one Governor Coolidge had recently addressed, that the AFL had pledged their "full moral and financial support" to the Boston Policemen's Union.[36] They were bolstered even further when more officers began to arrive asking to become members. Those who received the greatest cheers were the members of a delegation from the Metropolitan Park Police, representing most of the 53 officers who had refused to serve as strikebreakers the previous evening.[37] They had good reason to become members, for upon notifying their supervisors that they refused to abide by the order for emergency duty, they were immediately suspended and were "required to surrender their badges, revolvers and other paraphernalia."[38] When they left the station, a crowd, seeing them without their badges and guns, cried out, "Run them down."[39] Despite their hopes, however, of immediately gaining membership, President McInnes advised them that they needed to form their own organization and affiliate with the AFL.[40]

As the striking policemen celebrated throughout the morning, business owners slowly began assessing the damage done to their property.[41] After cleaning up the broken glass, many business owners began removing any valuables still remaining in their stores in preparation for further rioting. Others, however, took a different approach and decided to fortify their businesses. Employees from Huyler's and Mark Cross's stores on Tremont Street began erecting barriers and stringing barbed wire across them. "They were vicious-looking contrivances and looked capable of checking anyone," wrote one reporter who overheard a man remarking, "Gee, that looks like France."[42] Still others took an armed approach; owners of the Old South Trust Company on Washington Street decided to leave their doors wide open, although one only had to glance inside to see a half dozen armed men sitting with rifles and handguns at the ready.[43] Some store managers had all of their lights turned on, while others left their stores completely dark.[44] The managers of most of the department stores told their female employees arriving for work that morning to turn around, go home, and stay at home.[45]

People also began coming out to see the damage caused by the mobs, while others began walking the streets to see if there would be any more excitement or if the state guard had been deployed. Like the day before, the numbers continued to rise, sometimes rapidly in certain popular areas, with one of the major concentrations of people being located at Scollay Square. It was there that the trouble started once again.

Boston Police Sergeant Michael Sullivan was in charge of the square where there was a handful of volunteer officers working the area, but the crowds were growing too large for anyone to control. Then someone threw a rock at the window of Walton's Lunchroom on Tremont Row and broke the glass. This drew attention of not only the police but the crowds as well. As the volunteer officers tried to make their way to Walton's, they were attacked by people throwing sticks at them. It is estimated that within 15 minutes, the crowd had swelled to 5,000 people, all drawn to the unfolding excitement.[46] "The crowd was so dense," reported the *Boston Globe*, "that hundreds climbed on top of the subway entrances."[47] Feeling he needed to regain control, Sergeant Sullivan drew his revolver and pointed it at the crowd. That caused an immediate stampede as people fled for their lives down Brattle and Cornhill Streets.[48]

Then, with poor timing, a coal wagon began making its way across Scollay Square through the masses of people. The mob swarmed the wagon. Now armed with ready ammunition, they began throwing the black coal at the sergeant and the volunteer officers.[49] One of the volunteers, Arthur H. Morse, who was an attorney, "sustained a badly bruised and blackened eye when he was hit by a lump of coal."[50] This created a sense of desperation on the part of the volunteers, and they hatched a plan in the hopes of outmaneuvering the mob. Five of them, acting as decoys, ran down Brattle Street with the intent of drawing the crowds after them and away from Scollay Square.[51] It worked, for as the *Boston Herald* reported,

> These volunteers, hotly pursued by the mob, stopped from time to time and leveled their weapons against the crowd. Their would-be captors momentarily drew back, only to surge forward again and hurl a shower of missiles. The five decoys finally turned to make their stand and their assailants overwhelmed them. Two police sergeants and Superintendent Crowley ran to rescue these men from a brutal pummeling.[52]

It was an incredible risk to take, especially for Crowley, the man who was responsible for directing all of the police throughout Boston. Had they not received some assistance, it is doubtful any of them would have come out of the incident unscathed.

As it was, General Parker wanted the entire square cleared of people upon learning of the crowds gathering in Scollay Square.[53] He was thinking militarily of clearing an area and then sealing it off to prevent the enemy from returning, thus controlling the geographical domain. The general dispatched cavalry troops to begin sweeping through the square. Their arrival was fortuitous for the commander who was witnessing what was happening from atop horseback; he immediately ordered his troops into line formation and to draw sabers. This certainly had to have had a psychological impact on the crowd, but that was not all the cavalry commander was seeking. Having raised his own saber, he let it drop—the signal for the troops to charge. "The sight of a saber-swinging adversary bearing down on enemy troops at a gallop was horrifying," reported the *Boston Herald*, and upon seeing this, the mob panicked and ran in all directions.[54] The cavalry, having rescued the officers being beaten, had literally saved the day.[55]

Elsewhere in Scollay Square, the crowds were smashing more windows, bats were swung to damage property, mud was flung that spattered anyone and everyone, and occasionally someone would fire off a gun. Vehicles were overturned, stores were looted, and a US mail truck was ransacked by the frenzied crowd.[56] The situation had degraded in Scollay Square, while elsewhere it was only beginning.

"All day long the city was in an uproar," Rezneck wrote. "Gambling proceeded openly on all the streets—and whiskey was sold freely everywhere in spite of all prohibition."[57] The majority of the crowds milling about in the street were either playing craps or watching the craps games being played.[58] It was reported that two elderly women on Tremont Street, near Parker Street, saw a huge crowd gathered in front of the YMCA, the Salvation Army, and the Knights of Columbus storefronts. The crowd seemed very attentive to something going on along the sidewalk in front of the stores, so the ladies thought it might have been a religious service. It was not uncommon on Sundays for such meetings in the area, although usually they were held on the Boston Commons. "Let's go over to the meeting," suggested one of the ladies to her friend, and they crossed the street. As the *Boston Globe* reported, "Suddenly the women turned back and scurried across the street. They had heard the jingling of silver that sounded louder than a prayer-meeting collection. It was a game of craps, in fact 12 games of craps."[59]

In addition to the mass of people who had come out to walk the streets of Boston, another problem arose when people began trying to drive through the city. There were no traffic police on duty, for they had either gone on strike or were helping to control the mob activity, and the streets soon became gridlocked with vehicles.[60] The confluence of both people and automobiles made the problem even worse. One boy by the name of Frank Cassell saw the problem in front of the old State House, stepped into the middle of the intersection of Devenshire and State Streets, and began directing traffic. He apparently was quite successful as he managed to get traffic moving again, at least in the immediate vicinity. By early afternoon, however, a volunteer policeman was forced to chase him away. When asked by a reporter "Why?" he replied, "O, I had no fault to find with the boy, but we had to clear the streets of the crowd that gathered to see him perform. The streets were clear, but no one could walk on the sidewalks."[61] Recognizing the traffic problem, Chester I. Campbell, secretary of the Boston Automobile Dealers' Association, announced that his organization would assume the task of directing traffic. They eventually deployed 50 volunteers.

There were reports of aggressive crowds in the afternoon, although none equaled the violence experienced in Scollay Square. One demonstration of about 300 was located in front of Fay Hall, but the group was not destructive and appeared to be voicing their pro–police union sentiments.[62] One large crowd that possibly intended violence attempted to enter the courthouse building but were quickly turned away. Sheriff John A. Keliher had his deputies well prepared, and none of them had joined the strike. The crowd was immediately repelled, which left them to taunt the deputies from outside the courthouse until the Boston police managed to clear Courthouse Square.[63] Still another crowd that had gathered in Pemberton Square maintained a constant chorus of boos as they followed the volunteer officers on patrol there.[64]

There was often a distinct difference in the respect shown by the crowd toward the regular policemen versus the volunteers. The former were often given some degree of courtesy and respect, while the latter bore the brunt of the crowd's anger and animosity. For the working class, this was generally because the volunteers were seen as strikebreakers, while others simply felt the volunteers had no real authority over them, other than that which they could assert through the end of their nightstick or revolver. For whatever reason, the volunteers were the favorite target of the mob.

Most of the men who had already volunteered to serve as policemen had been told to report for duty Wednesday morning. Others, however, volunteered that morning after seeing the destruction the mob had committed Tuesday night. The surge of volunteers had become so great at the Chamber of Commerce office that they had to wait around in the library room until they could be processed. Although the numbers of volunteers were clouded in mystery, it was estimated that 500 recruits were added September 10, bringing the total to 825 volunteers.[65]

The largest increase that morning came from a delegation of Harvard University men who had arrived at 8 a.m. They had been motivated by President Lowell's call for service, and by 10 a.m. there were 150 Harvard students present.[66] Even President Lowell and Dean Chester Greenough showed up to encourage the Harvard volunteers, and later they would tour the streets of Boston doing the same.[67]

There were also many Harvard University alumni who volunteered, but the one the reporters were most interested in was former Harvard football player Huntington E. "Tack" Hardwick.[68] He was interviewed and followed by reporters for some time. Tack had asked to be placed on night duty, and when the reporters asked why, he responded, "I want night duty so I can attend to my business in the daytime."[69] When he began patrolling, his first assignment was to disperse a crowd across the street from the police station. As he was yet unarmed, the *Boston Globe* reported, "He doubled his fists and started toward the crowd as he used to start for the Yale rush line. The crowd broke up rapidly."[70]

When a volunteer was finally called for processing that morning, there was a request for basic information such as their occupation and where they lived. The volunteer's name was then placed on a list, and they would wait once again. One of the volunteers was General Francis Peabody, a lawyer and a member of one of Massachusetts's most distinguished families who had served as the judge advocate general to Governor William E. Russell (hence his title).[71] He was 65 years old, but he did not let that bother anyone else, although he, too, still had to wait for his name to be called.

When he finally heard his name, Russell went before a lieutenant's desk, announced his name, and the lieutenant checked it off a list. He then received his equipment: a badge to be worn on his lapel; a billy club to be placed in his coat pocket; and a revolver, fully loaded. Once so accoutered, he waited for his assignment. He was eventually paired with patrolman Murray, and they began walking their beat. One reporter wrote:

[General Peabody] strode down the north side of State [Street] wearing a natty, blue serge and golf cap and puffing away at a cigar. From his side pocket projected a billy. A few stopped to look in wonder at the badge shining on his coat lapel, but on the whole the crowd was kept moving.[72]

A short time later, he came across another volunteer, and one he knew well: Admiral Frances T. Bowles.[73] When Peabody asked him what he had been doing lately, he responded, "A little dusting and cleaning" for the Emergency Fleet Corporation (EFC), so he decided to volunteer. Bowles was actually in charge of the EFC, which had been created in 1917 to reestablish the Merchant Marines. After they conversed for a bit, Patrolman Murray then showed Peabody how to ring into the station at a nearby call box.

And so it went for many of the other volunteer policemen. Some, however, quickly found themselves in precarious situations depending upon where they were assigned. Thomas D. Cabot, a US Army lieutenant during the war, had been one of the officers on duty in front of Walton's Lunchroom. He and another volunteer had become the target of the crowd after the plate-glass window was broken; feeling overwhelmed, they were forced to run to the Court Square Police Station, where they were able to bring back help.[74] Although there were not as many incidents throughout the day, save in Scollay Square, it appears the volunteer police were the ones dealing with many of the situations before the state guard came on duty that evening. Indeed, the volunteers were the ones left to handle the resurgence of mob violence in Scollay Square.

Although the square had been cleared, General Parker did not have enough troops on hand to hold ground, and people began returning throughout the afternoon. Most of the state guard who had received their orders and were currently mobilizing would not reach the streets until early evening. In the meantime, the crowd had grown significantly by 5 p.m. The police were of the opinion that many of the criminals and gang members were now back out on the street looking to cause trouble, and as a result, they once again used the crowds to their advantage.[75] Since the coal from the wagon was gone and no longer useful after repeated use, the crowd now turned to anything that could serve as a projectile. Sergeant Sullivan, still on duty, dodged a bottle that was thrown at him, but was not quick enough to dodge the potato that followed.[76] Angered by the insult, he chased the youth who had thrown it, but as he did so, he fell on the stone pavement. It was reported that he "rose unsteadily with a gash in his face, from which the blood spurted," as the crowds began to rush him. "He then pulled his revolver, brandished it in the air, and rushed the crowd down Brattle [Street]. Other officers on duty also drew their revolvers and the volunteer police used their clubs on some of the youngsters."[77]

The crowds, however, just kept returning, and this back-and-forth between the police and the mob continued. At a few minutes past 6 p.m., a group of six volunteer officers who had been on the chasing end of the crowd found themselves in the middle of Scollay Square.[78] The mob almost immediately surrounded them on all sides. They were then pelted by sticks and stones and spattered with mud, as the mob viciously taunted the volunteers, encouraging them to pull their guns or use their nightsticks. So angered at this treatment, one of the volunteers rushed at some of the members of the mob, breaking from his fellow officers. This was an incredible mistake, for he was immediately overwhelmed and beaten to the ground. The others, however, came to his rescue by moving together and using their clubs.[79] All six were no doubt left wondering where the State Guard was at that moment.

The first visible sign of the state guard deployment came at approximately 1:30 p.m. when the fire alarm system for the Central Fire Station began sounding the "7-7-7" alarm.[80] Most people did not know what the alarm meant, naturally assuming there was a fire somewhere. The "7-7-7" call, however, was one of the means by which members of the state guard were alerted to report for duty. All afternoon, across the city, state guardsmen began reporting to their armories, where personnel would soon place them on the streets of Boston as a military force instructed to restore and preserve order.

The units being activated consisted of the 4th Brigade with its three components: the 11th, 12th, and 15th Infantry Regiments. Additional units mobilized included the 10th and 20th Regiments, the 15th Infantry, the 1st Motor Corps, the 1st Cavalry Troop, and the 1st Ambulance Company, comprising approximately 6,000 men reporting for duty.[81] It would take all afternoon for the state guard troops to report to either the East or South Armories, and their deployment onto the streets did not come about until early evening.[82] For instance, Delta Company of the 10th Regiment received their orders "by telephone at noon, to report to the East Armory immediately for active duty during the strike."[83] They were not on active duty at the time, so the troops were either at home or at work. By 3 p.m. three officers and 49 men had reported for duty, and their early arrival meant they were actually fed before assembly was called. The bugle sounded at 4:30 p.m. and the regiment (at least those who had reported) took their positions on the drill floor, while the officers received their instructions from Colonel T. F. Sullivan.[84]

At 5 p.m. Delta Company was loaded onto trucks. A convoy composed of four other companies left the armory heading for South Boston. The company was to report to Police Station 6 for duty.[85] As the trucks began driving down the crowded streets of Broadway, the troops saw the equally crowded sidewalks and received their first sign of what to expect—it was not a docile one. Rather, the crowds began voicing extreme hostility at the arrival of members of the state guard, and "amid hoots of derision the trucks made their way down Broadway as far as D Street."[86] At D Street the throng of people was so dense they left no path for the trucks to pass, so the drivers turned off Broadway and made their way down D Street before turning onto Third. When the trucks arrived in front of the station house, the officers reported for orders. Meanwhile, the troops left in the backs of the covered trucks began being pelted with rocks. The tension among the troops was rising quickly.[87]

Under the circumstances, the officers took abbreviated orders and quickly returned to their soldiers. Because it was believed they were in the greatest state of readiness, Delta Company, along with Charlie, were sent to the worst section of Broadway, ranging from Dorchester Avenue to Dorchester Street. They were to post sentinels at the intersections and patrol the sidewalks on both sides of the street in pairs. Their orders were to "keep the throngs moving."[88] When the trucks arrived on Broadway, they were immediately descended upon by the mob who threw any object that could serve as a missile. One of the things that took the troops aback was the fact that not only were men the source of these projectiles, but so too were women and children. Each time the trucks stopped to unload two soldiers, they immediately were showered with projectiles, causing some of them to be "so badly cut as to need medical attention," and "Private Emery was so badly injured that he was sent to the City Hospital."[89] When he arrived there, the doctors examined him and diagnosed he had received a skull fracture. He was listed in serious condition.[90]

Captain Swallow did the best he could in organizing his men into a line. Once they were assembled, "bayonets were ordered to be fixed."[91] "This had the desired effect" and very quickly "the crowd scattered and ceased its missile throwing."[92] Although the area was cleared, as soon as the captain resumed the march to deploy the men along the street, they were set upon again.[93] As Captain Swallow stopped the march to deploy a pair of men as sentinels or to patrol in pairs along each city block, he advised the men that "unless it became absolutely necessary, they were not to use their firearms."[94] They were also told to keep the people moving and to break up any threatening crowds.[95] Once left on their own, the soldiers began ordering the people to move along, go back home, and stay inside. "In almost all instances," Delta Company later reported, "their efforts were met with ridicule."[96]

The deployment of Alpha Company of the 11th Infantry Massachusetts State Guard, located in Newton, just west of the city, had a slightly different deployment. They were already serving on active duty when they received their orders to mobilize for riot control. Their numbers were not strong, explained the unknown author of the A Company memoirs, because their "original two-year enlistments were continuously running out."[97] "The ranks thinned," he continued, "but we were asked to recruit and carry on in spite of the fact that there seemed to be no place to carry to and no honor in carrying anywhere."[98] All they had been ordered to do was to drill and he lamented, "Drill—drill—drill—month after month—Sudbury, Framingham, and Boxford—when we might have been off having a good time somewhere else."[99]

They were drilling the day they received the phone call ordering them to report for service in the city. At 4 p.m. the bugles blew the call for assembly, and their company commander informed them in his strong Bostonian accent, "It seems that things are a bit 'nawsty' in town and apparently worse to come."[100] They were then marched to the train station from which they were transported to Huntington Avenue, and from there they marched to the South Armory. They arrived later than Delta Company, for it was now 5:45 p.m., and what they found on arrival was mass confusion and no time for a meal.[101] They were quickly loaded into trucks without being told where they were going. It seems the company was split—half were sent to Roxbury Crossing and the other half to Dudley Street.[102] The author of the memoir had gone with the latter group.

When they entered Station 9, he recalled, they were greeted by Captain Skilling. "Fudge," said the captain, with the author noting that "this wasn't the word he used."[103] Tipping his chair back from the desk, the captain said, "I didn't expect to see any of you fellows before midnight."[104] He then proceeded to give them some basic instruction about the use of police call boxes, and he showed them the area they were to patrol on a map. They were then quickly ushered out, loaded back onto the trucks, and driven to their drop-off points. Unlike the troops in Delta Company, those in Alpha quickly realized how hungry they were because they had not been fed.[105] However, they had little time to think about it, for when they reached each intersection or block to patrol, two of the troops were dropped off, and the truck continued on its way.[106] Like Delta Company, they were met with howls and invectives and all manner of projectiles, including rocks, tin cans, and sticks of wood.[107]

Captain Skilling's comment regarding not being prepared for the state guard's arrival was the same everywhere. Most of the police captains did not believe the guardsmen would be able to deploy until later that, and as a result, their early arrival created complications. The soldiers needed to be trained on at least a few things, as Skilling had done for Alpha Company, but the real fear came in having so many armed men deploying into the crowds of people. Captain Joseph Harriman of the Jamacia Plain station also had the same fear, which proved to be well founded after one of the state guardsmen accidentally shot him. "The rifle of private Joseph F. Fitzpatrick of Concord was accidentally discharged," read the *Boston Globe* the next morning. "The bullet passed through the thigh of Police Capt[ain] Joseph Harriman. Dr. W. A. Perrions was called and treated the wound, after which the captain was removed to the Faulkner Hospital."[108]

Still, the timing of the state guard's arrival proved fortuitous, for across the city of Boston, the mobs had turned ugly much earlier that Tuesday evening. Part of the explanation for this was that much of the goods had already been looted from stores the previous night, and businesses had prepared better earlier that day by removing valuables from the stores or by posting armed guards in their establishments. The result was that the mobs turned more violent, whether targeting other people in the mob or anyone in authority, including the volunteer police and the state guardsmen. Even the young teenage boy, Frank Cassell, who had been chased away for directing traffic, did not escape the violence of the evening. He had returned later to an intersection farther down the street near the Ames Building and began directing traffic to help keep vehicles moving. One of the thugs in the crowd approached him and pushed him. Cassell was "driven against an automobile" and then "knocked down and kicked by several thugs in the crowd.[109] He was forced to flee, taking refuge in a neighboring doorway.[110] He gave up trying to help.

The worst violence, however, came at about 7 p.m. that evening. Arthur McGill was 31 years of age and living at home with his mother. He had been drafted in September 1918, but the war ended before he ever went overseas, and since then he had been working at Page & Shaw's shipping.[111] He had dinner with his mother and afterward decided to go downtown to watch all the excitement. The small-statured man made his way through the crowds along Howard Street and managed to see some of the police officers and cavalrymen on horseback trying to control the crowds. "Suddenly the sound of shots was heard and the crowd scattered," one of the newspapers reported, leaving McGill "stretched on the ground."[112] He was transported to Relief Hospital but was dead on arrival. Almost immediately after, Mrs. Gertrude Lewis was brought into the hospital with a bullet wound to her right arm.[113] She, too, had been out to watch the excitement and wound up being shot. Unlike McGill, Lewis survived.

In light of the jam-packed streets and the violence of the crowds so early in the evening, as soon as a unit gathered at least some of their soldiers, they were deployed onto the streets of Boston. Very quickly, the following day's papers would report, "Mischief had become looting; recklessness had brought out force, and for the first time in the memory of any living man, troops controlled the city as the consequence of a strike."[114] The state guard, however, had to resort to violence in many cases in order to reassert that control.

Despite the state guard's deployment in South Boston by 7:30 p.m., the mob there had nearly doubled in size.[115] Monsignor Patten of St. Vincent de Paul Catholic Church on E Street near West Third Street tried speaking to the crowd, imploring them to orderliness.[116] But it had no effect. Three men then came out of the nearby station house, and someone in the crowd assumed they were volunteer police. A cry rang out, shouting, "Strikebreakers!" and immediately the crowd rushed at the three men. "In less than a minute there was a 'free-for-all' in the middle of West Broadway. The three 'volunteers' were getting the worst of it when suddenly a State Guard officer appeared on the scene."[117]

The state guard was starting to assert some control over the mob, however minor, but that all ended at about 8 p.m. when the sound of a plate-glass window shattering was heard on Dorchester Street near the intersection with Broadway. That sound proved to be the firing of a starter gun, for "this outbreak started a systematic smashing of windows from that point down Broadway."[118] On both sides of the street could be seen the smashing of glass, the crowds flooding into the store, loot then being carried out, and the mob moving on to the next store down the street. Delta Company made an attempt "to get men together to clear the street and it succeeded in driving the crowd down Broadway."[119] The only problem was it was proving "impossible to keep the street clear as there were not enough men to station at the intersecting streets and the crowd came back as soon as the troops had passed each intersection."[120] This continued for approximately a half hour, when Delta Company, seeing the destructive mob coming their way, "made preparations to fire a volley. Its men were extended across the street facing Dorchester Avenue," and after the mob ignored "every warning to stop the work of destruction, a volley was finally fired."[121] In a terrible frenzy of fear, the people fled in all directions, and in less than a minute, the streets, at least along Broadway, were clear. They had fired two volleys but hit no one—they had purposefully fired over their heads.[122] Still, the outcome proved to have little effect; the mob became ever more destructive and began placing obstacles in the path of the electric trolley cars in the hopes of either stopping or derailing them.[123]

More violence ensued around 9 p.m. when the mob began throwing rocks at the storefront window of Burdick's Jewelry store on West Broadway.[124] The owner, Stephen Burdick, rushed out to confront them. "He swept his right hand around toward his hip pocket," and someone in the crowd yelled, "He's got a gun."[125] The crowd fled.[126] Not seeing a gun displayed, the mob returned and began throwing rocks at the window. Burdick repeated his actions, but the crowd did not fall for the trick again and began throwing rocks at him. Burdick wisely retreated into his store, locked the door, and turned off the lights. He then unwisely exited onto the street through a back-door alley, where someone in the crowd recognized him. The mob set upon him, and he was "beaten, kicked and robbed" then "left on the ground almost unconscious."[127]

The smashing of plate-glass windows continued. Around 11 p.m., with the crowd still moving down West Broadway and smashing store after store, including O'Keefe's grocery store, Shay's hat store, and then the A&P grocery store, the state guardsmen established themselves into a riot formation to meet them.[128] They then rushed the crowd, who dispersed but gathered themselves for another push down the street in less than 20 minutes.[129] The reason it had taken them so long was because they had been gathering up stones to throw at the guardsmen. The mob then advanced, throwing the rocks at the soldiers. When Captain Thomas Hardy of Charles Company of the 10th Regiment was struck in the head by one of the rocks, someone ordered the men to draw their pistols and fire. They did so, once again, firing over their heads. This time, however, the crowd did not retreat, and someone from within the mob fired a pistol at the guardsmen. The state guard again unleashed a volley, but this time they fired directly into the crowd. Five members of the mob fell to the ground, while the rest fled.[130]

Those in the crowd who were shot were transported to area hospitals, while others who had been wounded but were still able to flee went to the hospitals on their own. One of the men, 19-year-old Robert Sheehan, was taken to Carney Hospital, where he was declared dead. He had been shot through the back. Another man, Joseph Flaherty, 38, had been transported to City Hospital, where he was diagnosed with a fractured left leg from his bullet wound. Still another, a man who called himself Thomas Carr but was really Anthony Czar, a 38-year-old

Russian, had been shot through the chest. He, too, was pronounced dead. The mystery of his death, however, came from the fact he had been standing in the doorway of his home, not in the street where the state guard had fired their volley into the crowd.[131]

Still more mysterious was the fact that many of those shot—including Walter Kratz, 17, Gertrude Sullivan, 16, and Helen Kelley, 16—had all arrived at the hospital with buckshot wounds.[132] The state guardsmen all carried rifles, and the officers had pistols. None of them carried shotguns. Moreover, Captain Hadley stated later in an investigation that he had not ordered the volley because he had been injured by the rock, and no one near him had heard him give the order to fire. The order had come from someone else.[133]

Outside of South Boston, the worst violence continued in Scollay Square, as it had already been occurring all afternoon. In the afternoon the volunteer police had been dealing with the situation, but by 6:30 p.m. the state guard had arrived. They had little effect, other than to draw the jeers and taunts of the crowd. It was when the 1st Cavalry Troop, commanded by Captain Fred Hunneman, arrived that the mob demonstrated some concern.[134] It was about 7 p.m. when the horseback soldiers arrived, and immediately they were ordered into columns of four. The captain issued the order to draw sabers, and the sight had a chilling effect on the crowd. The commander lowered his sword, "The horsemen began to urge their mounts to gallop" and instantly, "the mob broke in all directions," fleeing down Hanover, Howard, Sudbury, Brattle, and Court Streets.[135] It was mass panic. For the next 15 minutes, the cavalry made repeated sweeps across the wide-open plaza, leaving very few people left in Scollay Square. It did not last long.

The crowds began rushing back into the square 15 minutes later, numbering an estimated 10,000 people. They had come in so fast and crowded the square so much, there was no longer any room left to maneuver the horses. The mob controlled the square, and the sound of plate-glass windows breaking once again filled the air. One of the first was the window at

Woolworth's, and it is said that "at 5-minute intervals thereafter the crashes of glass continued."[136] With the cavalry out of commission due to the lack of maneuverability, the state guard and volunteer policemen were sent back in on foot, but they became little more than targets of every conceivable object that could be thrown.[137] It was said that the volunteers and the guardsmen gave as good as they got for "heads were beaten and faces smashed on both sides," with only occasional charges by the volunteer police with their revolvers drawn having any effect.[138]

One 18-year-old who was there that night in Scollay Square recounted his experiences to the *Boston Globe*. "Wednesday night I hears about the excitement in Scollay Square," he explained, "so I collects a couple of friends and goes down there, thinking, you know, to have a little fun—yell around some and maybe sass some of them Harvard cops."[139] He and his friends were in the square "when up blows one of them state's guards and tells me to move along." He defiantly told the soldier, "You've gotta heluva nerve, I gotta right here, who's goin' to make me move?" "Well," the soldier replied, "if I keep my health, I think I am." The young man admitted that he talked back to the guardsman when he told him, "Why, you little tin soldier, if you're so damn brave why didn't you enlist and go over with the regular guys? You ain't got the nerve of a watermelon—" And that was as far as he managed to get in his sassy tirade, when the soldier interrupted him and tiredly asked, "Are you goin' to move on?" The man shouted, "No," and the soldier replied, "Well, move down then," at which point he hit the 18-year-old on the head, knocking him to the ground. He hit several more times and moved on. The man was unconscious, and his friends had to carry him out of the square. When he was roused out of his stupor minutes later, he explained, "My head felt like it had been kicked by a mule, and I goes home and goes to bed still dizzy." He then wisely added, "And that's just where I keep on going till this thing's over."[140]

Whereas Tuesday night had been primarily marked by all of the looting, Wednesday night turned violent. The outcome of the violence was felt by mob and Boston police replacements alike. James Sullivan, 35, who had been at Haymarket Square that evening, was hit by a bullet that was deflected from the sidewalk.[141] Patrolman Richard D. Reemts of Station 10 in Roxbury Crossing was shot, and numerous members of the state guard, including Arthur H. Morse, a lawyer in civilian life, was hit in the eye with a piece of coal. H. M. Chamberlain, also a lawyer, was hit in the head with a stone that peeled back his scalp.[142]

By midnight a majority of the state guard had been deployed onto the streets of Boston, and most of the skirmishes continued with both sides pushing back and forth. For instance, on Washington Street, near Bromfield, the mob began using tactics to push against the state guardsmen.[143] Several members of the crowd claimed to be ex-soldiers, and they taunted the militia members, telling them they were not holding their rifles correctly. They tried baiting them by telling them to give them a rifle so they could show them the proper way to hold it. The guardsmen did not comply. The rabble-rousers then encouraged the mob, and they began crowding the guardsmen, who immediately began pushing back. This tactic was also abandoned. One man walked up to the soldiers, who responded by holding their rifles up, crossing bayonets, and blocking his way. The man reached into his coat pocket and pulled out his honorable discharge papers and showed them to the guardsmen, claiming he was one of them. He then pushed the guardsmen's rifles aside and walked on by. That was apparently the signal for the mob to follow, which they did en masse. The guardsmen retreated, and the mob followed them, "hooting and jeering."[144] When they reached the next corner, however, more guardsmen were there blocking the way, and the officer in charge drew his revolver on the mob. One of the men in the lead walked right up to him, and the officer struck him "over the head with the butt, sending him sprawling into the street."[145] The mob's advance was halted.

The streets began clearing around 1 a.m. the following morning, and by 2 a.m. they were nearly empty. It was at this point the state guardsmen who were still on the street were overcome by their hunger. The only company that had had any time to eat dinner was Delta; the rest had not had a meal since lunchtime. The commander of A Company, "with directness of purpose and clearness of vision, set out to hustle up a chuck outfit."[146] In light of the situation, he commandeered one of the local restaurants called the Waldorf Lunch System. The dining establishment was one of the earliest restaurant chains in America, when, in 1904, "its founder Henry conceived of standardized restaurants serving volumes of reliable food at good prices in clean, white-tiled lunch rooms."[147] By 1919, the year the company went public, there were 38 restaurants, 10 of which were in Boston. And the location on Dudley had just gone into the business of feeding the very hungry members of the Massachusetts State Guard.

Soldiers posing for a photo at Faneuil Hall, the headquarters of the Massachusetts State Guard during the Boston Police Strike.

Photo courtesy of the Boston Public Library, Arts Department.

11

Quelling the Violence
September 11, 1919

If Tuesday could be said to have been marked by shattered glass and looting, and Wednesday by mob violence, Thursday could assuredly be said to have been marked by death.

On Tuesday evening, when the officers went on strike, the commander of the Roxbury Crossing Station, Captain Jeremiah F. Gallivan, was saddened by the whole affair. Gallivan did not want the officers to walk out on strike, and he feared for what might happen to them should they do so. In the roll call room, Gallivan voiced his disappointment after the officers had announced their decision and offered them one piece of advice before they left. "Keep cool and keep out of crowds; you know what they lead to," he told them.[1] "I have no further advice to you men who have maintained peace and guarded property, and you should know how to act."[2] Unfortunately, a small group of the officers did not take the message to heart.

On Wednesday several of the striking officers banded together and went out driving late that night to harass the strikebreaking volunteer police officers. They should have stayed home. Among the group of officers was Arthur Shea, who was in one of two cars they drove that night while they were out on the prowl. Shea was a native Bostonian, born there on July 16, 1885; he was 34 years old at the time of the strike.[3]

He was five feet, eight inches in height, weighed 195 pounds, and had blue eyes. The striking officer had apprenticed young as a machinist and found employment in the Thomas Edison plant. He married Madeline Theresa Girard, and by the time of the strike, they had one son, John Arthur. Shea filled out his World War I draft registration card in September 1918, but there is no evidence he ever served in the military.[4] The following month, on October 10, 1918, he was appointed a patrolman with the Boston Police Department. Shea was involved in the May Day rioting in Roxbury and was one of the officers injured when he was shot in the thumb.[5] He had not been present at roll call on Tuesday evening because he was still convalescing at home.

The other known officer in this group was patrolman Richard Reemts, who was slightly older than Shea, having been born on April 2, 1883. Unlike Shea, Reemts was not a native of Boston.[6] He had been born in Woodstock, Maine, and was a tall, stout man, with blue eyes and light-colored hair.[7] On May 15, 1912, he married Katherine F. Brosnahan, a Boston native, and at the time of the strike, they had no known children.[8] Reemts had more seniority on the force than Shea did, for he had become a reserve officer in Division 6 on March 21, 1910, and had been working out of the Roxbury Crossing station longer than Shea had been a police officer.

How many other volunteer police officers—"strikebreakers" as they saw them—they harassed on Wednesday night is unknown, but at 2 a.m. early Thursday morning, September 11, the group spied two of the volunteers on the corner of Columbus Avenue and Buckingham Street.[9] The volunteers were both young—John Reid was 24 years old, and Thomas H. Gammack, one of the Harvard University students in his senior year, was 23.[10] One of the men in the group stepped out of his car and approached Reid and Gammack to ask them for directions to Auburndale, a village in the town of Newton, located west of the city. As the volunteers started giving them directions, Reemts and others in the group quickly descended upon the men, disarmed them of their weapons (both revolvers and billy clubs), and began abusing them. According to reports, "they were roughly treated."[11]

Seeing the two volunteers in trouble, Sergeant John D. McDonald of Station 5, located on East Dedham Street, ran to their aid.[12] When the striking officers saw the full-time supervisor running toward them, all of the men panicked and scattered. Shea ran for his car in hopes of being able to flee, but he only managed to get behind the wheel of the vehicle before he was stopped. Sergeant McDonald pulled his revolver as he was running and leaped onto the car, pointing the gun at Shea, ordering him to halt.[13] Wisely, Shea did not try to drive away.

Reemts, however, did not run to the cars. Rather, he began running down Columbus Avenue. As he did so, he ran straight toward Abraham M. Karp, who was standing in front of 199 Columbus Avenue. Karp was the 33-year-old proprietor of a store located at that address. He had heard the commotion outside his store, so he had grabbed his pistol and stepped outside to see what was happening. As he did so, he saw Reemts charging directly toward him. Fearing he was under attack, Karp raised his pistol and fired one shot. Reemts, hit in the stomach, collapsed to the ground.[14]

Meanwhile, Sergeant McDonald was holding Shea at gunpoint and ordered him out of the vehicle. After identifying Shea, McDonald ordered him to wait as he tended to Reemts. The sergeant then went to a nearby call box and called for an ambulance. Within minutes, Lieutenant Cundy of the Ambulance Company arrived on the scene. Reemts was placed in the ambulance and driven to City Hospital, where he arrived at 2:15 a.m.[15] Reemts was still conscious, and when asked what happened, he accused Sergeant McDonald of having shot him.[16] Reemts was declared to be in critical condition for "the bullet had perforated the stomach, intestines and duodenum."[17] He immediately underwent surgery.

Once Reemts was taken to the hospital, McDonald placed both Shea and Karp under arrest. He then had Shea drive all of them to the East Dedham Street Station. When they arrived there, both men were searched, and it was discovered that

Shea was still carrying his service pistol at the time. It was immediately confiscated, and they soon learned that because he had been home convalescing from his injury, he was not present Tuesday night to turn in his pistol and other equipment. Both men were then interviewed, and Shea was forthcoming with what he had done, while Karp admitted he had shot Reemts out of fear he was about to be assaulted. Karp was then charged with assault with intent to kill and Shea with robbery.[18]

As the investigation ensued, McDonald learned that Reemts had accused him of firing his pistol, but after a quick check of McDonald's handgun, it was evident the gun had not been fired. Once he finished the necessary paperwork, Sergeant McDonald left for the City Hospital, where he arrived at 7 a.m. There, he found Reemts was out of surgery and seemingly recovering well, so they were able to talk. McDonald explained what had happened, and it was reported that "Reemts, after he and the sergeant had the talk, said that it wasn't McDonald who shot him and that the only reason he had said so before was that McDonald was the only man in uniform that he saw in the immediate vicinity."[19]

Not long after speaking with Sergeant McDonald, Reemts began to develop a fever, and he was soon listed in critical condition again. He was suffering from "acute peritonitis and gas bacillus infection," and his wife called for a priest.[20] Reemts, who was not Catholic, made a deathbed conversion, which was prudent, for Reemts died that evening. His funeral services were held several days later at Saint Joseph's Church on Circuit Street.[21] Reemts's senseless death could have been avoided had he taken Captain Gallivan's advice. Because he did not, he now holds the dubious distinction of being the only striking police officer to die during the strike.

The next death came late that same morning at the hands of the state guard and involved one of the rioters. The guardsmen were ordered not to have a repeat of the previous day, and sweeps were ordered through the many squares and the Boston Common for mob activity.[22] Lieutenant James L. Dooley, who commanded a platoon of 40 men from Company F, 12th Regiment, had received orders "to clean up the Common."[23] At 10:50 a.m. the soldiers began their sweep through Boston Common and came across a large group of men shooting craps behind the cottages near Park Street.[24] The troops surrounded the men and placed them under arrest. Once they organized the men into a line, the gamblers were to keep their hands in the air while being marched toward Station 4 on Lagrange Street.[25]

When the line of men and their military guards set out, large crowds on the Common began swarming the soldiers as they marched the prisoners away, and a line of soldiers was positioned to hold the mob back. Still, the rioters pushed up against the soldiers, began yelling in their faces, and taunted them to fire their rifles, while others were throwing objects at them. As if this was not enough to incite the soldiers, many in the crowd physically rushed at them trying to invoke a response.[26] Several times, the soldiers fired their rifles in order to keep the mob back, but this had little effect on the crowd because they had become inured to the guardsmen firing above their heads.[27]

One man in the crowd who was wise to this tactic, Raymond Barnes, an 18-year-old sailor in the Merchant Marines, shouted, "They're only shooting in the air! It doesn't amount to anything."[28] With great excitement, he rushed forward at a line of six soldiers trying to hold the crowd back. It is believed that Barnes closed the gap with one of the soldiers faster than he had anticipated, and that "the soldier was probably as much surprised as Barnes himself."[29] In defense, the soldier dropped to one knee and with his rifle pointed upward, fired a shot at Barnes. According to the *Boston Globe*, "The shot struck the sailor in the neck, making a terrible wound."[30] Barnes's momentum caused him to fall toward the soldier, who shoved the end of his rifle with its sharp bayonet toward Barnes's chest. When the guardsman realized his assailant was no longer attacking but falling, he swept his rifle to the side and tried to catch Barnes in his arms. He did so, "easing him to the ground."[31]

The firing of the rifle had the effect of dispersing the crowd almost immediately, with many stampeding toward the capitol.[32] The sight of the mob stampeding toward guardsmen in that direction also elicited a response, although in that case no one was injured. Since the area was now clear and the scene relatively safe, the guardsmen began examining Barnes's wound. It was a horrendous wound, for "the shot tore away part of the man's throat."[33] Quickly, the soldiers lifted the Merchant Marine and carried him into Liggett's Drug Store on the corner of Tremont and Boylston Streets.[34] An ambulance was called, the store was cleared of people, and the guardsmen tried to control the bleeding.[35]

A large crowd had gathered outside Liggett's, with people pressed against the store windows trying to see what was happening inside. When the ambulance arrived, the street had to be cleared of people, but the crowd "fell back in quick obedience when the State Guard officers ordered them to clear the way for the ambulance."[36] Barnes was then transported to Relief Hospital, but shortly after his arrival, he was declared dead.[37]

Barnes had made an error in judgment that caused the needless end to his life. Had he not been trying to elicit a response from the soldiers, he would likely not have been killed. Many were quick to criticize the state guardsman for firing his rifle at an unarmed man, but one witness who was there, Edward C. Boyington, came to the soldier's defense. He argued that as fast as Barnes came at the soldier, he had no choice but to believe he was under attack and was "rightfully doing his duty," despite the horrific outcome.[38] Barnes, however, would not be the last to die on Thursday, September 11, for the next death came later that night.

As for the crapshooters under arrest, all 44 of them continued their march down the street toward the police station with their hands held high in the air. "That's the way to handle them!" one man was heard shouting, "A little more of that and the city will be quiet."[39] Nevertheless, after arriving at the police station, they were then taken over to the Municipal Court. When Chief Justice

Bolster heard the case before him, it did not take long before he dismissed the charges against all 44. The guardsmen were not trained police officers, so they did not realize they had to be able to positively identify the men and their activities, otherwise the charges would be dropped, as they were.[40]

In light of the presence of so many soldiers on the streets of Boston, reporters wanted to know if the city was under martial law. There were now over 5,000 guardsmen deployed, since most of them had reported for duty by sometime Wednesday evening. In fact, there were so many guardsmen available by early Thursday morning, units were able to rotate off the street and rest at one of the two armories. For instance, Delta Company had been relieved at 2 a.m., and after making their way to Station 6 on D Street in South Boston, they were trucked to the East Armory, where they could eat and sleep.[41]

At the first press conference of the morning with Mayor Peters and Brigadier General Samuel D. Parker, the question of martial law was put to the general. "The city is not under martial law," he told them. "We have been called out to assist in the preservation of law and order and are at the disposal of Mayor Peters. As I understand the situation, Sup[erintendent] of Police Crowley has been designated by the Mayor to direct the policing of the city and under his direction we are assigning guardsmen to the various police stations."[42] This was, in fact, true, for Peters had made sure that when Parker moved his operation's headquarters to the police department, he would work with the police through Crowley and not Curtis. As for Curtis, he worked long hours during the day handling administrative duties, such as reviewing men eligible for hire as full-time police officers, but otherwise he had gone home in the evening, having been given no operational duties.[43]

General Parker was also asked if martial law would be declared in the near future, and the general deferred the question to the mayor. "I don't think it would be advisable to ask me that question," came Mayor Peters's quick reply. "Present and prospective conditions do not seem to me to warrant it."[44]

Peters hoped the presence of the state guard would be enough to restore peace without having to declare martial law. There was no certainty that a decision like that would be well received by voters, and it was, after all, an election year.

After the press conference, Mayor Peters went back to his office. Since he had assumed control of the situation, he knew the rumors were circulating that he would be meeting with the striking officers and would likely hire them back. The fact that he was meeting with the leaders of the AFL after lunch did not help quell the rumors. With an eye toward the political ramifications of these rumors, Peters worked on a statement that was released at noon that began:

> In the difficult crisis through which we are passing, it is well that the community should remember the great obligation which it owes to those of the police force who have remained true to their oath of office and who have continued to assist in the preservation of law and order.[45]

By demonstrating his support for the 600 remaining police officers, Peters hoped to show that his allegiance was with them and not with the striking officers. The officers, he continued, "have faced not only physical danger, but, what is harder to a red-blooded man, the reproach of their lifetime associates that they have not stood by them."[46] Again, he was trying to acknowledge the difficulties faced by the officers who remained on duty by sympathizing with their situation.

In addition, there was another rumor that had a far more serious ramification, and that was the possibility of a general strike. If every member of every labor union in the city of Boston went on strike in solidarity with the Boston Policemen's Union, the infrastructure and economics of the city would be devastated. This remained present in the minds of nearly everyone, for Seattle had witnessed a general strike in solidarity with the shipyard strikers only seven months prior. Although the general strike proved to be a complete failure from a labor standpoint, it did, nonetheless, devastate the city.[47] Therefore, when Mayor Peters met with the labor leaders at 1 p.m., that was the most important thing on his mind, not hiring the striking officers back.

Four of the leading labor leaders of the AFL had come from their ongoing convention in Greenfield to talk with the mayor. They met behind closed doors and were likely not forthcoming on information regarding a general strike, primarily because they did not know what was being planned. Many of the labor unions in Boston were still debating the topic, while some had actually had votes, but even those results were not made publicly known. The primary issue for the AFL leaders was to deal with the entirety of ramifications of the strike. They brought two proposals before the mayor. The first was a list of recommendations stating the mayor should "abrogate Rule 35" and "reinstate the patrolmen suspended by Commissioner Curtis." He should then "order all the policemen back to their work" and consequently "dismiss the military."[48] After that, the entire dispute should be "left to arbitration."[49] Their second proposition was that "the Policemen's Union should be recognized—that is, that the original demand, on which the policemen struck, should be granted."[50] It would seem their proposal was to roll back time and allow the Policemen's Union to move forward without any consideration for what had happened.

Peters was incredulous, and it would not be the last time that day that he was taken aback by what he heard. As the mayor was readying his statement for release to the press, the governor sent a formal message to both the secretary of war, Newton Baker, and the acting secretary of the navy, Josephus Daniels.[51] "The entire State Guard of Massachusetts has been called out," Coolidge explained. "At the present time the city is orderly," but he added that there were "rumors of a very general strike."[52] Governor Coolidge was also well aware of the threat this would cause to not only Boston but to the entire state of Massachusetts. His request to Secretary Daniels was simply to be prepared to "render assistance from forces under your command immediately upon application, which I may be compelled to make of the President."[53] It was a prudent action to take because of the possibility of a general strike occurring, and Coolidge certainly did not want to be caught unprepared for such an eventuality.[54]

Next, the governor acted on what had been at the forefront of his activities that day. "Thinking I knew what to do," Coolidge recorded in his autobiography, "I consulted the law as is my custom."[55] By mid-morning he had found one of his own statutes that he thought suitable for the situation.[56] As Coolidge explained, "I found a general statute that gives the Governor authority to call on any police officer in the state to assist him."[57] He then proceeded to show the statute to the Massachusetts attorney general for his opinion. At the same time, he shared the statute with Police Commissioner Curtis and ex–attorney general Herbert Packer, who was personally advising Curtis on the situation.[58] After all three men agreed that Coolidge was accurate in his reading of the law, the governor went one step further and consulted "a profound judge of law," another ex–attorney general, Albert E. Pillsbury, a friend from his Amherst days.[59]

Once Pillsbury acknowledged his agreement that Coolidge could employ the statute and that he had no doubt it would trump Mayor Peters's recent executive order assuming control of the Boston Police, Coolidge set about issuing his own executive order.[60] He drafted the order as Mayor Peters began meeting with the labor leaders and directed it to Police Commissioner Curtis, after having the same men review it for its legal accuracy; it was sent at 3:45 p.m. The executive order, labeled "Number 1," read:

> You are hereby directed, for the purpose of assisting me in the performance of my duty, pursuant to the proclamation issued by me this day, to proceed in the performance of your duties as Police Commissioner of the city of Boston under my command and in obedience to such orders as I shall issue from time to time, and obey only such orders as I may so issue or transmit.[61]

At the same time, Coolidge had drafted a proclamation for the people, which read, in part,

> The entire state guard of Massachusetts has been called out. Under the constitution the governor is the commander in chief thereof, by an authority of which he could not, if he chose, divest himself. That command I must and will exercise.[62]

Coolidge also called upon "all citizens to assist me in preserving order, and especially directed all police officers in Boston to obey the orders of Mr. Curtis."[63]

The governor had effectively removed Mayor Peters from being in charge of the entire response regarding both his assertion of authority over the Boston Police Department and his authority to direct the state guard response.[64] He had given back the authority of running the police department to Police Commissioner Edwin Upton Curtis and made it absolute that he was now to report directly to the governor.[65] In addition, by asserting his authority over the entire state guard, he completely removed Mayor Peters from having any responsibility other than his mayoral duties. "Coolidge's procedural mastery again demonstrated value," explains his biographer, Amity Shlaes, for "exercising his own authority under the statute he had found, Coolidge made clear it was Curtis who was in charge."[66]

Coolidge then released both the executive order and the proclamation to the press. When Herbert Packer suggested to him that it might also be prudent to send a copy directly to Mayor Peters, for he was relieving him of his command, Coolidge is said to have responded, "Let him find out in the papers."[67]

And that was, indeed, exactly how Mayor Peters learned of his loss. One of the reporters had contacted the State House to see if the mayor had any response to the governor's actions, and his staff had to inquire what he was referring to before requesting they send a copy right over. While the mayor was still in his meeting with the labor leaders, a messenger brought him a copy of the document. As the *Boston Herald* remarked, "One can only imagine the shock Mayor Peters must have felt when he found out."[68]

When Coolidge met with reporters immediately following the release of his proclamation, he also threatened to take further action if the situation was not cleared up immediately. He threatened to use another statute, Chapter 108, Section 9, Volume 1 of the Massachusetts state laws, which stated the following:

222 / Chapter 11

Constables, city marshals, chiefs of police and all other police officers shall within their respective cities and towns aid the Governor in the performance of their duties whenever called upon for that purpose; and any such officers who refused so to do when called upon shall be punished by a fine of not over $100 or imprisonment for not more than three months.[69]

What Coolidge was threatening to do was to call upon all of the striking policemen to aid him in the performance of his duties by returning to work. If not, the law allowed him to order they be punished by potentially sending each and every last one of them to jail. A question people had at the time and still often do today is why Coolidge decided to respond when he did. Many have pointed out that Coolidge was slow to act in regard to the Boston Police Strike and that he waited too long before finally taking charge of the situation. The simple question, then, is why did he wait so long?

Perhaps the simple answer is that Coolidge's nature was not to overreact to any problem, believing that most problems tend to work themselves out before ever needing executive action. While true, that does not quite fully answer the question. Richard Lyons, perhaps, has provided the most sensible answer to the question when he explained that he believed the answer is found in Coolidge's own autobiography.[70] From the beginning, Coolidge did not believe the policemen had a right to strike, and the man in charge of the situation, Commissioner Curtis, was in agreement. Therefore, Coolidge had a like-minded person in place to deal with the situation. However, when Mayor Peters took charge of the Boston Police Department and had already signaled his interest in the Storrow plan, not to mention his meeting with labor leaders, Coolidge was afraid that Peters might reinstate the officers, thus making his position on the issue more difficult. "If he was to be superseded," Coolidge wrote of Police Commissioner Curtis in his autobiography, "I thought the men that he had discharged might be taken back and the cause lost."[71] Thus, Coolidge was motivated to ensure that "the cause" was not lost, the cause being the issue of whether police officers have the right to unionize and strike.

After finding a means in the law that allowed him as governor to call on any police officer to assist him, he called upon Commissioner Curtis for that assistance, and his man was once again in charge and Coolidge's control over the situation restored. "The cause" was not lost.

As if to confirm his fears, the reporters asked Mayor Peters if he would have hired back the police officers, and the mayor told them he had not made a decision either way. In so saying though, he acknowledged that he might have a position that was untenable to Coolidge. Of course, the mayor accurately added that the governor's proclamation made the entire thing a moot point, or at least it did for him.[72]

Upon receipt of the executive order, the police commissioner and General Parker immediately went to the State House to meet with the governor. They were there for 15 minutes and left without comment.[73] It was not until later in the evening, when the governor left for the day, that the press was able to get a comment from him. "Everything is very harmonious," he told them,

> There is perfect cooperation between all the authorities of the State and city. There is nothing more to be said about the proclamation than appears in it. It was merely made so that there should be no confusion in the public mind.[74]

The mayor did not meet with reporters until later that evening as well. He simply acknowledged he had received the order and proclamation without comment. However, in regard to the governor's call upon the citizens to aid him, he did state, "As Mayor of the city I urge the utmost cooperation of the people of our city in the maintenance of law and order, and pledge my loyal, earnest and complete support."[75] Again, asked about police affiliation with the AFL, he realistically responded, "No compromise is possible."[76]

In their editorial the next morning, the *Boston Globe* perhaps summarized all the political maneuverings best when it remarked, "Yesterday the police situation was in the hands of Mayor Peters. Today it is in sole charge of Gov[ernor]

Coolidge."[77] It then voiced what most citizens likely felt regarding the change in leadership: "Only those able to negotiate corners rapidly are able to make their minds follow the course of this strange maze."[78] The editors then concluded, "But, whatever the demerits of these rapid transfers, the real point is that the Governor is now in charge."[79]

Throughout the day, there was much activity in the city. The courts proved tremendously busy sentencing looters, crapshooters, burglars, robbers, and larcenists. Because the state guard could not identify any of them, the afternoon release of the 44 crapshooters was one of the most talked-about events in court that day, as was the trial of two of the rioters from the previous day in Scollay Square. Walter Allen and Charles F. Hayes were both tried by Judge Creed, but another surprise came from this case.[80] The judge found Allen guilty and sentenced him to serve one year in the House of Corrections. He then turned to Hayes and asked, "Is there anything you want to say before sentence is imposed?"[81] Hayes replied, "Yes, sir. I do. I'm not old enough."[82] Stunned, the judge asked him, "How old are you?" and Hayes said, "I'm not yet 15 years old."[83] The judge then asked when he was born, and his reply confirmed he was 14 years old. After being advised that the boy's father was in the courtroom, the judge asked the father how old the boy was. "My boy will be 15 years old next month," he replied. The judge asked the police if they wanted to accept the word of the boy and his father, and under the circumstances they did. The case was dismissed.

The hospitals remained just as busy as the courts, for many were presenting with various cuts and lacerations, most caused by flying objects and broken glass; there were several injuries from falls as well. The most sensational piece of news, however, came from Medical Examiner Leary of the City Hospital, who had performed the autopsy on Anthony Czar (Thomas Carr).[84] He had extracted the bullet from the body and presented it along with his report to Captain Murphy in the afternoon. The findings were significant. The bullet was a ".25 caliber automatic type," and as Murphy explained to the press, there was not "an officer or noncommissioned officer who had a weapon which used the .25-caliber bullet. Their pistols were all of much larger caliber."[85] This meant that Czar was likely killed from another person somewhere in the mob who had fired their gun, striking Czar dead.

Captain Murphy received a report from the Carney Hospital as well. Buckshot had been found in several of the victims from the tragedy that had occurred with the state guardsmen on West Broadway. The doctors had extracted shotgun pellets from four people—Charles C. Shea, Mary Stanton, Gertrude Sullivan, and Helen Kelley. The latter two were 16 years of age. Once again, the captain told the press that "no man in Co C of the 10th Regiment, which was on duty and fired the shots, had a riot gun and therefore, none of the buckshot wounds could possibly have been inflicted by the men under the command of Capt[ain] Thomas E. Hadley."[86] Once again, it appears it had been a fellow rioter who had used the concealment and noise of the crowd to cover their actions.

Union activity continued apace throughout the day. The first thing in the morning, the newspapers reported, "Nine patrolmen applied for admission to the union," and the atmosphere at Fay Hall remained positive, if not festive any longer.[87] The release of the governor's executive order, proclamation, and threat, however, brought a chilling effect over those in attendance later that afternoon. The Boston Policemen's Strike and their union were clearly in jeopardy. President McInnes appealed to the AFL representatives for guidance. They themselves began consulting with their superiors and the Boston Central Labor Union.

The first response came from the Boston Central Labor Union leaders, who called an emergency meeting for later that evening in Wells Memorial Hall, a workingmen's club located at 987 Washington Street and named for the Reverend E. M. P. Wells of the Episcopal City Mission of Boston.[88] The call went out to all affiliated local labor unions in the city to send representatives to the meeting in order to make their decision regarding support of the Boston Policemen's Union. They were effectively planning to take a vote on whether or not to call for a general strike.[89] If they voted to support the patrolmen's union, then all of the members of unions affiliated with the Central Labor Union would walk off their jobs in a sign of solidarity. The "secret roll call" was in actuality a canvass of the 125 locals who represented 100,000 union members to see whether they had already voted to support the patrolmen or not.[90] Each local "stated in writing whether a strike vote had been taken by their local" and if so, what had been the results. Although the canvass was conducted, "The result of the ballot was not announced."[91] Everyone nervously waited for the Central Labor Union to call for a press conference or to release a statement.

In addition to Governor Coolidge changing the political dynamic of the Boston Police Strike, President Woodrow Wilson also brought the power of the "bully pulpit" to bear on the situation.[92] While giving a speech in Helena, Montana, he defiantly voiced his position on the matter:

> I want to say that a strike of police in a great city like Boston, leaving that city at the mercy of an army of thugs, is a crime against civilization. The obligation of the policeman is as sacred as that of the soldier. He is a public servant. He has no right to prefer private advantage. I hope this lesson will be burned in so that it will never be forgotten.[93]

As Police Commissioner Curtis had an ally in the State House, Governor Coolidge had an ally in the White House.

When the *Boston Globe*'s evening edition was released late that afternoon, it stated in bold letters, "Keep Moving! Keep Off the Streets Tonight! There Is No Such Thing as an 'Innocent Bystander.'"[94] The state guard had been ordered earlier in the day to stringently enforce the rule of not allowing any crowds to gather. Anyone not willing to move along on their own accord would be forced to do so. It appears the guard was asserting more control than at previous times, for the newspapers wrote that some citizens reported "the guardsmen were a little too zealous at first in moving traffic when everybody was going about their business."[95] When asked by the reporters, the guardsmen explained that "loitering sightseers, who had shielded the young ruffians on the previous nights, had caused a lot of trouble for the volunteer police and others."[96] This second night the state guard took to heart the old proverb that an ounce of prevention is worth a pound of cure. It quickly became evident there was wisdom in the proverb for the next morning's paper headlined "Disorder Vanishes Before Military. State Guard Puts End to Rioting and Hoodlumism."[97] "By the iron grip of the military forces," the article noted, "Boston last night became once more a city of orderly recreation and sleep in the downtown section."[98]

General Samuel D. Parker was making sure the state guard's presence was felt, and both he and Superintendent Crowley ensured their presence was also noticed by the guardsmen, police officers, and volunteers.[99] Crowley, who had continued overseeing the police at night while Commissioner Curtis took that responsibility during the day, worked closely with the general. "Last night in an automobile," it was reported, the two men took "a tour of the city, paying special attention to places where trouble had previously developed."[100] It was said that they were "pleased with the conditions they found."[101]

In addition to the two armories in town, the state guard also took over Faneuil Hall, using the historic landmark as a barracks. The last time it had housed soldiers had been when British soldiers had occupied it the day after the Boston Massacre in 1770.[102] There were now enough troops to be able to work in shifts, but nearly all of the soldiers were on the street that night, and it showed. "Plenty of young toughs circulated about the city" on the night of September 11, but the *Boston Globe* reported, "the Guardsmen were planted so thick along the curbs that the crowd never had a chance to clot up into the turbulent masses that made the trouble on Wednesday."[103] In Scollay Square it was said the guardsmen there were "stationed every six feet" and "there were no craps games in progress," not "even in the alleys."[104]

In South Boston a Delta Company historian said in his memoirs that the guardsmen had assembled and marched back to Station 6 on D Street "with feelings of foreboding."[105] They were not looking forward to another night of constant struggles. However, as they began to deploy on the streets, the author explained, "The reception was in great contrast to that of the previous day . . . there was very little comment and no missile throwing."[106] There were some problems, such as a small group of teenagers who attempted to start trouble on West Broadway at C Street, but just as they had started assaulting several men, "the guards soon were busy and with the bayonets quickly subdued the rebellious gang."[107] A few others tried throwing bricks through store windows, but they were quickly subdued as well.[108]

It was the same everywhere. The craps games were mostly ended, and stores were predominantly boarded up; people were not allowed to stand still and were kept moving. There were no navy men on the streets, because their liberty had been revoked, and there were fewer people out in general.[109] The *Boston Herald* reported the next morning that "Rioting, suppressed by the rigorous rule of 7000 patrolling soldiers, their authority backed by loaded rifles, fixed bayonets, mounted machine guns, vanished almost completely last night, the only serious disorder being at Jamaica Plain."[110]

However, in a day marked by death, it closed with one more.

A group of men had gathered on Lamartine Street near Paul Gore Street, just down from Boylston Street in Jamaica Plain, around 8 or 8:30 that night to play craps. The crowd had grown rather large, and among the many people was 20-year-old Henry Grote. A tall, stocky man, Grote was a truck driver for Alfred G. Burkhardt, who owned a furniture moving company. Grote was a graduate of Sisters Parochial School of South Boston[111] and was on Lamartine Street with a friend, J. Carson McWilliams, a shorter, skinnier 18-year-old who had graduated from the Agassiz School. McWilliams was employed in the cutting rooms of the very large and imposing brick building that was home to the Thomas G. Plant Shoe Factory.[112] A third man in the crowd was John J. Powers, 25, but little else is known about him.

A 16-year-old named Arthur English joined the crowd watching the craps game just before 9 p.m. "I came from the cobbler shop on Lamartine [Street]," he later explained, "and walked over to a few of my friends who were standing near a craps game, which was in progress."[113] "We remained standing for a few moments," he continued, "when an automobile containing police sergeants came in our direction."[114] English then stated that on seeing the police, "We ran."[115]

The men nearly all ran down Lamartine toward Boylston Street, but when they arrived at the intersection, they split up. English, Powers, Grote, and McWilliams joined the group of men running down Boylston; they turned onto Armory Street and kept on running. The men were moving fast and happened to be heading directly toward two state guardsmen on patrol. Seeing the men running hard in their direction, the guardsmen possibly perceived them as a threat and ordered the men to halt. English verified this when he said, "The guardsman shouted halt," but he did not heed the warning and, as he told the reporter, "I kept on running."[116] And that was when two shots rent the air.[117]

John DeLang, who lived at the corner of Armory and Porter Streets, heard the two shots and ran out of his home and into the street. He saw Powers and English "lying on the ground," and the two guardsmen were still holding their rifles. He went up to the guardsmen and asked why they had shot the two men, and he told the reporters the next day that one of the guardsmen said to him, "I did not shoot, he did the shooting."[118] The other, DeLang, had told him, "He had lost his head and fired."[119] Further back down the street, perhaps because he had not been able to keep up with his more powerful friend, lay Henry Grote. Unlike Powers and McWilliams, however, Grote was not moving.

There is some confusion over who fired the two shots. DeLang said one guardsman had fired both shots. However, there were reports of both guardsmen having fired once each.[120]

Further confusion came about when the police filed their report for the incident that stated, "Two guardsmen noticed a gang of young men on Porter [Street], apparently fooling with a manhole."[121] The youths were told to halt because they were trying to lift a manhole cover, not because they were fleeing from the police for gathering around a craps game. Unless in their flight, for some reason, the men tried to remove a manhole cover, which is unlikely, the statement was given to provide a reason for the shots having been fired.

Ambulances were summoned to the scene, and Powers and McWilliams were taken to the City Hospital. The body of Henry Grote was also taken there. English had continued running all the way home, but it was there he realized he had been shot. The family's doctor, Dr. Broughton, was summoned to the house and took English to Faulkner Hospital.[122] English had been shot in the left thigh, but it healed quickly. The nature of John Powers's wound is unknown, but he was doing well by the next day. McWilliams, like English, was shot in the left thigh, but evidently it must have been an arterial wound, for he was still listed in critical condition several days later, although on his way to recovering.

The Jamaica Plain shooting proved to be the last tragic death of the day and of the Boston Police Strike. With help from the remaining police officers and volunteers, the state guard had the city under control, and by late that night, there were almost no citizens on the streets. The excitement was over, and most people by this point just wanted the whole affair to be over. It seems most people were growing tired of the strike.

Close to midnight that night, a woman phoned police headquarters and said she wanted to speak to her husband. The desk sergeant told her that was not possible for it was against departmental policy since personal calls were not allowed on an official police business phone. The lady persisted and asked when her husband would be home. The sergeant inquired who her husband was and learned that he was a volunteer police officer working out of the Lagrange Street Station. The sergeant was able to inform her that those men would be off duty early in the morning the following day, Friday, September 12. She thanked the sergeant and asked him to relay a message to her husband: "Tell him he had better throw up this job and get back to his regular job. I have got all I propose to stand of this staying out all night."[123]

Governor Calvin Coolidge inspects soldiers of the Massachusetts State Guard before they go on duty, patrolling the streets of Boston.
Photo courtesy of the Boston Public Library, Arts Department.

12

Coolidge Takes Charge

September 12, 1919

In the early hours that Friday morning, Harry Sparks was parked in his own personal vehicle alongside a sidewalk in the vicinity of Court Square.[1] He was one of the volunteer police officers working out of Station 2. Sparks had decided to join the volunteer police because although he was an amateur welterweight wrestler, he had no immediate bouts scheduled and had the time to help out.

At 2 a.m. that morning, he heard a "touring car" driving slowly along the street.[2] Thinking they might be the type looking for trouble, he became suspicious and began watching the vehicle closely. As the car continued in this manner, Sparks started to follow, without his headlights on. When the vehicle finally came to a stop, Sparks threw on his emergency brake, hopped out of his car, and ran up to the passenger side of the vehicle, leaping onto the running boards. As the window was rolled down, he reached through the opening and began patting down the passenger. Feeling what he thought might be a weapon, he reached into the man's coat and pulled out a revolver. Now armed with two guns, he ordered the men out of the vehicle. Since there were five men in total, Sparks kept a close eye on them knowing he was vastly outnumbered. Fortunately, two state guardsmen out walking their own patrol saw what was happening and helped Sparks place the five men in custody. Now that the suspects were secured, Sparks searched the vehicle and "found two jimmies and other burglars' tools, a flashlight with extra batteries and a big handful of cartridges."[3] He placed all five men under arrest and with the guardsmen's assistance took them to Station 2 for booking. Once word spread among the command staff, Sparks was "highly complimented" for his actions.[4]

Another volunteer officer who was praised that day was former Boston patrolman Edwin Piper. He had joined the Boston Police Department in 1872, and after walking a beat for 42 years, he retired at the age of 65 on December 18, 1914.[5] He was currently on the pension rolls and was receiving a yearly income of $700.[6] Despite being 69 years old, he decided to report for duty at nearby Station 16 in Back Bay first thing that morning. When he arrived he apologized to the commander and said he would have been there sooner, but he had been on vacation in Ludlow, Vermont.

Perhaps the most surprising action on the part of Boston's police that morning came when a handful of striking officers returned to work. Police headquarters proved to be a little vague on just how many officers returned to work, for when the reporters asked them this question, their initial response was, "Several."[7] When the reporters pressed how many that entailed, the police official replied, "Well, several means more than one, doesn't it? It also means more than two. That is as far as I will go in answer to the question."[8] It is believed that there were, in fact, four officers who had requested to return to work.[9] Each of these men was issued back their gear, and by about 9:20 a.m. that morning, they resumed patrolling the streets of Boston.

Despite the many volunteers and officers who had remained on duty, what had really turned the tide against the rioters was the strong presence of the state guard. By early morning Friday, however, the guardsmen were exhausted. Nearly all of the men were on duty Thursday night into Friday morning, and most of them had been working the previous night and a good portion of the day. Now that the security of the city was largely under

control, the state guard leaders working with station commanders were finally able to begin rotating soldiers off duty. One
guardsman at Station 2, seeing some of his fellow soldiers going
off duty, said to the reporters present,

> Gosh! I wish they would relieve me. I've got to get some sleep.
> I went on duty at 8 p.m. on Wednesday, went off duty at 5 a.m.
> Thursday; went on again at 1 p.m. the same day, and I'm still
> on duty. I'm going on again at 1 p.m. no matter when I get
> through this morning.[10]

The guardsmen of Delta Company fared somewhat better,
for they had already started rotating soldiers off duty earlier
that morning, since the battalions were moving toward limit-
ing each company to one 8-hour shift in a 24-hour period.[11] The
biggest problem the state guard faced, however, was not the
tired soldiers but the hungry soldiers. The state guard's logistics
capabilities had not kept up with the soldiers' deployment, and
they proved woefully behind in mobilizing their mess sections.
According to Delta Company's historian, "Most of the men of
D company ate at the Waldorf Lunch on Broadway where the
management very generously gave everyone in uniform of the
State a discount of 50%."[12] That meant they only had to pay 15
cents for each meal they ate. There is little doubt the men found
this agreeable, for the cost was low, they knew they would eventually be reimbursed for the expense, and they did not have to
eat Army chow.

Not long after Governor Coolidge, Mayor Peters, and Commissioner Curtis arrived at their offices, word arrived of
a speech President Woodrow Wilson had given in Coeur
D'Alene, Idaho, that Friday morning. He spoke inside a large
tent that was only partially filled, and after being introduced
by Idaho's governor D. W. Davis, he spoke about the peace
treaty currently on the table, the Treaty of Saint-Germain-en-
Laye between the victorious Allies and Austria. He said that
if it was not accepted, Americans would see "a world again
aflame with war."[13] In addition to the Great War, he also

addressed the situation in Boston, calling it "an intolerable crime against civilization."[14] He railed against the police going on strike, abhorring the fact government could not do its most important job if "every man is looking out for his own selfish interests."[15] He then reproved the striking police officers when he declared,

> I want to say this, that a strike of the policemen of a great city, leaving that city at the mercy of an army of thugs, is a crime against civilization. In my judgement the obligation of a policeman is as sacred and direct as the obligation of a soldier. He is a public servant, not a private employee, and the whole honor of the community is in his hands. He has no right to prefer any private advantage to the public safety. I hope that the lesson will be learned to that it will never again be forgotten, because the pride of America is that it can exercise self-control.[16]

The sentiment was certainly not lost on Commissioner Curtis.

At about the time the words of the president's speech were received in Boston, Commissioner Curtis was releasing his own directives that reflected the president's words. He directed Superintendent Crowley to notify the command staff and all division captains of his decision. The method of delivery was initially by phone, but by early afternoon each of the station houses had received the order in writing. The message stated, "None of the patrolmen who failed to report for duty on Sept 9, 1919, or since that time may return to duty under any circumstances; nor are they to be allowed to remain or loiter on the premises of the different station houses."[17] He also ordered all division commanders to report directly to him if any officer who had been on vacation or sick leave during the strike reported back for duty. Curtis wanted to ensure that each of those men's circumstances was personally vetted by him so he could determine if their leave had been genuine or used as a means to show support for the strike without actually joining the union or abandoning their post themselves. In the case of the few officers who had returned to duty after participating in the strike, they were recalled to their respective stations until clarification of their status could be received from police headquarters. Those patrolmen really did not have to await an answer from the police commissioner, for when the governor spoke at the State House soon after, their status became all too clear.

At 10 a.m. that morning, Mayor Peters met with Governor Coolidge to discuss the current situation in Boston and the change in leadership from the mayor to the governor. As he left the meeting a short time later, the reporters at the State House asked why the two men had met. "I have called on the Governor," Peters answered, "to assure him of my loyal personal support and of the cooperation and support of all the citizens of Boston."[18] When asked what he thought of the situation, Peters answered, "Better, much better," but then after a quick reflection gave this further explanation: "That is, so far as protection is concerned. As to the general strike, your guess is as good as mine."[19] The threat of a general strike by all the unions in Boston remained a potential threat to the city.

Governor Coolidge also met with the State House reporters a short time later to essentially release his decision on how he planned to address the strike now that he was in charge. According to his biographer Amity Shlaes, "Coolidge confronted a choice."[20] The biographer explained that the most "obvious move would be to declare victory and then give ground a bit, finding a way to reinstate the policemen on his own terms."[21] This would communicate that he was in charge of the situation, but it would also effectively return the patrolmen to their beats, thus allowing him to quickly demobilize the state guard. "The second option," Shlaes explains, was for the governor to "stand firm a few more days, and then give in and negotiate with the striking police."[22] This would allow for the restoration of order; the governor could assert his authority and yet show mercy to the patrolmen's union. He could have allowed them to retain the union, while at the same time weaken their powers and force them to revoke their affiliation with the AFL. Both decisions would have asserted his authority but allowed for a compromise. However, as Shales stated, "Coolidge chose neither."[23]

Instead, Governor Coolidge decided that both of these politically viable and astute decisions would have placed him in a position to take the striking officers back and so, "the cause lost."[24] He did not want to lose the cause by allowing police officers to unionize, so he stayed the course by keeping the state guard deployed on the streets of Boston and refusing to allow any of the patrolmen to return to work. When he was interviewed later, he made his support of the cause abundantly clear when he explained that the State of Massachusetts did not support, nor would it recognize, the police officers' affiliation with the AFL.[25] "Governor," one reporter asked, "will you tell us why the State objects to affiliation of the police with the A.F. of L.?"[26] Coolidge was somewhat evasive when he replied, "That is something that the State has nothing to do with. Internal direction of the police department is wholly in the hands of the Police Commissioner."[27] After several more questions were asked as the reporters tried to get the governor to respond to the state's position on union affiliation, one reporter asked him, "Would you permit the men to return with the understanding that they will form an organization not affiliated with the A.F. of L.?"[28] To this Coolidge answered, "You are now coming into the question of whether the action of the police was as a matter of fact a strike, and whether the men who left their places might under any circumstances be taken back."[29] Coolidge was moving the reporters closer to divulging his decision, but still, to this he added, "That, of course, is for the Police Commissioner alone to determine."[30]

The reporters were likely frustrated with his responses, but one finally asked if he would negotiate with the strikers if they returned. This was the word Coolidge wanted to hear. To this the governor replied, "The present situation should not be called a strike. There is no strike on. These men are public officials, not employees. It is improperly referred to as a strike."[31] Naturally, the reporters asked if the police officers were not strikers, then just what would he call their actions. "Desertion of duty," Coolidge quickly replied.[32]

With that statement, the governor's position became clear. It was not unusual for governments and corporations to negotiate with strikers—it was a common occurrence in the Progressive era. However, if the state would not recognize the patrolmen who walked off duty as "strikers" but rather "deserters," then the officers were derelict in their duty and could thus be fired for failing to perform their sworn duty. Government did not negotiate with deserters.

Nevertheless, the reporters pressed the issue, asking Coolidge if he would allow the 19 suspended policemen to be reinstated and the entire matter sent into arbitration. "We cannot think of arbitrating the Government or the form of law," he replied.[33] "There can be no opportunity for any compromise in respect to either."[34] Realizing that Coolidge was now of the mind the police officers should not be allowed back on the job, the reporters asked if he could see any circumstances under which that could be taken back. The governor stated, "I do not think of any conditions under which they should be reinstated, but I must say again that it is a matter wholly beyond my control."[35]

Once again, Coolidge shifted the responsibility for the situation back to Commissioner Curtis. However, he knew that Curtis held the same positions as he did, so Coolidge, once again, was in a position to leave the matter entirely to the police commissioner. The cause was not lost.

The press scrambled over to Pemberton Square to obtain a quote from Commissioner Curtis regarding his intentions since they realized the plight of the striking officers rested in his hands. When they were finally able to question him, they were disappointed in his response. "I would gladly furnish the public through the press a statement as to my future plans in regard to the police department," he began, "but in all these matters I act according to law as expressed to me by the Attorney General."[36] The only problem was the question Curtis had posed to the attorney general, for Henry A. Wyman was currently being investigated by his office. Curtis, however, assured the press that when he received his answer, "I will make a statement of my intentions."[37]

As word of the interview with the governor began to circulate and made its way back to Fay Hall and all of the striking officers, all their hopes and dreams were beginning to vanish.[38] The reality for the officers who walked off the job on Tuesday evening was starting to become clear—they would never be Boston police officers again. Despite this, they were still hoping against hope they would still win the day.

The words of Governor Coolidge were heard across the nation, for the strike in Boston, Massachusetts, had implications for every state in the union. Every state governor and most large city mayors watched the situation closely, knowing full well what unfolded there could potentially affect them. When Governor Carl Milliken of Maine read of the interview with Governor Coolidge, he sent him a telegram. "Speaking, as I confidently assume to do, for the people of Maine," Milliken began,

> I congratulate you heartily upon your prompt and vigorous action for the restoration of orderly and lawful government in Boston. We are watching you with intense interest, because we believe that the maintenance of free institutions in America depends upon the firm and courageous handling of every crisis like the existing desertion and mutiny of the Boston police force.[39]

Not everyone, however, was as supportive of the governor's position.

Samuel Gompers, the president of the AFL, had been publicly quiet about the Boston police strike for the most part. Between his travels and his father's death, he was under a lot of strain and left the matter to his subordinates, particularly the representatives of the AFL working directly with the Boston Policemen's Union. However, upon receipt of the governor's interview, he realized that there was a good chance his own cause would be lost, and he began working in earnest to salvage the situation.

After being brought up to date on the state of affairs, Gompers realized things were worse off than he had thought. The strike had proven to be a disaster, and it was doing little to help the members of the Boston Policemen's Union or the AFL. The riots, the looting, the injuries, and the deaths had done nothing to advance the union's cause, and with Coolidge asserting his authority and calling the police officers "deserters," Gompers knew quick and drastic actions were needed. Therefore, he sent a telegram to Mayor Peters, and in doing so, as historian Frederick Koss wrote, "organized labor [had] sounded its first official call for a tactical retreat."[40]

"No man or group of men more genuinely regrets the present Boston situation than do the American Federation of Labor and I," the message began.[41] Gompers framed his telegram as a response to a request President Wilson had made in regard to a similar situation occurring in Washington, DC, with the Metropolitan Police. The policemen of that department had called for the right to unionize, and their leadership, in turn, issued an order stating that police officers were not authorized to hold membership in a union affiliated with the AFL. Wilson had called for a conference to be held on October 6 and had asked that any actions be deferred until after the conference.[42] The president was trying to prevent a repeat of the Boston Police Strike in the nation's capital. Although the situation in DC had little bearing on what was occurring in Boston, for the police in DC had not actually gone on strike, Gompers hoped to use the president's request as a means of salvaging the situation regarding the Boston Policemen's Union by trumping the governor's decision with the president's request.

Gompers told the mayor in the telegram, "I am telegraphing the representative of the American Federation of Labor in Boston, Mr. Frank McCarthy . . . to appeal to the Policemen's Union to cooperate and return to their posts."[43] Gompers simultaneously sent a copy of the message to McCarthy, and added a personal note:

> I strongly appeal to you and to the policemen to cooperate in having the spirit and purpose of the above-quoted telegram

242 / Chapter 12

carried out, and that the policemen will whole-heartedly do their duty in the premises. Please give this your immediate attention.[44]

Gompers was seeing that perceptions had changed. Whereas the strikers seemed to be in the right at the beginning of the week, the devastation caused by the strike had turned both citizens and government officials against the police union. Now, instead of trying to earn a pay increase and obtain better working conditions, Gompers had become concerned about whether they would just be able to keep their jobs. This is why he encouraged McCarthy to act fast, before anyone in Boston fired the officers.

Rather than appeal to the governor or the police commissioner, however, Gompers sent the telegram to Mayor Peters, asking that the policemen be permitted to return to work.[45] Despite knowing that Coolidge had taken charge of the situation, Gompers could not appeal to the governor because he knew Coolidge would not be sympathetic to his request. The only person left was to appeal to was the mayor, who had no control over the situation. Gompers's true hope was that the message would be published in the newspapers (which it was), and that the people would be sympathetic to his request.

Mayor Peters replied to Gompers, acerbically writing him, "The situation in Boston differed from that of the District of Columbia as the policemen here left their posts and gave the city over to forces of disorder."[46] "The governor as commander-in-chief of the state's forces has now charge of the Police Department," he told Gompers, ending with the terse statement, "Your communication should be directed to him."[47] Before Gompers read the mayor's telegram, he learned of Peters's response in an Associated Press news release.[48] The mayor had given his telegram to the local newsmen. Of course, taking the governor's repeated stance in the interview, Gompers should really have sent the telegram to Commissioner Curtis, but Curtis had already stated his position, and Gompers knew he would not be sympathetic to the request either. Seeing no alternative,

Gompers sent the same request to the governor but issued no reply to the mayor's telegram.

The governor also learned of the telegram being sent to him by Gompers through the press. Since he had not officially received the message, he decided not to comment on it directly.[49] It would not have mattered anyway, for Henry Long, the governor's secretary, believed that "nothing at the State House on Friday indicated a change in the Governor's attitude toward the police union."[50] Indeed, his attitude had not changed.

McCarthy received the request from Gompers and immediately began working with Boston Policemen's Union president John F. McInnis to determine how best to act on Gompers's request. After they conferred, McInnis agreed they should ask the members to return to work, for as he told the reporters, "That is a logical step."[51] In addition to calling for a meeting of the membership later that night, McCarthy also requested a conference with the governor for the next day. It was granted.[52]

As McInnis and the union's leadership, as well as their AFL representatives, began working on the resolution and calling the members to Fay Hall for a vote on Gompers's proposal, the state guard, volunteer officers, and remaining members of the Boston Police Department continued to secure the city.[53] General Parker felt confident that the "worst had passed," and with the combination of forces and their ability to prevent crowds from gathering in any one location, they had the situation under control.[54] In addition to the number of volunteers rising to 1,300 in total, other sources of assistance were beginning to solve additional problems the city faced.

While trying to control the people who flooded the streets and sidewalks, little attention had been paid to monitoring and directing traffic. By Friday morning, however, the automobile dealers of Boston had organized their members as a volunteer traffic squad to regulate motor vehicles at dangerous intersections in the downtown area. The men deployed at exactly noon that Friday and all wore suits and white armbands as a means of identification. Crowds soon formed to watch the volunteer traffic men at work shortly after noon, with numerous cheers, praise, and encouragement for what they were doing. "I hope you get a good job when you are through here, boy," one man yelled as he passed one young volunteer. "It sure looks good to see things getting orderly again."[55] There were, however, some complaints over the new "traffic cops," for some of the drivers felt the men got a little "saucy," and the state guard had more work in trying to keep crowds of spectators from forming to watch the new traffic squad at work.[56]

The majority of the craps games had disappeared off the streets because the state guard no longer tolerated any kind of gatherings, but they still came across some recalcitrant gamblers. One volunteer police officer and former army soldier was patrolling along Washington Street around noon when he heard what sounded to him like a carnival barker shouting in the streets. "Come on, gentlemen, come on. You all know it," he heard the man call out.[57]

> This is the old army game. We pay even money for under seven and even money for over seven. Three to one if seven come out on the little dice. Every one can play. Come on, gentlemen, it's the old army game.[58]

Moving through the crowd, he saw before the barker a piece of cardboard with piles of coins and dollar bills. He had seen numerous craps games throughout the city during the strike, but this, he said, was the first time he had seen the "old army game."[59] The phrase has held many different meanings over the years, going from a card game like three-card monte to the three-shells-and-a-pea game. All were meant to swindle people out of their money because these were confidence games or games of deception. At the time, this game was likely what was also referred to as "chuck-a-luck," where bets were placed on the outcome of three dice rolled in a small birdcage-like contraption.

By evening it began to drizzle outside, and Friday night turned dreary. There were few disturbances that night, in part likely due to the weather. And with so few pedestrians and automobiles on the streets, there were fewer people for the guardsmen and volunteer officers to have to deal with. There were some minor gatherings that had to be broken up from time to time, and general crimes that had little to do with the strike itself still had to be dealt with. One incident, however, reminiscent of the first two nights of rioting, occurred in South Boston along West Broadway near Dorchester at about 8:50 p.m. The state guardsmen were patrolling the area when someone threw a brick through the plate-glass window at the Waldorf Lunch Company. The brick was reported to have "landed about 10 feet inside the store and missed the cashier's head by less than five feet."[60] At first it was thought the target was the cafeteria itself, as they had been feeding the state guardsmen since Wednesday. But it was later reported to have been "to revenge the many arrests made in the lunch room in the past few weeks."[61] Either way, the state guard responded in force, quickly formed a skirmish line, and then repeatedly swept the streets clear of anyone in the area.

The worst incident that night occurred just after midnight along Washington Street at Northampton Street. Robert P. Nolan was out on patrol in the area when two men walking toward him suddenly assaulted him.[62] In the fight Nolan pulled his firearm and fired one shot. The bullet did not strike either of his assailants but hit James McCourt, 29, an "innocent bystander," who happened to be in the area.[63] The sound of the gunshot stunned the two men, and they were quickly overpowered by Nolan with assistance and taken into custody. The two men were identified as Thomas McCormack, 29, and George A. Berkhardt, 31, and taken to the East Dedham Street Station. Nolan was transported to a hospital for his wound.

Gompers had meant to try to ameliorate the situation with his message, but he faced opposition from many fronts, including from those within his own AFL leadership. Vice President Matthew Woll spoke that evening to reporters, making several contradictory statements such as "The American Federation of Labor discourages all Government employees from striking" and "The American Federation of Labor cannot tell any body of men not to strike." But the brunt of his interview was to place the blame for the strike on Boston city officials.[64] "The very influence that could be of vast assistance to the public in preventing such a disaster and condition as now obtains in Boston could have been avoided by the officials of Boston and Massachusetts," he argued, "if they had permitted the police to belong to the American Federation of Labor. The fact that they refused to permit the police to come into the American Federation of Labor is the reason we find that condition prevailing."[65] In his speech Woll avoided mentioning how the AFL had failed to discuss whether or not police unions could go on strike when collective bargaining failed. It was one thing to recognize police affiliation with the AFL, but it had become clear by then that their ability to strike was an entirely different question and one that should have been resolved before voting to bring them into the fold. Still, whether out of anger or frustration, the message he conveyed ran counter to the one Gompers was trying to convey.

At Fay Hall, meetings and discussions were ongoing as the members of the union assembled for yet another historic vote— on whether they would return to work or stay the course. By late evening there were over 1,000 patrolmen assembled for the vote. As they gathered, it was reported that while they did not break out into song, and there was not much cheering, the men were still enthusiastic about their prospects.[66]

The executive committee and the AFL representatives had spent most of the afternoon and early evening crafting the resolution the members would vote on. The resolution included five "whereas" statements that provided the facts and reasons for the resolution. They addressed the statement made by President Wilson and the request by Samuel Gompers, but boldly inserted a statement "that the status of the Boston police remain the same as before the issuance of orders of Sept 8, 1919, suspending the following named officers," at which point it listed the name and division of each of the officers Curtis had suspended.[67] The resolution then "resolved" the following:

It is in the good sense and judgement of the executive committee of the union in executive session assembled, we respectfully request Calvin Coolidge, Governor of Massachusetts, and
now in control of the Police Department of the City of Boston,
to reinstate said members in said Police Department of the City
of Boston on date to be agreed upon by both parties pending
the adjustment of grievance at issue.[68]

One source of debate in crafting the resolution had been
focused on the 19 officers under suspension. The issue was
whether or not to include their return to duty as a condition
for all of the striking officers to return to work. On one hand,
it would have been a harder sell to the union members if the
suspended officers were not included in the return to work, but
on the other hand, placing a condition on the governor for their
return to duty was risky, especially in light of Coolidge's earlier
words to the press. They decided to incorporate the condition
into the resolution and so, once finished, it next had to be presented to all of the union members.

When the meeting began, there were a number who
explained the reason for the resolution and why the members
should support its passage by voting in favor. Frank M. McCarthy, representing the AFL, read Samuel Gompers's telegram to
those assembled and, speaking on his behalf, addressed the need
for the police officers to return to work.[69] President Michael J.
O'Donnell of the Boston Central Labor Union spoke about the
support the patrolmen were receiving by all the other unions but
acknowledged it would be best to return to work in light of the
situation. Edward F. McGrady, who was a member of the strike
committee for the Central Labor Union, also referred to the
patrolmen returning to work considering the use of strikes by
labor unions and their effectiveness. And both Misses Mary A.
Mahoney and Annie Molloy of the Telephone Operators' Union
had just come from an executive board meeting to announce
that their membership would be holding a vote on Tuesday con-
cerning whether they should go on strike in solidarity with the
police.[70] Oddly, the only person not noted to have spoken that
evening was John F. McInnis.

After the many addresses were over, the wastepaper basket was once again put to use as the ballot box. Members of the union began filing up to present themselves before the election-eers, their names were checked off a list, and they placed their pieces of paper in the ballot box. When the votes were later can-vassed, it was unanimous. The members had voted to pass the resolution and agreed to return to work.

Frank H. McCarthy immediately released a statement at 10:30 p.m. "The members of the Boston Policemen's Union," it read, "have accepted the suggestion of President Samuel Gomp-ers of the A. F. of L., and have instructed their committee to act in accordance."[71] A copy was sent directly to Governor Coolidge, but since he had already retired for the evening, it was received by his secretary, Henry Long. He responded that the governor would receive the telegram in the morning.

What is striking about the flurry of telegrams that day is that they were all sent to either Governor Coolidge or Mayor Peters. Gompers had sent his telegram to the mayor and later the governor, while McCarthy only sent a copy of the resolu-tion to the governor. The mayor had said to send the telegram to the governor, while the governor repeatedly said he was not in charge of any decision regarding the Boston Police Depart-ment, stating that person was Commissioner Curtis. Neither representative of the AFL bothered to send their messages to Police Commissioner Curtis, who just so happened to be the person who held the officers' fate in his hands. However, even if McCarthy had sent the last message to the commissioner, it would not have mattered, for Curtis had already reached his decision.

What no one knew at the time was that Commissioner Cur-tis had requested a ruling from state Attorney General Wyman regarding the state's opinion on whether or not the policemen had vacated their positions, and he had already heard back. Wyman phoned the commissioner that evening, and although he wanted to revisit the law first thing in the morning before giving his official opinion, he was confident enough to tell Curtis informally that the police had abandoned their posts. Wyman told the commissioner he could come to his office in the morning for his official ruling. Curtis now knew administratively how to proceed. The officers would *not* be allowed to return to duty, and he would begin the process of dismissing every last police officer who had abandoned his post.

Governor Calvin Coolidge and Boston Police Commissioner Edwin Upton Curtis review the Boston Police in 1930 after more than 1,000 new police officers were hired to replace the striking officers.

Photo courtesy of the Library of Congress.

13

Firing and Hiring a Police Department

September 13, 1919

The rains from the previous night had stopped, and Saturday morning dawned warm and humid. As the state guardsmen and volunteer police officers on duty were thinking more and more of sleep, their replacements were making their way to the station houses to prepare for what would hopefully be an uneventful day. One of the station house captains was reported to have been personally handing out refreshments to the men before they went on duty, as a way of thanking the volunteers for their service.

The *Boston Globe* shared an anecdote of an exchange between one of the volunteer officers and the captain, although the paper stressed it was only an "alleged" story, having been reported by a "witness."[1] As the volunteer approached the table where the captain was dispensing beverages, the captain asked him, "Coffee?" The volunteer was said to have replied, "No. Give me tea. Coffee keeps me awake."[2] The story, probably true, was likely called "alleged" so as not to shame the good work the volunteer police officers had been doing.

The morning edition of the *Globe* reported on the prospect of some good news to come later that day. "The possibility that the police strike might be finished by this morning," it explained, "caused a good deal of excitement in the city, where scores of meetings and conferences looking to a further and perhaps

251

long-continuing contest were going on."³ While there had been numerous meetings on Friday, most had failed to resolve anything. That would not prove to be the case on Saturday.

The first meeting was the one held by Governor Calvin Coolidge with the union representatives. That morning, Coolidge looked over the collected correspondence awaiting him, and among the pile was the telegram from Samuel Gompers. He read the message but laid it aside to see what additional arguments would come forth during the 10 a.m. meeting.

Upon arriving at the State House, Coolidge held some brief consultations before sitting down with the union representatives as promised. AFL liaison Frank McCarthy was in attendance, as was President John F. McInnes of the Policemen's Union, along with five other members of the executive board. In addition, pro-union City Councilor James T. Moriarty and two representatives of the Central Labor Union were also present. As was typical of a meeting with Coolidge, the participants did most of the talking, while "Silent Cal" simply listened.

McInnes explained to the governor the many reasons why members of the police department joined the AFL, citing their poor salary that could not keep up with inflation and the horrible working conditions. The labor representatives then explained that it was their desire that the Boston policemen be able to retain their affiliation with the AFL, and they assured him there were no plans to call for a general strike.⁴ When Coolidge finally did speak, it was brief. He stated that the ruling on the men who had not reported for duty was now merely "a question of law," and that Commissioner Curtis should be "guided by the opinion of the Attorney General."⁵ He also stated that he did not know what, if any, decision the police commissioner had reached. In the end, the union delegation asked Coolidge if he could arrange for them to meet with Curtis, and he agreed only to relay the request.⁶

Meanwhile, as that meeting was underway, Commissioner Curtis also made his way to the State House for what proved to be the most important meeting that day, the one with Attorney General Wyman. It was only a brief meeting, for after some discussion of the situation, Wyman formally declared the state's position. "Confirming the oral opinion expressed to you yesterday upon the statement of facts as presented," he began, "I beg to advise you that the situation amply warrants a finding by you that the policemen in question have abandoned their offices."[7]

That confirmed what Wyman had told him by phone the night before, so to Curtis, that issue was now closed. Perhaps the more important question for Curtis entailed what exactly this statement meant administratively speaking, and Wyman provided the answer: "In the event of your decision that such abandonment has taken place, the offices abandoned are to be treated as vacant, to be filled by you as provided by law."[8] According to Wyman's interpretation of the law, not only did the officers who walked out on September 9 abandon their posts, but in light of the officers' posts now standing vacant, Curtis could immediately begin hiring new officers without having to wait for the abandonment paperwork to be processed.[9] In other words, Curtis could now administratively dismiss one set of officers and hire a new set of officers at the same time without one having any bearing on the other.

Curtis returned to Pemberton Square while the governor's meeting was still ongoing, since that meeting did not end until just before noon. The reporters had assembled before the meeting even began and were outside waiting to receive statements from the attendees. When the union representatives came out, the reporters managed to obtain several statements from one of the members of the police union, although which board member was not specified. "The situation is now in the hands of the Governor," he is reported to have said.[10]

> You can make it plain that John F. McInnes, president of the Policemen's Union, will never go back on the police force of Boston except as a union policeman, and that is the sentiment of the policemen. The American Federation of Labor charge will never leave my hands.[11]

By the time the reporters heard from McInnes, however, there was apparently already a rumor going around that someone from the union had said the strikers would return to work and were willing to drop their affiliation with the AFL. How or who started the rumor is unknown, but this was the first thing McInnes addressed in his meeting with reporters, calling it "a dangerous and contemptible lie."[12]

With regard to McInnes's own statement about the meeting, he explained that he would announce the governor's position on the resolution to the policemen at Fay Hall later that evening.[13] He also reaffirmed that they were still determined to retain their AFL affiliation, although they were willing to return to work while awaiting the outcome of the conference in Washington, DC. "My men," McInnes defiantly stated, "still cling to the hope they can win."[14]

After the union representatives left the State House, the reporters received a statement from Governor Coolidge regarding the meeting. "At a conference with labor leaders, held at their request, details were presented to me of the conditions under which the policemen in Boston performed the duties of their office," he began in that matter-of-fact manner in which he wrote.[15] Because they had spoken about Gompers's telegram to the governor, Coolidge included the following in his statement: "I told the committee that the matter suggested in the telegram was entirely in the hands of the Police Commissioner," and added, "I understand the matter of the telegram has been conveyed to Mr. Curtis."[16] He also mentioned the delegation's request to meet with the police commissioner and noted he had taken the efforts to "transmit that request."[17]

As the pressmen gathered their news from the State House, Curtis was back in his office, where he was having a meeting with Mayor Peters.[18] Curtis asked to speak to the mayor about his proposal to hire new police officers to fill the vacant posts. He was not asking for the mayor's permission, for he did not need that. What he was asking for was a pay raise for the new officers, and for that, he needed the mayor's approval. The plan he laid out before the mayor was to increase the pay of all entry-level officers to $1,400, which would apply to every patrolman on the force.[19] What is so stunning about this request is that it is approximately the same amount the members of the Boston Policemen's Union had requested. Peters's reaction during the meeting is unknown, but he immediately called the city auditor, J. Alfred Mitchell, and the fire commissioner, John F. Murphy, for a meeting after arriving and hearing the plan.[20] The auditor explained what it would cost, while the fire commissioner pointed out that if the policemen were granted an increase, the same would have to be done for the firemen.[21] The mayor set about finding a way to make the proposal work.

After his meeting with the mayor, Curtis drafted a general order, and by early afternoon he released it for dissemination. The press obtained a copy as well. "It is manifest that the places in the police force of Boston, formerly held by the men who deserted their posts of duty, have by this action been rendered vacant," the general order began.[22] Commissioner Curtis made the attorney general's opinion official on the matter, and by including the statement in the general order, he had also made official the status of the officers and their positions.

After noting the attorney general's ruling on the law, Curtis divulged his intent: "I shall accordingly proceed in accordance with law and in strict compliance with the requirements of the Civil Service laws to fill these vacancies with new men."[23] The police officers who walked out on strike would be replaced, and he then made mention of the new pay, explaining, "I have submitted to the Mayor of Boston recommendations for immediate adoption relating to a revision of salaries for the lowest paid members of the Police Force; and I shall later submit recommendations for a revision of the entire salary list."[24] Any hope the striking men would be able to return to work under any circumstances had just been crushed by the police commissioner's order.

Curtis then began the laborious administrative process of dismissing approximately 1,400 patrolmen. He began with the 19 who were still under suspension orders pending his final decision. Starting with McInnes, he detailed the charge against him, "Violation of Section 19 of Said Rule," then laid out the specifications for the charge and detailed the outcome of the administrative hearing process that had placed them on suspension. Finally, he concluded, "The Commissioner finds and adjudges him guilty as charged in the complaint, and on the thirteenth day of September, 1919, sentenced him, the said John F. McInnes, to be dismissed from the Police Department of the City of Boston."[25] This template was then followed for each of the other 18 leaders of the police union who were under suspension. After that, Curtis began the process of removing all of the other striking policemen from the department's rolls; each officer's duty card was stamped with the simple notation, "Abandoned his duty September 9, 1919."[26] This also included the four policemen who had returned to duty on Friday. All four were dismissed from the force for having abandoned their posts.

Curtis then began the process of hiring new police officers. Before looking over the better candidates among the volunteer police officers who had applied or been recommended for full-time positions, he first drew upon the applications from military veterans, since he could expedite their hiring. The process for not only firing 1,400 officers but hiring that many was now underway.

When the policemen gathered inside or outside of Fay Hall heard the news of Commissioner Curtis's general order, they were, needless to say, shocked. The *Globe* reported their collective response later that evening when it reported, "Fay Hall and its vicinity are two of the quietest spots in the city today."[27] While most of the members of the Boston Policemen's Union were already assembled waiting to hear President McInnes's report about his earlier meeting with the governor, upon hearing the commissioner's decision, any who were not present quickly made their way there. The men met quietly, both in groups and as a whole, but in the end, they reaffirmed their decision to retain their membership in the AFL.[28] There really was little else they could do.

After the reporters heard the news, they contacted AFL President Gompers for his comments on the police commissioner's order. Gompers testily replied, "I suppose he is willing to assume the responsibility for the consequences of his action."[29] When asked to elaborate, he stated he had no further comments.

By midmorning, as the weather was turning warmer, the crowds began to return. Many people were simply out shopping, but others were on the streets looking for excitement, and some wanted to resume their taunts of the state guardsmen and volunteer police.[30] One such man was Gustave C. Gaist.[31]

Gaist was 25 years old, Russian born, and had immigrated to America with his parents. During World War I he enlisted in the US Army and after training was assigned to the 30th Engineers and deployed to France, where he spent 13 months before being discharged in February 1919. He first worked for Fore River as a boilermaker, but after beginning his studies to be an electrical engineer, he obtained a job with the North Packing and Provision Company working in their engine room. He lived with his parents, two brothers, and a sister in Dorchester on Monadnock Street, and he is believed to have been sympathetic to both the communist cause and the workers' movement.[32]

Out walking on the south side of Boston Common at approximately 11:30 a.m. that Saturday morning, he stopped at the northeast corner of Boylston and Tremont Streets. Why he stopped is disputed, for one account states he stopped to talk to his brother, while according to others, he stopped to taunt the guardsmen who were telling people to keep moving.[33] What happened next, however, is not disputed.

Because Gaist had stopped, the guardsmen specifically told him to move, and a "dispute" ensued in which Gaist is reported to have "expressed a dislike for the guardsman's tone of voice and manner" and told him "he talked too loud."[34] As a show of force, the guardsman pointed his rifle at Gaist, possibly "levelling" it "against Gaist's breast," and he told him to move on.[35] Gaist did not. Instead, he pushed the bayonet away and attempted to grab the soldier's rifle. A struggle ensued.

The guardsmen shouted for the corporal of the guard, who was stationed on the opposite corner across Boylston Street, and who, upon seeing the commotion, began running to assist. Gaist, realizing he was about to be outnumbered, let go of the rifle and started running diagonally across the street toward the Hotel Touraine. One bystander, William P. Pembroke, a recently discharged soldier, was standing near the hotel and later told reporters, "I was just crossing the street when I heard a commotion and saw a man running toward me, followed by a guardsman."[36] The corporal had turned to follow Gaist, shouted for him to halt, then raised his rifle and fired.

Immediately, there was pandemonium on the streets as the crowds in the area began to scatter. Pembroke was lucky, for as he stated, "I stepped aside and a moment later the State Guard fired."[37] He was not hit, but Gaist was. The bullet struck Gaist in the chest, passing completely through him. Though slowed and directed downward, the bullet still had enough velocity to continue traveling, and it struck a passerby, Mrs. Mary Jacques, age 42, in the thigh.[38] She, too, collapsed in the street. Pembroke, who had watched the entire incident, went immediately to her assistance. "I picked her up and carried her into the store, where they took care of her until we could get an ambulance."[39] An ambulance also came for Gaist, but he was already dead.

Mrs. Jacques and the body of Gustave Gaist were taken to City Hospital, and Inspector Dennessy reported there to begin the investigation. He spoke with Jacques, who was in good condition, and he recovered Gaist's possessions as evidence. He is reported to have found a pair of brass knuckles and some "Red literature."[40]

Also at the City Hospital at the time were John Powers and Arthur English, who had been shot by a state guardsmen early Friday morning in the incident in which Henry Grote was killed. They were both reported to be doing well and would recover from their wounds.[41] In addition, Captain Joseph Harriman, who had accidently been shot by a state guardsman, was recovering nicely at Faulkner Hospital.

There was one additional shooting later that afternoon associated with one of the few craps games still going on in the city. Word had been received by the state guard that there was a large craps game taking place in North Square. Together with the volunteer police officers, they descended upon the large game from all directions and "ordered everybody to put their hands up."[42] There were several who tried to escape and when grabbed by the guardsmen and police, they put up a fight. Shots were then fired, reportedly in the air as a threat, but one of the bullets struck a bystander. Michael Russo, a nine-year-old boy, let out a yell and staggered into the street with "blood pouring from his hand."[43] A passing automobile was stopped, and the driver transported Russo to the hospital, where he was treated and released.[44]

This proved not to be the last shooting incident of the Boston Police Strike. The last would come later that night.

As Saturday afternoon progressed, the fallout from Commissioner Curtis's decision continued. The first salvo came from AFL President Samuel Gompers, who sat down to write a more detailed public statement regarding the decision, after making his curt reply to the media. "The unionizing of policemen is not of the seeking of the American Federation of Labor," Gompers wrote, stating that it was they who came seeking affiliation with the AFL because of poor pay and working conditions that the city would not address.[45] He then placed blame for the week of rioting. He first argued that "sound public opinion will make the authorities in Boston admit and share their own full responsibility for it," before directing most of his blame on the commissioner, stating, "The situation in which the policemen find themselves today was provoked and practically forced upon them by the autocratic action of Police Commissioner Curtis."[46] In closing, he reiterated his earlier sentiment to the press upon hearing the commissioner's decision: "If the authorities give no consideration to the human side of the question or to the advice and suggestion which I had the honor to make, then whatever betide is upon the head of the authorities responsible thereof."[47]

Coolidge, meanwhile, was working on his own response to Gompers's earlier message, which he had received Friday night but had not read until early Saturday morning. In typical Coolidge fashion, it was short and direct:

> Under the law the suggestions contained in your telegram are not within the authority of the Governor of Massachusetts, but only of the Commissioner of Police of the city of Boston. With the maintenance of discipline in his department, I have no authority to intervene. He has decided that the men have abandoned their sworn duty and has accordingly declared

their places vacant. I shall support the commissioner in the
execution of law and maintenance of order.[48]

As he finished his response to Gompers, Coolidge received
a quick reply from Commissioner Curtis regarding his meeting
with the union representatives. "I am of course, willing at any
time to confer with Your Excellency," he wrote Coolidge, "but
I do not deem it advisable, under the existing circumstances, to
join in the suggested conference."[49] Coolidge must have spoken
with Curtis by phone regarding his desire to not meet with the
union representatives and advised Curtis that it would likely be
more prudent to do so, for the police commissioner evidently
changed his mind. Coolidge's secretary, Henry F. Long, released
a statement a short time later stating,

> I am authorized to say for Mr Curtis that he is willing to confer
> in his own behalf with Mr O'Donnell, Mr McCarthy and Mr
> McInnes and that an appointment may be made for that pur-
> pose on Monday morning, as he has engagements which take
> up his time until that date.[50]

By that time, Coolidge no doubt felt it would be too late.

Having received the telegram from Coolidge, Gompers did
not waste time in sending a reply. In it he argued, "The question at issue is not one of law and order, but the assumption of
an autocratic and unwarranted position by the commissioner
of police, who is not responsible to the people of Boston, but
who is appointed by you."[51] What Gompers disagreed with was
the commissioner's "order in which the right of the policemen
to organize has been denied," which was precisely the "cause"
that Governor Coolidge had been fighting for. Coolidge did
not believe police officers should have the right to unionize
and affiliate with the AFL. "May I not further appeal to you, to
Mayor Peters and the police commissioner," Gompers pleaded,
"to take a broad view of the entire situation and thus give the
opportunity for cool, deliberate consideration when the passions
aroused shall have subsided?"[52] Once again, Coolidge laid the
telegram aside, deciding that he would wait to reply the following morning.

Despite Gompers's last-minute attempts to thwart the loss that would not only impact the Boston Policemen's Union but the AFL as well, Commissioner Curtis moved forward with his administrative duties of firing the 19 suspended police officers who had abandoned their duty Tuesday night. Curtis dispatched Captain King and Sergeant Augusta to Fay Hall armed with the general order and the 19 official discharge papers. They arrived at 5:45 p.m., in what had become a most symbolical time. The majority of the men were not present, for they had been on a break for dinner and were only starting to return at that time. Therefore, the captain and sergeant waited at the entrance to Fay Hall to meet each of the 19 men as they returned.[53] It was certainly a somber affair.

By the time President John F. McInnes gaveled in the after-dinner meeting, all 19 officers had received their papers. In the first order of business, McInnes announced to the packed hall that he could no longer preside over the meeting, "owing to the fact that as a private citizen the rules of the union forbade his acting."[54] An individual had to be a police officer in order to be a member of the Boston Policemen's Union. The men shouted their disagreement and "by a voice vote, amid cheers, the members re-elected him and the other officers of the union."[55]

The meeting then continued; the men spent the majority of the time discussing the decision by Commissioner Curtis, or, actually, criticizing him. In the end, one final piece of business was to raise concern for the widow of patrolman Reempts, the only police officer killed during the strike. They agreed to pass a hat and managed to raise $900 to help support her (the equivalent of raising $14,750 in today's dollars). The meeting was then adjourned, and perhaps to try and recapture the excitement over the strike they had felt on Tuesday, the men left the hall singing "Pack Up Your Troubles in Your Old Kit Bag and Smile, Smile, Smile."[56]

President McInnes, however, was not smiling. He was angry with the police commissioner's decision, and he remained defiant before the press:

> The members of the Boston Policemen's Union are not wavering in the face of the false reports of the money interest now

trying so hard to deprive us of our American freedom. In the homes and the hearts of the policemen we are undaunted in our efforts to retain our union and gain recognition.[57]

Despite his bluster, McInnes knew they had been defeated.

As the sun began to set, the state guard became more assertive in keeping people moving, hoping to ensure another mostly peaceful night. The peace was called into question when there was a "two-alarm fire" along Abbottsford Street in Roxbury, where a barn had been set on fire.[58] The fire department responded, fire lines were established, and eventually the fire was extinguished. The cause of the fire was found to have been an incendiary device. It was suspected that it may have been caused by individuals hoping to stir things up for Saturday night.

The last shooting that day, and the last shooting that took place during the Boston Police Strike, is only *suspected* of being connected with the events of the strike. It took place late that Saturday night while there were still crowds about, at the intersection of Washington and Beach Streets, merely a block east and south of the earlier day's shooting near the Boston Common. There was a commotion there in the middle of the street, and the guardsmen went to clear it out. At that point, both Sergeant Edwin B. Taylor and Private Edward Harney of the 12th Regiment saw a man attempting to steal a car, and they went to confront him.

The man was James Donnelly, 22, who had served in the army at Camp Devens for one year in support of the war effort and was then working for the Boston Auto Gage Company.[59] Both soldiers confronted Donnelly by ordering him out of the vehicle, thinking he was possibly using the commotion as cover to steal the car. It is reported that "when the man failed to obey," the soldiers "fired on him."[60] A total of three bullets were fired, and one struck Donnelly in the left shoulder. It then penetrated downward and passed through one of his lungs.

Donnelly was taken out of the car and into the nearby Beach Street Café. There, his wound was dressed, and he was placed under arrest. After an ambulance arrived, he was transported to City Hospital where he underwent surgery and was listed in critical condition. By Monday, however, he was out of danger and on his way to recovery.[61]

In the end, nine people were killed during the Boston Police Strike, and 23 more, like Donnelly, were wounded. Eight of the nine people killed had been involved in confrontations with the state guard. The only other killing was that of striker patrolman Reemts, who was shot and killed by a frightened storekeeper.

The formal portrait of Governor Calvin Coolidge, who soon became the 30th president of the United States for his handling of the Boston Police Strike and taking the position that "There is no right to strike against the public safety by anybody, anywhere, any time."

Photo courtesy of the Library of Congress.

14

. . . Is Paved with Good Intentions

On Sunday morning, September 14, 1919, church bells rang out across the city of Boston, breaking the peaceful stillness that had settled on the city overnight.[1] From church house to church house, preachers, pastors, and priests gave thanks to God that order had been restored. The Reverend John F. Burns of the Gate of Heaven Church recalled, "We have witnessed deplorable scenes in this district this past week," while Reverend George J. Patterson of St. Vincent's Church said in his homily that everyone in the district must stand up "against any such outbreak of lawlessness."[2] The Reverend Edward Cummings of the Arlington Street Church perhaps summed it up best when he told his flock, "Boston has had a taste of Hell."[3] Still, others such as Dr. Alexander Mann of the Episcopal Trinity Church, were more accusatory, for he placed the blame for the previous week's lawlessness on the police, although he did add, "I believe that their acts are more the result of muddy thinking than of deliberate disloyalty."[4]

The newspapers that morning all conveyed the hell the city had been through, writing of their hopes for a better future. "It has been a strenuous week for Boston—a chapter in her history never to be forgotten," the *Boston Sunday Post* editors expressed by way of example. They continued,

Boston is not proud of the record. . . . But the darkest days
have passed . . . perhaps it is well that the issue has been
fought out, rather than that the menace should continue to
hang over the city. It will be a long time before there will occur
another strike of the Boston Policemen. The lesson has been
learned in the hard school of experience. It is a severe lesson
and it will be long remembered. . . . Thus, law and order win
out in our good old city, and it will be many a day before it is
threatened in like manner. Boston is herself again.[5]

The words proved prescient, for the Boston Police never went
on strike again, and the next police strike in the United States
did not come about until nearly 50 years later, in Youngstown,
Ohio, in 1967. What truly brought the Boston Police Strike to
its end and prevented any police strikes for the next two generations was Governor Calvin Coolidge's reply to AFL leader
Samuel Gompers's telegram from the night before. "Soon,
Samuel Gompers began to telegraph me," Coolidge recalled in
his autobiography, explaining how Gompers had asked him for
"the removal of Mr. Curtis and the reinstatement of the union
policemen. . . . This required me to make a reply."[6] In terms of
Coolidge's sparse use of words, his reply to Gompers's telegram
was a somewhat lengthy one for the governor, but it was only
one simple, direct sentence that would bring the entire event to
an end.

Coolidge began by addressing Gompers's repeated call for
the removal of Commissioner Curtis. "I have already refused
to remove the Police Commissioner of Boston," he reiterated,
before explaining, "I did not appoint him. He can assume no
position which the courts would uphold except what the people
have by the authority of their law vested in him. He speaks only
with their voice."[7]

Coolidge then directed his attention to Gompers's wording
regarding "the question at issue," which the AFL leader had
claimed was the fact that the "right of the policemen to organize has been denied—a right which has heretofore never been
questioned."[8] Coolidge disagreed for, as he quite succinctly
stated, "The right of the police of Boston to affiliate has always
been questioned, never granted, is now prohibited."[9] To this,

he added that President Wilson's suggestion for waiting to see how their conference turned out before taking any action did not apply to the situation in Boston, primarily because the Washington, DC, Metropolitan Police had not actually gone on strike and walked off their posts.

Coolidge then turned to Gompers's complaints about the police commissioner. Gompers described the police commissioner's decision to remove the police officers who had walked off the job as an "autocratic and unwarranted position" and expressed his belief that Curtis was wrong and "not responsible to the people of Boston."[10] Coolidge's reply to that was to tell Gompers that his "assertion that the commissioner was wrong cannot justify the wrong of leaving the city unguarded" and that action had "furnished the opportunity" for violence, while "the criminal element furnished the action."[11]

It was the next line Coolidge delivered that Koss called his "coup de grace."[12] The governor stated, "There is no right to strike against the public safety by anybody, anywhere, any time."[13] As ever, using an economy of words, Coolidge captured not only his own sentiment but the sentiment of the majority of people in Boston as well as Massachusetts and throughout the United States. That one sentence became the most repeated line of the Boston Police Strike and was asserted by newspapers, politicians, and people all across America.[14] As Amity Shlaes writes, "The repeated line found in papers across the country capturing the sentiment of the people" became "a *vox populi*."[15] Coolidge very quickly became aware of just how much that line resonated with the people, and he later wrote in his autobiography,

> This phrase caught the attention of the nation. It was beginning to be clear that if voluntary associations were to be permitted to substitute their will for the authority of public officials the end of our government was at hand. The issue was nothing less than whether the law which the people had made through their duly authorized agencies should be supreme.[16]

It was that line that eliminated any more threats to Coolidge's "cause."

There was more to the telegram Coolidge sent, but in 24 hours the rest became immaterial. Coolidge had, however, added that he did not agree with returning the striking officers to work because it would mean placing the public safety of the people of Boston back "in the hands of these same policemen" who had abandoned their duty, and he, like Gompers, wished to take a "broad view of every situation."[17]

The reason the sentence resonated with many individuals is because the majority of people at the time agreed with the sentiment. The people of Boston who had endured the chaos of the previous week and had their lives disrupted by the strike certainly were in agreement. For some, it was because of the looting of their stores. For others, it was because they had become victims of violence. For many families, it was because one or more of their members was absent because they were either protecting stores from looting, serving as volunteer policemen, or had been called to duty in the state guard. For most, it was simply their inability to move about the city as they had done so before to accomplish their more mundane tasks such as shopping or going to work. The people largely supported the concepts of law and order, especially those involved in church and civic groups, and so they were fully on the side of Curtis and Coolidge in the handling of the strike. Outside Boston, the desire for law and order was the same, coupled with fears that something similar might happen in their own town. Equally pressing were the fears of the "Reds" and the fear of a possible communist uprising in America that was intricately tied to the issues of immigrants, minorities, and labor unions. Fear has always been a motivating factor that has driven American policy.

This does not mean that the strike did not divide people, for in Boston, Thomas O'Connor explains, "The Boston police strike went a long way toward solidifying the division between the Boston Irish and the Yankee blue bloods."[18] The deep-seated hatred of the Irish Catholics by the Yankee Protestants was simply confirmed by the actions of the Boston patrolmen, most of whom were Irish, as well as the rioters, many of whom were also Irish but were overwhelmingly from the immigrant class. The strike did little to persuade what was already the prevailing attitude toward foreigners in Boston and throughout America; rather, it reinforced it. To drive home their point, many made note of the fact the worst-hit sections of Boston during the riots were immigrant neighborhoods, the very same neighborhoods in which many of the rioters lived. Therefore, the public at the time, both progressives and conservatives in Boston, the state of Massachusetts, and across the nation, applauded the stand taken with regard to the police and their unionization. Although Robert Sobel goes so far as to say it was only later that those who sided with the stance of the governor and commissioner were "perceived as being anti-union and even reactionary," a perhaps more honest read of the situation would be to say there were more people at the time who agreed with the leadership in the crisis. However, due to immigration and changing attitudes in America, more and more people came to see the decision as both anti-union and reactionary in nature.[19]

By Monday morning, with the strike over, the threat of a general strike removed, and a police force largely expunged of police officers who had abandoned their duties from their rolls, the most important task that remained was to hire a new police department. Once that was achieved, a second important task could be accomplished and that was having the state guard stand down. Commissioner Curtis began moving as fast as he could to hire an all-new police force, for this action required the hiring of over 1,000 police officers and proved to be no easy task. Many members of the Boston Policemen's Union, disgruntled over losing their jobs, began finding ways to sabotage the commissioner's plans.[20] "The discharged men," Richard Lyons explains, "circulated rumors that the courts would soon order their reinstatement, making the positions offered by the Commissioner only temporary."[21] This made recruiting men to even apply for a position difficult, thus frustrating the commissioner's plans for a large candidate pool from which to hire. Some of the men who did apply reported they had threats made against them, and when offered a job, some of the fired officers made sure to "intimidate applicants from accepting positions."[22] Once new police officers were hired, the disgruntled union members put pressure on other unions not to accept contracts from the police department. This meant that when Curtis ordered new uniforms and equipment for his recently hired policemen, he had trouble finding businesses willing to manufacture the uniforms or sell the equipment to the police department, thus delaying the fielding of the new officers.[23] Commissioner Curtis had little choice but to have these contracts filled by out-of-state vendors, thus depriving Massachusetts state tax dollars from being used in-state.[24] Fortunately, General Parker and the Massachusetts State Guard remained on duty, and Curtis was guaranteed they would remain so until his new patrolmen were fully deployed.[25]

Although there have been many questions about the Boston Police Strike since it ended, the most prevalent question in the immediate aftermath of the strike was why the state guard had not been called out sooner. In addition, many people were asking why the volunteer police were not put on duty Tuesday rather than waiting until Wednesday morning to be in place. Because the mayor defended himself so often by stating that he had asked Commissioner Curtis if they were needed, and he had said no at the time, most of the attention shifted toward Curtis (although much of the responsibility for calling the guard did rest with the mayor). In addition, Curtis had coordinated the call for police volunteers, and he knew that there were at least several hundred at his disposal by Tuesday of the strike. Curtis remained rather silent on the matter, dedicating most of his time to his administrative duties and hiring a new force. However, he finally answered his critics' charges later that fall.

Curtis chose to use his annual *Boston Police Commissioner's Report*, released on November 30, 1919, as his forum to publicly state his reasoning at the time. After explaining that there were "facts which apparently are not generally known," he presented three justifications.[26] The first was a matter of law in regard to the volunteer police officers. Curtis could not field the volunteer policemen until after the Boston patrolmen left their posts, otherwise he would have been violating the law.

Second, he explained that he had been monitoring the situation in the field; he had consulted with the police department's captains who had presented him with information that led him to believe 800 officers would remain on duty, rather than only approximately 400 officers who actually did remain, all of them officers with rank or close to retirement. Thus, he felt that with a force of 800 police officers, he would still be able to maintain law and order in the city.

The third, again, was an instance of law. He explained that the city could not, by statutory authority, call out the state guard unless "a tumult, riot, or mob" existed or was threatened. Until there was clear evidence of such a threat, or those activities became real, he could not, by law, call for the state guard. When 5:45 p.m. arrived, and the officers had left their posts, there was no "tumult, riot, or mob" and disruptive behaviors did not develop until later in the evening. Although Curtis did a poor job of monitoring the situation that night (for he went home to bed), even if the state guard had been called out at the first signs of any of those three categories, their deployment would not have occurred until early Wednesday morning, likely the same time as the volunteer police officers were finally deployed. Of course, the volunteer police could have at least been deployed at the first signs of trouble.

Curtis also added one more justification when he made the statement, "The secrecy of the proceedings on the part of the men, and the frequently reiterated statement that the word 'strike' had never been mentioned, made it impossible to have the troops on the scene before they actually got there."[27] Clearly, this is a disingenuous statement, for the *Boston Globe*, among other papers, was actively reporting the activities of the Boston Policemen's Union in both the morning and evening papers, and on September 9, the *Boston Herald*'s banner headline read, "Police Vote to Strike Today: To Quit at 5:45 p.m. Rollcall."[28] It was no secret that the police were at least saying they were going to strike.

One thing the commissioner did not state in the report was the fact he had not believed the officers were going to actually walk off their jobs. Curtis could not conceive of someone, especially a government official like a police officer, failing to do their promised duty. Because of this, even up to the final hour,

Curtis believed the union officers were bluffing, and he intended to call their bluff.

Years later Coolidge agreed with the commissioner. Again, from his autobiography, Coolidge wrote, "Such action probably would have saved some property, but would have decided no issue."[29] Once more, Coolidge shows more concern for his "cause," giving it more importance than the destruction of property, not to mention the loss of lives and injuries that occurred. And Coolidge continued by stating,

> In fact it would have made it more difficult to maintain the position Mr. Curtis had taken, and which I was supporting, because the issue was not understood, and the disorder focused public attention on it, and showed just what it meant to have a police force that did not obey orders.[30]

In other words, if it had not been for rioting in the wake of the police walkout, the people might not have been supportive of his cause, thus rendering support for the Boston Policemen's Union and their right to unionize and affiliate with the AFL.

By the end of October, the 10th Regiment started to draw down, reducing the number of soldiers on active duty, including those in D Company.[31] By mid-November the company only had nine soldiers and their commander remaining on duty, and they were attached to another company. A Company of the 11th Regiment had also seen their numbers reduced, and by November 23 they were ordered home and placed on reserve.[32] The entire state guard was finally relieved of duty on December 16. They were completely gone from the streets of Boston by Christmas.[33]

Although the mayor's role in the Boston Police Strike was seen by the people of Boston as being somewhat mixed, they were apparently forgiving enough to reelect him to office the following year. However, he only won by a narrow margin. Two years later, in 1922, the rising tide against the Boston Brahmin began to encroach upon their political powers. The irascible James Michael Curley returned to the mayoral office having won by a narrow margin with the support of the Boston Irish and other Boston ethnic groups. "From that time forward," explains Jack Tager, "Boston was to become an Irish domain, a protected fortress against outsiders unsympathetic to an ethnic, working-class community."[34]

On February 6, 1922, Mayor Andrew James Peters left office, and he never held a political position again. In the late 1920s he was considered as a possible candidate for governor but was not nominated to run, and after the scandal with 11-year-old Starr Wyman broke, he was never considered again. He died of pneumonia on June 26, 1938, when he was 66 years old.

When Commissioner Curtis held his first day of recruiting for new officers on September 22, 350 men turned out for a job. This was not surprising, for there were still economic problems in the aftermath of World War I that included widespread unemployment, and there were plenty of veterans eager to find a job.[35] However, after that day, some of the former patrolmen began sabotaging his plans, and between the spread of rumors and threats, the number of applicants dwindled. Still, Curtis persevered, and by November he managed to hire 1,343 new patrolmen.[36]

During all of this, Commissioner Curtis's health continued to decline, but he was determined to rebuild the Boston Police Department, and so he remained. It is reported that during the hiring, he suffered several heart attacks, but whenever retirement was suggested as an option for him, he would reply, "No, I'm going to stick as long as I have strength."[37] On March 28, 1922, he reported to work at the usual time in the morning, but he left early that day due to what he claimed to be indigestion. He died at home later that afternoon from a major coronary heart attack. He was 60 years old.

Although Peters ultimately lost office, and Curtis his life, perhaps the greatest loss in the Boston Police Strike were the unions. The American Federation of Labor lost control of the situation, and the strike gave them bad press. The AFL had to go back on their plans to charter police departments because members forced them to revoke the charters of the 37 police unions they had recognized since July. The AFL continued the fight by

274 / Chapter 14

appealing the decision in the Boston courts, but on November 7, 1919, all hope was lost when the Massachusetts Supreme Judicial Court upheld the dismissal of the officers.[38] There were few grounds upon which the AFL could appeal to the US Supreme Court, so Gompers was forced to admit defeat.

Samuel Gompers himself was never quite the same leader after the Boston Police Strike, and his situation was made worse when he contracted influenza in February 1923. He never fully recovered, and his health continued to decline. In addition to suffering from diabetes, he experienced congestive heart failure in June 1924. On December 6 that year, while in Mexico City attending the Pan-American Federation of Labor meeting, he collapsed. He was taken by train to San Antonio, Texas, where he died on December 13. He was 74.

The members of the Boston Policemen's Union suffered first from the loss of their jobs and then from their crushing defeat in the courts. Despite those defeats, they continued to plead for their old jobs back, and those appeals lasted for decades. Whenever a new governor or mayor came into office or a new police commissioner was appointed, there was always the hope that they would overturn the decision allowing them to resume their careers as police officers in Boston. Although all heard their cries, none were willing to answer them.

The president of the policemen's union, John McInnes, lost his position as the head of the union as well as his job as a police officer. By the next year, according to the 1920 Census, his occupation was bricklayer.[39] Perhaps more than anyone, he initially fought against the decision, soon grew tired and sick, and began to fade away. After enduring a long illness, McInnes died in his home on May 16, 1924, at the age of 52.[40] Ironically, his obituary stated that he was the "man who did more than any other to make Calvin Coolidge President of the United States."[41]

For every Boston police officer who had gone on strike in solidarity with the Boston Policemen's Union, each had their own tragic story in the aftermath of being fired. In one family, both John Halward Boyle and his brother Thomas H. Boyle lost their jobs as police officers.[42] In another family, the strike divided family members. Frederick Joseph Wheeler was the son of a Boston police officer who joined the department in July 1919 and two months later went on strike. His father, Sergeant Frederick Nelson Wheeler, did not.[43] One can only imagine the division the strike had created in that family.

There were others who managed to make do by finding other jobs. William Patrick Wills, one of the 19 leaders of the Boston Policemen's Union who was dismissed for General Order 125 and had been with the department since 1904, had a wife and child to support. So, after the strike, no longer able to afford their own apartment, he was forced by the circumstances to move his family into his mother's home. He was fortunate when it came to employment, for one of the other striking officers, Edmund Burke, had become the proprietor of Duggan's Garage on the South End, and he offered him a job. For the rest of his life, Wills worked as a gas station attendant.

Another fired patrolman, Edward "Smokey" M. Kelleher, managed to find work as a collector for unpaid bills and later became a salesman.[44] He had only been a police officer for a short time since he had served in World War I with distinction, earning the Croix de Guerre, before coming home and joining the department on July 7, 1919. He then lost his job just over two months later. Smokey Kelleher gave an interview not long after the strike and likely voiced the sentiment of many of the other officers who lost their jobs. "I didn't want to strike," he explained, "and I don't know any other man who did want to."[45] He then elaborated:

> I went out when 19 men were discharged by the commissioner because I and the others had elected them officers of the union. They were no more guilty than I was, and I wouldn't be yellow enough to leave them to be the goats for all of us.[46]

Another officer echoed a similar explanation for why the police officers voted to strike. When asked how many actually wanted to go on strike, he responded, "How many wanted to go on strike? Less than 50 percent, but a lot were led to vote that way because they didn't want to desert the boys."[47]

When Smokey Kelleher was questioned about the strike that resulted in riots, property damage, and both death and injury, he replied,

> I wouldn't have gone on a strike if I had thought the city was undefended and there was going to be a riot. The papers said there were plenty of men to keep order and handle the crowd. The commissioner himself said so.[48]

Still, he was clearly bitter over the commissioner's actions, for he also commented, "Now the policeman's pay has been raised and the stations are to be fixed; the hours even may be made better."[49] He then pointed out, "It took a strike to do it."[50]

Yet, while the strike did perhaps bring about the change in Boston officer pay and working conditions, there was a higher price to be paid with regard to police unionism. "It can be unequivocally stated," concludes Jonathan White in his study of the Boston Police Strike, "that the major outcome of the strike was the defeat of police unionism."[51] Police historian Robert M. Fogelson once wrote that the Boston Police Strike's impact on police unions in America was that it "emasculated them" and that "By virtue of these efforts, the rank-and-file were represented only by their fraternal and benevolent groups and their political clubs down through the 1920s."[52] Having the advantage of a longer view of history, another police historian, Thomas Reppetto, explains, "The Boston police strike left a permanent legacy for the American police."[53] Among the impacts was the fact that "for a half century no American police department would consider striking" and "without the strike weapon they had no bargaining position," hence, like Fogelson said, they were emasculated.[54]

It seems there really was only one person in all of the fallout from the Boston Police Strike who came out ahead, and that was Governor Calvin Coolidge. As his biographer Amity Shlaes explains, after his handling of the strike and the release of his reply to Gompers, "Coolidge was suddenly a person to be followed."[55] In fact, Sobel relates, "In the weeks and months that followed, Coolidge received some seventy thousand letters, telegrams, and other communications praising his stand, many calling upon him to run for national office."[56]

Coolidge did not have any immediate plans to do so, for he faced reelection in the State House that November. Still, his handling of the strike no doubt bolstered his win that fall. Coolidge faced the Democratic nominee, Richard H. Long, at the ballot box on November 4, 1919, and by the time the votes were being counted, it was clear Coolidge was going to win by a landslide. In the end, he obtained 317,774 votes to Long's 192,673, giving him a plurality of approximately 125,000 votes, the greatest electoral victory in the state of Massachusetts up to that point in history.[57] Coolidge, however, claimed in an interview that the outcome was not necessarily a certain one. "I understood perfectly," Coolidge told reporters after the election,

My attitude in the police matter greatly endangered what at the time appeared my certain election. What I did then had to be done. It was of more consequence than my success in the polls. I should not have done otherwise had I known that it would bring about my certain defeat.[58]

Coolidge was now a national figure, and even President Woodrow Wilson, a member of the opposite party, telegraphed to congratulate him on his victory: "I congratulate you upon your election as victory for law and order. When that is the issue, all Americans stand together."[59]

The following year, at the 1920 Republican National Convention, the members of that party also stood together behind Coolidge. After nominating Harding as the party's nominee for president, the discussion turned to who would fill the vice presidency. The name Calvin Coolidge was brought up by Senator Irvine Lenroot of Wisconsin when Judge McCamant, a delegate from Oregon, shouted that Calvin Coolidge, "is big enough and sound enough to be President of the United States, should occasion arise."[60] A roar of approval went up, and Coolidge took the ballot on the first vote.[61] It was the same that November, for Harding and Coolidge won election in a landslide.

In his autobiography Coolidge knew what elected him vice president. "No doubt it was the police strike of Boston that brought me into national prominence," he wrote, before adding, "That furnished the occasion and I took advantage of the opportunity."[62] He was sworn into office on March 4, 1921, and began serving as the 29th vice president of the United States in which he truly earned his sobriquet, "Silent Cal."

A little over two years later, on the night of August 2, 1923, he received the stunning news. "I was awakened by my father coming up the stairs calling my name," he wrote in his autobiography.[63] "I noticed that his voice trembled. As the only times I had ever observed that before were when death had visited our family, I knew that something of the gravest nature had occurred."[64] Calvin Coolidge had just become the 30th president of the United States. Harding had died in San Francisco while on a tour of America in an attempt to gain favor for his upcoming reelection to office.

Calvin Coolidge had certainly gained the most from the Boston Police Strike. He had become the foremost political leader of the United States of America. "If it had not been for the Boston Police Strike of September 1919," Russell once observed, "Calvin Coolidge would no doubt have ended as just another in the succession of Republican Governors of Massachusetts."[65]

The most debated question regarding the strike, and the one question that was asked in the immediate aftermath of the strike and has been asked ever since is: Who is to blame? At the time, it is fairly evident who was blaming whom. The public, the governor, and Commissioner Curtis were most certainly blaming the police officers for abandoning their posts, brought on by their desire to retain their union affiliation with the AFL.[66] Gompers and most of the labor union representatives primarily placed their blame on Curtis, although many also saw Governor Coolidge as sharing in that blame. Mayor Peters was the only one who did not seem to have all the blame placed on him, in part because he did, after all, try to assert some authority after his police commissioner had failed him.[67] If he was blamed for anything, it was for being a weak leader and waiting too long to intervene and then failing at doing so when he finally took action. There were also some who blamed the AFL for suddenly chartering police unions after having resisted doing so for years, but when it comes to the union, again, most of the blame was placed on the members of the Boston Policemen's Union.

Those who have studied the Boston Police Strike over the years tend to take two different approaches. The first is generally in support of the views of their subject, such as Sobel, who blames the unions and the officers in his biography of Coolidge, while those entrenched in labor union research tend to blame Coolidge and Curtis.[68] The second group are those who explore the Boston Police Strike itself with more depth and less bias. These scholars tend to come away with conclusions that tend to spread the blame across the various actors.[69] For instance, while Russell places the blame mostly on Coolidge and Curtis, he also believes the AFL did not support the police enough, while Koss says they were victims—pawns in an organized labor game.[70]

There is, perhaps, another way of looking at the Boston Police Strike. The oft-quoted line "The road to hell is paved with good intentions" actually has two meanings. The first suggests that people who intend to do something for someone but fail to follow through are placing themselves on the road to hell. The other and more applicable perspective is that the decisions and actions of people, even when made and done with the best of intentions, can still set us on the road to hell. In this case, it would be the decisions made by all of the actors in the Boston Police Strike, even though made with the best of intentions, that created the tragedy Boston witnessed in September 1919. And it is perhaps another quote that emphasizes this particular point. It has been said that when two people—one good, one evil—oppose each other, we have melodrama. But when we have two people, both good, who oppose each other, we have a tragedy.[71] In the case of the Boston Police Strike, we have many actors, all of whom felt they were doing the right thing but who created a tragic event nonetheless.

The police officers who joined together to form the Boston Policemen's Union that then affiliated with the AFL were doing so because of the deplorable working conditions of the Boston

Police Department. The long work hours, the conditions of the station houses, and most importantly, the pay that was not keeping up with inflation—all of these were impoverishing every patrolman and his family. People have the right to a fair wage, one that affords them at least subsistence, but when inflation did not even allow them that level of human decency, they tried to redress their grievances. When they gained no traction on this front, they formed their union and affiliated with the AFL. As the events unfolded, and they voted to strike, the police officers were doing the right thing.

Commissioner Curtis was also doing the right thing. As an administrative leader, he understood that when leaders give orders, followers must obey those orders, or the organization fails. When the officers moved toward unionizing and affiliating with the AFL, he saw that relationship as one in which the patrolmen would effectively be following the leadership of others outside the department. The saying that no man can serve two masters is sound advice, and Curtis knew he had to issue the order to avoid losing control.[72] And when officers disobey orders, and in this case they moved forward with their AFL affiliation, he felt it only proper to charge them for their violation. Curtis followed all the rules and regulations to the very end; he fired the 19 officers and removed all the others from departmental rolls for abandoning their duty because it was the right thing to do.

Mayor Peters, as a politician and elected leader, understood both the need to do what was right for the citizens of Boston, while at the same time following the law. In trying to balance these competing interests, Peters searched for some form of compromise that could present a means for resolving the situation. When he followed the law and trusted his police commissioner, although he rightfully worried about the outcome, he was doing the right thing. Then, when the police commissioner failed him, and riots and looting occurred, he again did the right thing by taking charge of the situation. And after Coolidge asserted his authority and placed Curtis in charge once again, Mayor Peters did what was right in his support of both Coolidge and Curtis.

Samuel Gompers and members of the AFL were doing the right thing by finally allowing a police department to affiliate with their organization. They had been chartering public employees for years but had refused to charter public employees who worked as police officers. They were doing the right thing by avoiding discriminating against a particular category of public employees when they changed their policy and began accepting charters from police unions. And once order was restored, Gompers was right in making his appeals for the leadership to recognize the humanity of the officers who had gone on strike and calling for a peaceable settlement that was in the best interest of all parties.

Finally, Coolidge was doing the right thing by forcing the issue and staying focused on his cause, namely, to prevent police officers, or any public safety officers, from being able to unionize because of the bad precedent it set for future governance. Like Curtis, Coolidge agreed that if police officers were able to unionize, they would be serving two masters, and what may be in the best interest of the union members may not be in the best interest of the citizens of that city or state. For Coolidge, it was clearly about the power of government, the power of the State, and doing right by the people he represented.

There has been nothing in the historical record that has ever presented clear and incontrovertible evidence to suggest any of the principal actors in the Boston Police Strike were acting maliciously. Every actor in the strike was doing the right thing, and it is difficult to place blame on anyone for so doing. As has often occurred in history, there are simply those events in which all the principal actors are doing the right thing, but because of a confluence of competing circumstances, the events lead to collective failure. When the rioting turned violent and deadly, and Boston became hell on earth, the confluence of every actor's decision to do good, although in opposition to one another, caused the Boston Police Strike to become the tragedy it is remembered as today.

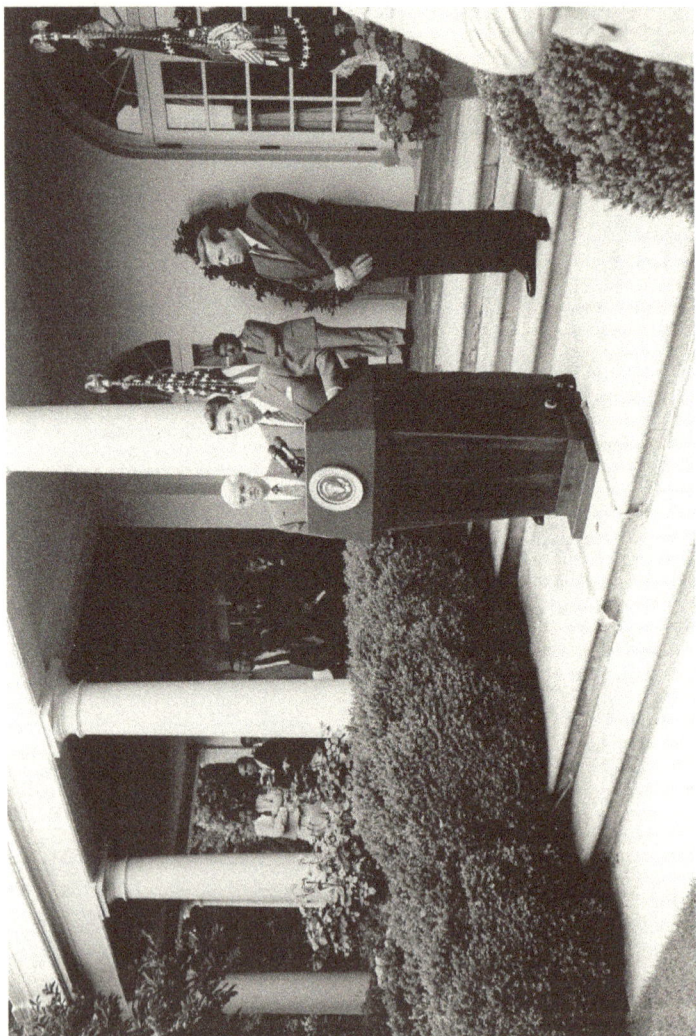

President Ronald Reagan on August 3, 1981, in the White House Rose Garden, where he delivered his remarks on the Air Traffic Controllers Strike, echoing the sentiments of Calvin Coolidge during the Boston Police Strike.

Photo courtesy of the Ronald Reagan Presidential Library, National Archives and Records Administration.

Epilogue
August 3, 1981

Not long after Ronald Reagan's inauguration as the 40th president of the United States, he entered the Oval Office, which, as was standard practice, had new carpeting and freshly painted walls. One of the first things he did was to hang a portrait of Calvin Coolidge. "I'd always thought of Coolidge as one of our most underrated presidents," he wrote later in his autobiography.[1] "He wasn't a man with flamboyant looks or style, but he got things done in a quiet way."[2] Calvin Coolidge was one of the president's heroes. On August 3, 1981, not yet six months since he had taken the oath of office, Ronald Reagan had the opportunity to emulate his hero when he held a remarks and question-and-answer session with reporters regarding the Air Traffic Controllers Strike.

America's air traffic controllers, the men and women who coordinate the planes in the sky and the use of airport runways for takeoffs and landings to avoid collisions, had felt the effects of 1970s inflation. It had left them with far less buying power in 1981 than they had had ten years earlier. Represented by their union, the Professional Air Traffic Controllers Organization (PATCO), they demanded higher pay. In addition to an increase in wages, they also sought better work conditions through a reduction in the number of hours worked per week from 40 to 32. Their reasoning was due to the high stress of the job.[3]

PATCO President Robert Poli and Transportation Secretary Drew Lewis had been in negotiations since the spring of 1981, and what they ultimately agreed upon was an across-the-board $4,000 raise for the 40-hour workweek. Although not exactly what the membership wanted, Poli thought it was a decent compromise. The membership disagreed.

Poli and Lewis continued negotiations, while the union threatened to strike on August 3 if their demands were not met. Reagan wrote in his diary, "I told Drew L[ewis] to tell their union chief I was the best friend his people ever had in the White House but I would not countenance an illegal strike nor would I permit negotiations while such a strike was in process."[4] Indeed, Reagan had once been the head of the Screen Actors Guild, representing the interests of its members. As the head of that union, and a lifelong member of the AFL-CIO, he had actually led the Screen Actors Guild on their first strike. This is why he wrote the statement of being their "best friend" in his diary.

Despite Lewis's passing Reagan's words along to the union, the membership refused to back down and kept to its threat. At 7 a.m. on Monday morning, August 3, 1981, the air traffic controllers declared they were officially on strike. Nearly 13,000 members of PATCO walked off the job. Flights were canceled, airports were shut down, and air travel snarled to a halt.

"Government cannot close down the assembly line," Reagan told reporters. "It has to provide without interruption the protective services which are government's reason for being."[5] He then read the oath each air traffic controller takes when accepting their job, which specifically states, "I am not participating in any strike against the Government of the United States or any agency thereof, and I will not so participate while an employee of the Government of the United States or any agency thereof."[6] Reagan then concluded his statement by clearly stating, "It is for this reason that I must tell those who fail to report for duty this morning they are in violation of the law, and if they do not report for work within 48 hours, they have forfeited their jobs and will be terminated."[7]

Although President Reagan had not used the specific words of Calvin Coolidge—"There is no right to strike against the public safety by any body, any time, any where"—he certainly incorporated their meaning into his statement.[8]

As historian H. W. Brands said, "many of the controllers didn't believe him," like the Boston policemen before them. But 48 hours later, for the 11,359 who had not returned to work, Reagan remained true to his word, as Commissioner Curtis did when the Boston Police Strike occurred, and he fired every one of them.[9] And like the Boston patrolmen, they were never hired back.

Afterword

In the mid-1980s, when I was a first-year college student at Radford University in Virginia, I took several classes with Dr. James N. Gilbert. In one of those courses on policing, he told us the story of the Boston Police Strike of 1919. Absolutely fascinated by the tragedy of what happened to the city of Boston when the policemen went on strike, I stopped off at the university library to read more about those events in September 1919. Although I found several articles, the only book I could find was Francis Russell's *A City in Terror: Calvin Coolidge and the 1919 Boston Police Strike* (Beacon Press, 1975), until now the only book ever published on these events. It was an enjoyable and fascinating read, and the book remains an engaging read to this day.

Having become a college professor, I often referred back to Russell's book as a citation for the strike and referenced it when I began writing more police history myself. As I started to look at Russell's sources more closely, this, for me at least, is where the glamor of Russell's book began to fade. There is no doubt he is a widely respected historian, and he wrote at a time when historians read voluminously on a subject and then told their readers what they had learned. What became maddening for me was Russell's system of citations. There were none. All his book had was a meager "selected bibliography" that presented no means by which to ascertain where Russell obtained his information for specific quotes, facts, and assertions. In many cases, the historian made his sources clear in the narrative, for he often made note of their origin in the text. In others, the quotes he used were searchable on the Internet, thus allowing someone to discover the original source with this added step. There were some, however, in which he presented no evidence, and no other author has ever verified Russell's statements, making some of the book's quotes and information questionable. To rectify this, I thought of one day writing a book that would present better documentation of sources, but it remained only that—an idea.

In 2017, as I was ushering my biography of Police Chief August Vollmer toward publication, I was already immersed in the research and about to start writing my next book project, which was set for publication in 2019: *The Birth of the FBI* (Rowman & Littlefield). At some point the date 2019 sparked my memory of the Boston Police Strike of 1919. Realizing the 100th anniversary of the strike was forthcoming and remembering I had always wanted to write a book on that subject, I spoke with my editor, Kathryn Knigge at Rowman & Littlefield, who was very supportive of the idea and encouraged me to do so. Of course, she was hoping to have it in time for the anniversary. I knew that would not be possible, and feared, more than likely, someone else was already hard at work on the book. She suggested we wait to see what happened on the anniversary, and if no one published anything, she would certainly be willing to move forward with that as my next project.

I delivered *The Birth of the FBI* in late 2018, and soon began gathering all of the sources I could locate on the strike. When the anniversary came and went, there were no books published, so by the end of the year, I was already hard at work on this book. Two of the sources I spent the most time with were Newspapers .com and Newspapersarchive.com, two wonderful databases for researchers. Through these, I began reading thousands of pages of newspaper articles on the strike. To help me in this endeavor, I put my research assistant, Jacqueline Nguyen, to work on the project. I must say her hard work and assistance proved invaluable to the project. As for those hard-to-find articles, I managed to keep Sarah Greenmyer in the Interlibrary Loan office at Sam Houston State University very busy. My many thanks go to her for tracking down all those old esoteric articles I requested quite frequently. Another source of information came about unexpectedly, and that was the University of Massachusetts at Boston's Roll Call project, in which they researched the "men behind the 1919 Boston Police Strike." My hope was to meet the directors, Joanne Riley and Margaret R. Sullivan, on a visit to Boston, but that was curtailed because of COVID. Still, their hard work and the work of the countless volunteers for the project who investigated the life story of each of the officers who went on strike for their biographical information and stories proved invaluable to my own project. I am deeply indebted to them and hope to one day meet some of those involved in the project.

There were so many other sources of help I received for this book that I would be remiss if I did not mention them. Aaron Schmidt, the curator of photography at the Boston Public Library, was incredibly helpful in researching the library's holdings on the strike. So, also, was archivist Julie Bartlett Nelson of the Calvin Coolidge Presidential Library & Museum, Forbes Library. And the many people who assisted me from the Library of Congress should also be recognized for their assistance as well, including Kelly Dyson, Erica Kelly, and Kenneth Johnson. Everyone was very gracious with their time.

There were also many who helped me bring this book to print. I would first like to thank my wife, Judy, for listening to me read the chapters aloud to her as I finished. She always has a knack for catching those little details I too often miss. I also wish to thank Ronda Harris for her excellent copyediting of the book. You are always a pleasure to work with, and my writing always improves under your skillful edits, although I should note here that any mistakes in the manuscript remain mine and mine alone. And, finally, I would like to thank the editors at Rowman & Littlefield: Kathryn Knigge, who helped move the project forward, and Becca Beurer, who helped usher it to publication.

Both of you have my heartfelt appreciation for your friendly and professional editorial guidance along the way. Everyone at Rowman & Littlefield has been very kind and easygoing to work with, which is something I very much appreciate.

Willard M. Oliver
Huntsville, Texas

Notes

Prologue

1. *Boston Globe*, September 9, 1919; Russell, *A City in Terror*, 112.
2. Boston Police Commissioner, *Fourteenth Annual Report*.
3. UMASS Boston, *1919 Boston Police Strike Project*.
4. Ibid.
5. *Boston Globe*, September 9, 1919.
6. Ibid.
7. Ibid.
8. Ibid.
9. Ibid.
10. *Boston Globe*, September 10, 1919; Koss, "The Boston Police Strike of 1919, 160.
11. Koss, "The Boston Police Strike of 1919," 160.
12. *Boston Globe*, September 9, 1919.
13. Koss, "The Boston Police Strike of 1919," 162.
14. Ibid.
15. Ibid.
16. Ibid.
17. Ibid.
18. Koss, "The Boston Police Strike of 1919," 162; Russell, *A City in Terror*, 113.
19. *Boston Evening Globe*, September 9, 1919.
20. *Boston Evening Globe*, September 9, 1919; Boston Police Commissioner, *Fourteenth Annual Report*; Russell, *A City in Terror*, 113. *Note:* Koss, in his dissertation, claimed 1,375 voted "yes" with no opposed votes (Koss, "Boston Police Strike of 1919," 162).

21. *Boston Herald*, September 10, 1919.
22. *Boston Post*, September 9, 1919; *Boston Traveler*, September 9, 1919.

Chapter 1. America's First Police Department

1. City of Boston, "A Brief History of the B.P.D."
2. City of Boston, "Symbols."
3. Roth, *Historical Dictionary of Law Enforcement*, 34.
4. Boston Police Department, "History"; see also Roth, *A History of Crime*.
5. McCaffrey, "The Boston Police Department," 672.
6. Boston Police Department, "History."
7. Diamond, *Guns, Germs, and Steel.*
8. Ibid., 268.
9. Ibid., 272.
10. Ibid., 273.
11. Ibid., 280.
12. Round, *Feudal England.*
13. Morris, *The Frankpledge System.*
14. Ibid.
15. Morris, *The Medieval English Sheriff to 1300.*
16. Harding, *England in the Thirteenth Century*, 92.
17. Ibid.
18. Statute of Winchester, 1285.
19. Ibid.
20. Ibid.
21. Pringle, *Hue and Cry*, 43.
22. Kappeler, Sluder, and Alpert, *Forces of Deviance*, 32.
23. Shakespeare, *Much Ado About Nothing*, 79.
24. Peterson, *The City-State of Boston.*
25. Bopp and Schultz, *A Short History of American Law Enforcement*; Fogelson, *Big-City Police*; Savage, *Police Records and Recollections.*
26. Winthrop, *Winthrop's Journal*, 62.
27. Savage, *A Chronological History of the Boston Watch and Police*, 12.
28. Oliver and Hilgenberg, *A History of Crime*; Savage, *Police Records.*
29. Boston City Council, *Ordinances and Rule*, 521.
30. Ibid.
31. Ibid.
32. Oliver and Hilgenberg, *A History of Crime.*
33. Bopp and Schultz, *A Short History*; Fogelson, *Big-City Police.*
34. Franklin, *The Autobiography of Benjamin Franklin*, 88.
35. Ibid.
36. Monkkonen, *Police in Urban America*, 32.

37. Burrows and Wallace, *Gotham*; Miller, *Cops and Bobbies*; Walling, *Recollections*.
38. Walling, *Recollections*, 32.
39. Ibid.
40. Burrows and Wallace, *Gotham*, 637.
41. Friedman, *Crime and Punishment*, 68.
42. Ibid.
43. Savage, *Police Records*, 42.
44. Lane, *Policing the City*.
45. Ibid.
46. Ibid., 11.
47. Ibid.
48. Harrison, *Police Administration in Boston*.
49. Lane, *Policing the City*, 16.
50. Lane, "Urban Police and Crime."
51. Quincy, *Municipal History*, 102.
52. Ibid., 104.
53. Ibid., 273.
54. Ibid., 272.
55. Ibid.
56. Lane, "Urban Police"; Tager, *Boston Riots*.
57. Prioli, "The Ursuline Outrage," 100.
58. Schultz, *Fire and Roses*.
59. Prioli, "The Ursuline Outrage," 102.
60. Tager, *Boston Riots*, 82.
61. Ibid.
62. Prioli, "The Ursuline Outrage," 103; Tager, *Boston Riots*, 112.
63. Lane, *Policing the City*, 30.
64. Ibid.
65. Davis, *Inhuman Bondage*, 263.
66. *Boston Commercial Gazette*, October 24, 1835.
67. Tager, *Boston Riots*, 91.
68. Lane, *Policing the City*, 32.
69. Levy, "The Abolition Riot," 88.
70. Eliot, "Being Mayor of Boston," 156.
71. Stevens, *Hidden History*, 44.
72. Lane, *Policing the City*, 33.
73. Boston, *Documents*, No. 15, 303.
74. Ibid.
75. Lane, *Policing the City*, 35.

Chapter 2. The Boston Police Department

1. Eliot, "Being Mayor."
2. City of Boston, *The Inaugural Addresses*, 236.
3. Ibid.
4. Gately, *Drink*.
5. Lane, *Policing the City*, 44.
6. Ferdinand, *Boston's Lower Criminal Courts*, 88.
7. *American Jurist and Law Magazine*, "Codification."
8. Augustus, *A Report*; Panzarella, "Theory and Practice."
9. Ferdinand, *Boston's Lower Criminal Courts*; Panzarella, "Theory and Practice."
10. Ferdinand, *Boston's Lower Criminal Courts* & "The Criminal Patterns."
11. Friedman, *Crime and Punishment*, 203.
12. Ibid., 204.
13. Lane, *Policing the City*, 57–58; see also Lane, "Urban Police."
14. Emsley and Shpayer-Makov, *Police Detectives*; Morton, *The First Detective.*
15. Silverman, *Edgar A. Poe.*
16. Beattie, *The First English Detectives*; Fairlie, "Police Administration."
17. Beattie, *The First English Detectives*; Emsley & Shpayer-Makov, *Police Detectives.*
18. Lane, *Policing the City*, 60.
19. Pearl, "Into the Shadows."
20. Ibid.
21. Lane, *Policing the City*, 60.
22. Ibid., 61.
23. Savage, *Police Records*, 90–91.
24. Friedman, *Crime and Punishment*, 70.
25. *Semi-Weekly Atlas*, September 17, 1851.
26. Lane, *Policing the City*, 66.
27. Ibid., 74.
28. O'Connor, *The Boston Irish*, 64.
29. Handlin, *Boston's Immigrants.*
30. *Semi-Weekly Atlas*, December 11, 1852.
31. Lane, "Urban Police," 9.
32. Savage, *Police Records*, 2–93.
33. Ibid., 93.
34. Lane, *Policing the City*, 96; see also McCaffrey, "The Boston Police Department."
35. Fairlie, "Police Administration"; McCaffrey, "The Boston Police Department"; Wells, *Boston Police Department.*
36. Savage, *Police Records*, 94.
37. Fairlie, "Police Administration."

38. Savage, *Police Records*, 97.
39. Lane, *Policing the City*; Savage, *Police Records*.
40. Savage, *Police Records*; Wells, *Boston Police Department*.
41. Monkkonen, "History of Urban Police," 551.
42. Savage, *Police Records*, 99.
43. Monkkonen, *Police in Urban America*.
44. Ibid., 45.
45. Ibid.
46. Lane, *Policing the City*, 105.
47. O'Connor, *Civil War Boston*; Kirkland, "Boston During the Civil War."
48. Hanna, "The Boston Draft Riot"; Walker, *A Critical History*.
49. Lane, *Policing the City*; Wells, *Boston Police Department*.
50. McCaffrey, "The Boston Police Department," 672.
51. Lane, *Policing the City*, 197.
52. Hill, *Argument Made Before*, 11; see also Ellis, *The Argument*; Phillips, *Wendell Phillips*.
53. Lane, *Policing the City*.
54. Abbott, "The Civil War"; Byrnes, *Professional Criminals*.
55. *Boston Herald*, February 15, 1870.
56. Walker, *A Critical History*, 37.
57. Walker, *A Critical History*, 35; Savage, *Police Records*.
58. Hoogenboom, *Outlawing the Spoils*.
59. Lane, *Policing the City*, 197.
60. McCaffrey, "The Boston Police Department," 672.
61. Lane, *Policing the City*, 198.

Chapter 3. Political Control of the Boston Police Department

1. Lane, *Policing the City*, 200.
2. Ibid., 199.
3. City of Boston, First Annual Report, 3.
4. Ibid., 4.
5. Boston Police Department, *1880 Annual Police Report*.
6. Lane, *Policing the City*; Monkkonen, "History of Urban Police."
7. Boston Police Department, *1880 Annual Police Report*, 13–14.
8. Lane, *Policing the City*, 210.
9. Ibid., 212.
10. Gusfield, *Symbolic Crusade*, 7.
11. Ibid.
12. Galvin, "The Dark Ages," 99.
13. *Boston Globe*, February 27, 1885.

14. *Boston Evening Transcript*, February 28, 1885.
15. Galvin, "The Dark Ages."
16. Fogelson, *Big-City Police*, 14; Fairlie, "Police Administration," 8.
17. Fogelson, *Big-City Police*, 14.
18. Galvin, "The Dark Ages."
19. Fogelson, *Big-City Police*, 21–22.
20. Lane, *Policing the City*, 224.
21. McCaffrey, "The Boston Police Department," 672.
22. Lane, *Policing the City*, 224.
23. Ibid.
24. Friedman, *Crime and Punishment*, 151–52.
25. Dilworth, *The Blue*, 35.
26. Ibid., 35–36.
27. Von Hoffman, "An Officer," 310.
28. Ibid., 311.
29. Ibid., 312.
30. Ibid.
31. Ibid., 317.
32. Ibid., 321.
33. Ibid., 322.
34. Ibid.
35. Ibid., 322.
36. Jeffers, *Commissioner Roosevelt*; Zacks, *Island of Vice*.
37. McCaffrey, "The Boston Police Department," 672.
38. Harrison, *Police Administration*, 22.
39. Lyons, "The Boston Police Strike," 151.
40. Koss, "The Boston Police Strike," 11.
41. Lyons, "The Boston Police Strike," 151–52.
42. Fogelson, *Big-City Police*, 14.
43. Koss, "The Boston Police Strike," 12.
44. Reppetto, *American Police*, 98.
45. Koss, "The Boston Police Strike," 12.
46. Ibid., 13.
47. Ibid.
48. Commonwealth of Massachusetts, *First Annual Report*, 7.
49. Commonwealth of Massachusetts, *Sixth Annual Report*, 5–6.
50. White, "Violence," 63.
51. Ibid.
52. King, "Police Strikes," 298.
53. Reppetto, *American Police*, 99.
54. Commonwealth of Massachusetts, *Third Annual Report*, 5–6.
55. Hopkins, *Our Lawless Police*, 60.
56. King, "Police Strikes," 302.
57. McCaffrey, "The Boston Police Department," 677–78.
58. White, "A Triumph of Bureaucracy," 115.

59. McCaffrey, "The Boston Police Department," 678.
60. Lyons, "The Boston Police Strike," 151.
61. Koss, "The Boston Police Strike," 26.
62. Slater, "Public Workers," 15–16.
63. Fosdick, *American Police Systems*, 230.
64. Reppetto, *American Police*, 101.
65. National Commission on Law Observance, *Report on Lawlessness*, 104–7.
66. Harrison, *Police Administration*, 23.
67. Ibid.
68. Ibid.
69. Reppetto, *American Police*, 106.
70. Koss, "The Boston Police Strike," 21.
71. Ibid.
72. Ibid., 21.

Chapter 4. The Great War's Impact on Boston

1. *Boston Globe*, July 26, 1919.
2. Puleo, *Dark Tide*, 95.
3. Ibid.
4. *Boston Globe*, January 16, 1919; Puleo, *Dark Tide*, 95.
5. Puleo, *Dark Tide*, 10.
6. Ibid., 11.
7. *Boston Globe*, January 16, 1919.
8. Ibid.
9. Puleo, *Dark Tide*, 95.
10. *Boston Globe*, January 16, 1919.
11. Puleo, *Dark Tide*, 95.
12. Ibid., 96.
13. *Boston Globe*, January 15, 1919.
14. *Boston Globe*, January 15, 1919; Puleo, *Dark Tide*.
15. Puleo, *Dark Tide*, 97.
16. Kennedy, *Over Here*, 250.
17. Ibid., 236.
18. Harding, "Inaugural Address."
19. Murray, *Red Scare*, 9.
20. Ibid., 5.
21. Bourne, *The War*, 4.
22. Bourne, *The War*, 4; Wilson, War Message, 7.
23. Wilson, War Message, 8.
24. Kennedy, *Over Here*, 11.
25. Walworth, *Woodrow Wilson*, 97.
26. Sykley, "Boston at War," 4.

27. Puleo, *Dark Tide*, 56.
28. *Boston Evening Globe*, April 2, 1917.
29. Sykley, "Boston at War," 4.
30. Ibid.
31. Ibid.
32. Ibid., 10.
33. National Lancers, "Our History."
34. Sykley, "Boston at War," 10.
35. A Company, *Dates, Data and Ditties*, 7.
36. Ibid.
37. D Company, *D of the Tenth*, 16.
38. Ibid.
39. A Company, *Dates, Data and Ditties*, 7.
40. *Boston Globe*, November 11, 1918.
41. Ibid.
42. White, "Violence During the 1919 Boston Police Strike," 61.
43. Douglas, *Real Wages*.
44. Murray, *Red Scare*, 7.
45. Ibid.
46. Ibid., 5.
47. Ibid., 7.
48. Juris and Feuille, *Police Unionism*.
49. Murray, *Red Scare*, 8.
50. Lyons, "The Boston Police Strike," 149–50.
51. Ibid.
52. Farmer, "The Boston Police Strike," 37.
53. Koss, "The Boston Police Strike," 3–4.
54. Koss, "The Boston Police Strike," 3–4; King, "Police Strikes," 310.
55. Koss, "The Boston Police Strike," 3–4.
56. Fitzgerald, "The Boston Police Strike."
57. Lyons, "The Boston Police Strike," 150.
58. Farmer, "The Boston Police Strike," 36.
59. King, "Police Strikes."
60. Lurie, "Government Regulation," 121.
61. Farmer, "The Boston Police Strike," 37.
62. Lyons, "The Boston Police Strike," 148.
63. Centers for Disease Control, "1918 Pandemic (H1N1 Virus)."
64. Ireland, *Medical Department*, 83.
65. Barry, *The Great Influenza*, 4.
66. Ibid.
67. Ibid., 183.
68. Ibid.
69. Ibid., 184.
70. Sykley, "Boston at War," 13.
71. Barry, *The Great Influenza*, 186.

72. Ibid., 186–87.
73. Ibid., 187.
74. American Experience, "A Letter from Camp Devens."
75. Barry, *The Great Influenza*, 221.
76. Tomes, "Destroyer and Teacher," 52.
77. Barry, *The Great Influenza*, 221.
78. History News Network, "Racial Violence and a Pandemic."
79. Migration Policy Institute, "U.S. Immigration Trends."
80. US World War One Centennial Commission, "Immigrants."
81. Ibid.
82. Kennedy, *Over Here*.
83. Pub. L. 65–150, May 16, 1918.
84. Murray, *Red Scare*.
85. Puleo, *Dark Tide*, 35.
86. Wilkerson, *The Warmth*.
87. Ibid., 8.
88. Tager, *Boston Riots*, 144.
89. Ibid., 145.
90. Ibid., 145.
91. Puleo, *Dark Tide*, 31.
92. Ibid.
93. Cromwell, *The Other Brahmins*, 72.
94. Wilkerson, *The Warmth of Other Suns*.
95. National Park Service, "From the Great Migration."
96. Amory, *The Proper Bostonians*, 12.
97. Jaher, *The Urban Establishment*.
98. Story, "Harvard and the Boston Brahmins."
99. Connolly, *The Triumph of Ethnic Progressivism*.
100. Rowland, "Irish-American Catholics."
101. Fried, "No Irish Need Deny"; Jensen, "No Irish Need Apply."
102. Handlin, *Boston's Immigrants*, 216.
103. 1920 US Census.
104. Connolly, *The Triumph of Ethnic Progressivism*; Ryan, *Beyond*.
105. Connolly, *The Triumph of Ethnic Progressivism*, 38.
106. Chernev, *Twilight of Empire*.
107. Murray, *Red Scare*.
108. Ellis, "J. Edgar Hoover," 40–41.
109. Watson, *Sacco & Vanzetti*.
110. Gage, *The Day Wall Street Exploded*, 27.
111. Ackerman, *Young J. Edgar*, 11.
112. Ibid.
113. Ibid., 12.
114. *Chicago Daily Tribune*, June 3, 1919.
115. Ibid.
116. Ackerman, *Young J. Edgar*, 13.

117. *Chicago Daily Tribune*, June 3, 1919.
118. US House of Representatives, *Attorney General A. Mitchell Palmer*, 159.
119. Watson, *Sacco & Vanzetti*, 10.
120. *Cordova Daily Times*, June 3, 1919.
121. Murray, "Outer World and Inner Light," 275.
122. Ibid., 276.
123. Federal Bureau of Investigation, "History."
124. Federal Bureau of Investigation, "History"; Ellis, "J. Edgar Hoover," 41.
125. Ackerman, *Young J. Edgar*, 385.
126. Murray, *Red Scare*, 16; see also *Boston Herald*, July 30, 1919; *New York Times*, July 28, 1919; Lynch, "'Red Riots.'"
127. Puleo, *Dark Tide*, 40.
128. Ibid., 41–42.
129. Ibid., 19.
130. Ibid., 78.
131. US House of Representatives, *Sedition*, 40.
132. White, *A Triumph*, 157.
133. Puleo, *Dark Tide*.
134. *Boston Globe*, June 3, 1919.
135. Ibid.
136. Ibid.
137. Ibid.
138. Walker, *Popular Justice*, 149.
139. Walker, *A Critical History*, 121.
140. Johnson, *Along This Way*, 168.
141. Ellis, "J. Edgar Hoover," 42.
142. Ibid.
143. Walker, *A Critical History*, 109.
144. Walker, *Popular Justice*, 148.
145. Tager, *Boston Riots*, 148.
146. Ibid.
147. Ibid.
148. Ibid.
149. Ibid., 152.
150. King, "Police Strikes," 312.
151. Officer Down Memorial Page, "Captain Hugh J. Lee."
152. King, "Police Strikes," 312.
153. Tager, *Boston Riots*, 152.
154. Boston Police Commissioner, *Twelfth Annual Report*, 18.
155. Ibid.

Chapter 5. Boston's Leadership

1. Lyons, "The Boston Police Strike," 152; see also Tager, *Boston Riots*, 157.
2. Sobel, *Coolidge*, 130.
3. Russell, "Coolidge and the Boston Police Strike," 406.
4. Russell, "Coolidge," 406; White, *A Puritan*, 149.
5. Boston Fire Historical Society, "Great Boston Fire."
6. The Arnold Arboretum, "Our History."
7. Goodman, *The Passing*.
8. Lyons, "The Boston Police Strike."
9. Harvard College, "Andrew James Peters," 361.
10. Ibid.
11. Ibid.
12. Ibid., 362.
13. Ibid.
14. Goodman, *The Passing*, 67.
15. Harvard College, "Andrew James Peters," 361–62.
16. Goodman, *The Passing*.
17. Ibid., 68.
18. Harvard College, "Andrew James Peters," 362.
19. Goodman, *The Passing*.
20. Beatty, *The Rascal King*, 9.
21. Goodman, *The Passing*, 68.
22. Hart, *Commonwealth History*, 7.
23. Peters, *Inaugural Address*, 4.
24. Harvard College, "Andrew James Peters," 362.
25. Fuess, *Calvin Coolidge*, 205.
26. Curley, *I'd Do It Again*, 138.
27. Goodman, *The Passing*, 70.
28. Russell, "Coolidge," 406.
29. Sobel, *Coolidge*, 130.
30. Tager, *Boston Riots*, 158.
31. Sykley, *Boston at War*.
32. *Boston Globe*, January 1, 1919.
33. *Munsey's Magazine*, "In the Public Eye," 487.
34. Lyons, "The Boston Police Strike," 152.
35. White, *A Puritan*, 149.
36. *Munsey's Magazine*, "In the Public Eye," 487.
37. Ibid.
38. Ibid.
39. Ibid.
40. Ibid.
41. Ibid.
42. Coolidge, "Edwin Upton Curtis," 536.

43. *Chicago Tribune*, December 12, 1894.
44. *Munsey's Magazine*, "In the Public Eye," 487.
45. Ainley, *Boston Mahatma*, 1.
46. Reppetto, *American Police*, 110.
47. Shlaes, *Coolidge*, 65.
48. Coolidge, "Edwin Upton Curtis," 536.
49. *New England Magazine*, "Edwin Upton Curtis," 113.
50. *Boston Globe*, December 14, 1918.
51. Russell, "Coolidge and the Boston Police Strike," 405.
52. *Boston Globe*, December 25, 1918.
53. *Boston Globe*, December 31, 1918.
54. Fuess, *Calvin Coolidge*, 204.
55. White, "Violence," 64.
56. Ibid.
57. *Boston Globe*, December 26, 1918.
58. *Boston Globe*, December 31, 1918.
59. Ibid.
60. Ibid.
61. Fuess, *Calvin Coolidge*, 204; *Boston Globe*, December 31, 1918.
62. *Boston Globe*, December 31, 1918.
63. Ibid.
64. White, *A Puritan*, 151.
65. Ibid., 152.
66. Lyons, "The Boston Police Strike," 152.
67. Coolidge, "Edwin Upton Curtis," 536.

Chapter 6. Governor Calvin Coolidge

1. Russell, "The Strike."
2. Coolidge, *The Autobiography*, 3.
3. Shlaes, *Coolidge*, 19.
4. Ibid.
5. Coolidge, *The Autobiography*, 7.
6. Shlaes, *Coolidge*, 20.
7. Ibid.
8. Coolidge, *The Autobiography*, 7.
9. Ibid., 9.
10. Ibid., 24.
11. Ibid.
12. Shlaes, *Coolidge*, 14.
13. Coolidge, *The Autobiography*, 13.
14. Ibid., 47.
15. Sobel, *Coolidge*.

16. DeGregorio, *The Complete Book*, 447.
17. Ibid.
18. Shlaes, *Coolidge*, 20.
19. Coolidge, *The Autobiography*, 33.
20. Whiting, *President Coolidge*, 10.
21. Sobel, *Coolidge*, 26.
22. Ibid.
23. Ibid., 27.
24. Ibid.
25. Shlaes, *Coolidge*, 26.
26. Sobel, *Coolidge*, 25; Shlaes, *Coolidge*, 26.
27. White, *A Puritan*, 29.
28. Coolidge, *The Autobiography*, 47–48.
29. Sobel, *Coolidge*.
30. Shlaes, *Coolidge*, 31.
31. Fuess, *Amherst*, 55.
32. Coolidge, *The Autobiography*, 62.
33. DeGregorio, *The Complete Book*, 449.
34. Sobel, *Coolidge*, 33.
35. Shlaes, *Coolidge*, 43.
36. Ibid., 48.
37. Sobel, *Coolidge*.
38. Ibid., 40.
39. Coolidge, *The Autobiography*, 71.
40. DeGregorio, *The Complete Book*, 449.
41. Sobel, *Coolidge*, 41.
42. Ibid.
43. Ibid., 43.
44. Ibid., 46.
45. Coolidge, *The Autobiography*, 85.
46. Ibid.
47. Sobel, *Coolidge*.
48. Ibid.
49. Ibid., 53.
50. Ibid., 54.
51. McCoy, *Calvin Coolidge*, 29.
52. Ibid.
53. Shlaes, *Coolidge*, 93.
54. Ibid.
55. Coolidge, *Grace Coolidge*.
56. Sobel, *Coolidge*, 56.
57. Ibid.
58. Ibid., 58.
59. Shlaes, *Coolidge*, 105.
60. Ibid., 106.

304 / Notes

61. Sobel, *Coolidge*, 72.
62. Ibid., 73.
63. Coolidge, *The Autobiography*, 100–1.
64. Shlaes, *Coolidge*, 109.
65. DeGregorio, *The Complete Book*, 451.
66. Current Opinion, "Coolidge," 38.
67. Shlaes, *Coolidge*, 111.
68. Ibid.
69. Coolidge, *The Autobiography*, 103.
70. Shlaes, *Coolidge*, 114.
71. Ibid.
72. Foner, *History of the Labor Movement*, 307.
73. Ibid., 115.
74. Ibid.
75. Ibid.
76. Ibid.
77. Fuess, *Calvin Coolidge*, 111.
78. Coolidge, *The Autobiography*, 108.
79. Shlaes, *Coolidge*, 120.
80. Coolidge, *The Autobiography*, 107.
81. Shlaes, *Coolidge*, 122.
82. Sobel, *Coolidge*.
83. Coolidge, *The Autobiography*, 111.
84. Shlaes, *Coolidge*, 135.
85. Current Opinion, "Coolidge."
86. Shlaes, *Coolidge*, 137.
87. Sobel, *Coolidge*, 101.
88. Ibid.
89. Ibid.
90. Coolidge, *The Autobiography*, 117.
91. Sobel, *Coolidge*, 107.
92. Ibid., 104.
93. Coolidge, *The Autobiography*, 121.
94. McCoy, *Calvin Coolidge*, 76.
95. Coolidge, *The Autobiography*, 124-25.
96. Ibid.
97. Shlaes, *Coolidge*, 120.
98. Russell, "Coolidge," 408.
99. DeGregorio, *The Complete Book*.
100. Current Opinion, "Coolidge," 38.
101. Lyons, "The Boston Police Strike," 154.
102. Sobel, *Coolidge*, 242.
103. Lyons, "The Boston Police Strike," 154.

Chapter 7. The Call for Unionization

1. Koss, "The Boston Police Strike."
2. Epstein and Prak, *Guilds*; Gies and Gies, *Cathedral*; Ogilvie, *Institutions*.
3. Green, *Death in the Haymarket*; Gage, *The Day Wall Street Exploded*.
4. Mandel, *Samuel Gompers*.
5. Gompers, *Seventy Years of Life*, 6.
6. Ibid., 44.
7. Ibid., 44–45.
8. Ibid., 45.
9. Ibid., 68.
10. Mandel, *Samuel Gompers*.
11. Green, *Death in the Haymarket*.
12. Ibid.
13. *New York Times*, May 5, 1886.
14. Green, *Death in the Haymarket*, 11.
15. Gage, *The Day Wall Street Exploded*, 56; Kennedy, *Over Here*, 71.
16. Lorwin, *The American Federation of Labor*.
17. Ibid.
18. Gage, *The Day Wall Street Exploded*, 78.
19. Ibid.
20. Lorwin, *The American Federation of Labor*.
21. Kennedy, *Over Here*, 28.
22. Smith, "Organized Labor," 265.
23. Lorwin, *The American Federation of Labor*, 170.
24. Kennedy, *Over Here*, 258.
25. Lyons, "The Boston Police Strike," 150; Murray, *Red Scare*, 8.
26. Sobel, *Coolidge*, 124.
27. Lyons, "The Boston Police Strike," 150–51.
28. Ibid.
29. *Boston Globe*, April 12, 1919.
30. *Boston Globe*, April 15, 1919.
31. Ibid.
32. King, "Police Strikes," 313–14.
33. Puleo, *Dark Tide*, 143.
34. *Boston Globe*, April 16, 1919.
35. Gutman, *Work, Culture*.
36. King, "Police Strikes," 313–14.
37. Shlaes, *Coolidge*, 154–55.
38. *Boston Globe*, April 21, 1919.
39. Ibid.
40. *Boston Globe*, April 18, 1919; Sobel, *Coolidge*, 126.
41. *Boston Globe*, April 22, 1919.
42. Ibid.

43. King, "Police Strikes of 1918 and 1919," 314.
44. *Boston Globe*, July 15, 1919.
45. *Boston Globe*, July 16, 1919.
46. *Boston Globe*, July 17, 1919.
47. *Boston Globe*, July 18, 1919.
48. *Boston Globe*, July 19, 1919.
49. Sobel, *Coolidge*, 126.
50. *Boston Globe*, July 21, 1919.
51. King, "Police Strikes," 314.
52. Sobel, *Coolidge*, 123.
53. Ziskind, *One Thousand Strikes*.
54. *Evening World (New York)*, April 5, 1889.
55. *Camden Daily Telegram*, April 9, 1889.
56. Ibid.
57. King, "Police Strikes," 315–16.
58. *Camden Daily Telegram*, April 9, 1889.
59. Herron, "The Police Strike"; King, *Police Strikes*; Ziskind, *One Thousand Strikes*.
60. *Atlanta Constitution*, September 15, 1918.
61. Herron, "The Police Strike," 190.
62. Ibid., 185.
63. *Atlanta Constitution*, September 15, 1918.
64. Ibid.
65. *Cincinnati Enquirer*, September 17, 1918.
66. *Lexington Herald-Leader*, September 17, 1918.
67. *Cincinnati Enquirer*, September 17, 1918.
68. Ibid.
69. Slater, "Public Workers," 10.
70. American Federal of Labor, *Report of Proceedings* 1917; Slater, "Public Workers."
71. American Federation of Labor, *Report of Proceedings 1919*, 216.
72. Slater, "Public Workers," 10.
73. Ibid.
74. *Boston Herald*, August 2, 1919; Slater, "Public Workers," 12.
75. Boston Police Commissioner, *Fourteenth Annual Report*, 8.
76. Ibid., 9.
77. Lyons, "The Boston Police Strike," 151.
78. Koss, "The Boston Police Strike," 35.
79. Ibid.
80. Ibid., 36.
81. Ibid., 33.
82. Ibid., 33.
83. Ibid., 331.
84. Ibid., 4.
85. Ibid., 7.

86. Ibid., 38–39.
87. Ibid., 39.
88. Ibid.
89. Boston Police Commissioner, *Fourteenth Annual Report*, 9–10.
90. Ibid.
91. Lyons, "The Boston Police Strike," 151.
92. Slater, "Public Workers," 11.
93. Lyons, "The Boston Police Strike," 151.

Chapter 8. The Road to Hell . . .

1. *Chicago Daily Tribune*, August 1, 1919.
2. Lyons, "The Boston Police Strike," 155.
3. *Los Angeles Daily Times*, August 6, 1919.
4. Ibid.
5. *Albuquerque Morning Journal*, August 11, 1919; *Times* (London), August 11, 1919.
6. Bean, "Police Unrest"; Reynolds and Judge, *The Night*; Taaffe and Mulhearn, *Liverpool*.
7. *New-York Tribune*, August 7, 1919.
8. Boston Police Commissioner, *Fourteenth Annual Report*, 5.
9. Ibid.
10. Ibid.
11. *Boston Globe*, August 12, 1919.
12. *Boston Globe*, August 16, 1919.
13. Ibid.
14. Boston Police Commissioner, *Fourteenth Annual Report*, 11.
15. *Boston Daily Globe*, August 16, 1919; *Boston Herald*, August 16, 1919.
16. *Boston Daily Globe*, August 16, 1919.
17. Ibid.
18. *New-York Tribune*, August 16, 1919.
19. *Boston Daily Globe*, August 16, 1919.
20. *Boston Evening Globe*, August 16, 1919; King, *Police Strikes*, 339.
21. King, *Police Strikes*, 339.
22. *Boston Evening Globe*, August 16, 1919.
23. *Boston Daily Globe*, August 18, 1919.
24. *Boston Daily Globe*, August 19, 1919; *Boston Herald* August 19, 1919.
25. Coolidge, *The Autobiography*, 127.
26. *Boston Daily Globe*, August 20, 1919.
27. King, *Police Strikes*, 344.
28. *Boston Daily Globe*, August 20, 1919; *Boston Herald* August 20, 1919.
29. *Boston Daily Globe*, August 20, 1919.
30. *Boston Daily Globe*, August 21, 1919; *Boston Herald* August 21, 1919.

31. *Boston Daily Globe,* August 21, 1919.
32. Ibid.
33. Ibid.
34. *Boston Daily Globe,* August 21, 1919; *Boston Herald* August 21, 1919.
35. *Boston Daily Globe,* August 21, 1919.
36. *Boston Herald,* August 21, 1919.
37. *Boston Daily Globe,* August 21, 1919.
38. Russell, *A City in Terror.*
39. *Boston Daily Globe,* August 23, 1919.
40. *Boston Sunday Globe,* August 24, 1919.
41. Ibid.
42. *Boston Daily Globe,* August 25, 1919.
43. Ibid.
44. Ibid.
45. *Passaic Daily Herald,* August 25, 1919.
46. *San Francisco Chronicle,* August 5, 1919.
47. Boston Police Commissioner, *Fourteenth Annual Report,* 11.
48. *Boston Globe,* August 26, 1919.
49. Ibid.
50. *Boston Globe,* August 27, 1919
51. *Boston Globe,* August 26, 1919.
52. *Boston Globe,* August 27, 1919.
53. *Boston Globe,* August 26, 1919.
54. Ibid.
55. Ibid.
56. Ibid.
57. Ibid.
58. Citizens' Committee, *Report,* 1.
59. Ibid.
60. *Boston Globe,* August 28, 1919; *Boston Herald* August 28, 1919.
61. Citizens' Committee, *Report,* Appendix 3.
62. Citizens' Committee, *Report,* Appendix 4; *Boston Globe,* September 1, 1919.
63. *Boston Globe,* September 3, 1919.
64. Ibid.
65. Boston Police Commissioner, *Fourteenth Annual Report,* 11.
66. *Boston Globe,* September 2, 1919.
67. *Boston Herald,* August 28, 1919.
68. *Boston Globe,* August 28, 1919.
69. *Boston Globe,* September 4, 1919.
70. Boston Police Commissioner, *Fourteenth Annual Report,* 12.
71. Citizens' Committee, *Report,* Appendix 7.
72. Ibid.
73. Lyons, "The Boston Police Strike."
74. Boston Police Commissioner, *Fourteenth Annual Report,* 12.

75. Ibid.
76. *Boston Globe*, September 6, 1919.
77. *Boston Globe*, September 5, 1919.
78. *Boston Sunday Globe*, September 7, 1919.
79. Ibid.
80. *Boston Globe*, September 8, 1919.
81. *Boston Globe*, September 6, 1919.
82. Citizens' Committee, *Report*, Appendix 9.
83. *Boston Globe*, September 8, 1919.
84. Citizens' Committee, *Report*, Appendix 10.
85. *Boston Evening Globe*, September 8, 1919.
86. Ibid.
87. Ibid.
88. Ibid.
89. Citizens' Committee, *Report*, Appendix 11.
90. Coolidge, *The Autobiography*, 127–28.
91. Ibid.

Chapter 9. In the Absence of Police

1. *Boston Evening Globe*, September 9, 1919.
2. *Boston Post*, September 9, 1919; *Boston Evening Globe*, September 9, 1919.
3. *Boston Evening Globe*, September 9, 1919.
4. Ibid.
5. Ibid.
6. *Boston Evening Globe*, September 8, 1919.
7. Boston Police Commissioner, *Police Records*.
8. *Boston Evening Globe*, September 9, 1919; Russell, *A City in Terror*, 142.
9. Ibid.
10. Pendergrass, "The Boys."
11. Lyons, "The Boston Police Strike," 160.
12. *Boston Evening Globe*, September 9, 1919.
13. *Boston Evening Globe*, September 9, 1919; Lyons, "The Boston Police Strike," 160.
14. Russell, *A City in Terror*, 141.
15. Ibid., 142.
16. *Boston Evening Globe*, September 9, 1919.
17. Ibid.
18. Citizens' Committee, *Report*, Appendix 12.
19. Ibid.
20. Ibid.
21. Ibid.
22. *Boston Evening Globe*, September 9, 1919; Russell, *A City in Terror*, 120.

23. *Boston Globe*, September 10, 1919.
24. Boston Citizens' Committee, *Report*, 19–20.
25. Russell, *A City in Terror*, 128.
26. *Boston Globe*, September 10, 1919.
27. White, *A Puritan in Babylon*, 158.
28. Ibid.
29. Fuess, *Calvin Coolidge*, 218.
30. Boston, *Documents*, vol. 1, 17.
31. Boston Citizens' Committee, *Report*, 19–20.
32. Coolidge, *The Autobiography*, 130.
33. Asinof, *1919*, 158.
34. *Boston Herald*, September 9, 1919; Koss, "The Boston Police Strike," 169.
35. Lyons, "Boston Police Strike," 161; Koss, "The Boston Police Strike," 189.
36. Coolidge, *The Autobiography*, 128.
37. Koss, "The Boston Police Strike," 189.
38. Lyons, "The Boston Police Strike," 162.
39. UMASS Boston, *1919 Boston Police Strike Project*.
40. *Boston Globe*, September 10, 1919; Russell, *A City in Terror*, 121.
41. *Boston Globe*, September 10, 1919.
42. *Boston Globe*, September 10, 1919; Koss, "The Boston Police Strike," 172.
43. UMASS Boston, *1919 Boston Police Strike Project*.
44. *Boston Globe*, September 10, 1919.
45. Ibid.
46. Ibid.
47. Koss, "The Boston Police Strike," 170; Lyons, "The Boston Police Strike," 147; *Boston Globe*, September 10, 1919.
48. *Boston Globe*, September 10, 1919.
49. Ibid.
50. Rezneck, "An Innocent Abroad," 441.
51. Ibid.
52. *Boston Globe*, September 10, 1919.
53. Ibid.
54. *Boston Herald*, September 19, 1919; see also Koss, "The Boston Police Strike," 171.
55. *Boston Globe*, September 10, 1919; UMASS Boston, *1919 Boston Police Strike Project*.
56. *Boston Herald*, September 10, 1919.
57. *Boston Globe*, September 10, 1919; Russell, *A City in Terror*, 126.
58. *Boston Globe*, September 10, 1919.
59. *Boston Herald*, September 19, 1919.
60. Russell, *A City in Terror*, 123.
61. *Boston Globe*, September 10, 1919; Koss, "The Boston Police Strike," 170.
62. *Boston Globe*, September 10, 1919.
63. Ibid.

64. Bartlett, "Anarchy," 460; Koss, "The Boston Police Strike," 173.
65. Bartlett, "Anarchy," 460.
66. *Boston Globe*, September 10, 1919; Russell, *A City in Terror*, 123.
67. Bartlett, "Anarchy," 460.
68. Bartlett, "Anarchy," 460; Koss, "The Boston Police Strike," 173.
69. Bartlett, "Anarchy," 460; Russell, *A City in Terror*, 125.
70. Russell, *A City in Terror*, 127.
71. *Boston Globe*, September 10, 1919.
72. Ibid.
73. Coolidge, *The Autobiography*, 129.
74. Boston Police Commissioner, *Fourteenth Annual Report*, 16.
75. Ibid.
76. Ibid.
77. Ibid., 5.
78. Russell, *A City in Terror*, 113.
79. *Boston Herald*, September 10, 1919.
80. *Boston Globe*, September 10, 1919; see also Russell, *A City in Terror*, 145.
81. *Boston Herald*, September 10, 1919.
82. *Boston Globe*, September 10, 1919.
83. *Boston Herald*, September 10, 1919.
84. *Boston Globe*, September 10, 1919.
85. Ibid.
86. Ibid.
87. Ibid.
88. *Boston Herald*, September 10, 1919.
89. *Boston Globe*, September 10, 1919.
90. Ibid.
91. Ibid.
92. Ibid.
93. Koss, "The Boston Police Strike," 317; *Boston Globe*, September 10, 1919.
94. *Boston Herald*, September 10, 1919.
95. Coolidge, *The Autobiography*, 129–30.
96. Ibid., 130.
97. Ibid., 131.
98. *Boston Globe*, September 10, 1919.
99. Tager, *Boston Riots*, 161–62.
100. Ibid.
101. Wood, *Reds*, 10–11; see also Koss, "The Boston Police Strike," 176.
102. Wood, *Reds*, 10–11.
103. Ibid.
104. Ibid.
105. Ibid.
106. Ibid.
107. Tager, *Boston Riots*, 161–62.

108. *Boston Globe*, September 10, 1919.
109. Ibid.
110. *Boston Globe*, September 10, 1919; Russell, *A City in Terror*, 133.
111. Shlaes, Coolidge, 157.
112. *Boston Globe*, September 10, 1919.
113. Ibid.
114. Koss, "The Boston Police Strike," 191; *Boston Globe*, September 10, 1919.
115. *Boston Globe*, September 10, 1919.
116. Ibid.
117. Ibid.
118. Ibid.
119. Ibid.
120. Pattullo, "The National Crisis."
121. *Boston Globe*, September 10, 1919.
122. Ibid.
123. *Boston Herald*, September 10, 1919.
124. *Boston Globe*, September 10, 1919.
125. Ibid.
126. Ibid.
127. *Boston Evening Transcript*, September 10, 1919.
128. Ibid.
129. Ibid.
130. Ibid.
131. Ibid.
132. *Boston Globe*, September 10, 1919.
133. Ibid.
134. Ibid.
135. Ibid.
136. Ibid.
137. Ibid.
138. Tager, *Boston Riots*, 162.
139. *Boston Globe*, September 10, 1919.
140. Ibid.
141. Ibid.
142. *Boston Evening Globe*, September 12, 1919.
143. Ibid.
144. *Boston Globe*, September 10, 1919.
145. Ibid.
146. Ibid.
147. Ibid.
148. Ibid.
149. Ibid.
150. Ibid.

151. Koss, "The Boston Police Strike," 177; *Boston Herald*, September 10, 1919.
152. *Boston Globe*, September 10, 1919.
153. Ibid.

Chapter 10. The Boston Riots

1. Rezneck, "An Innocent Abroad," 442.
2. Ibid.
3. Ibid.
4. *Boston Herald*, September 10, 1919; Russell, *A City in Terror*, 144.
5. *Wall Street Journal*, September 10, 1919.
6. *Boston Globe*, September 10, 1919.
7. Fitzgerald, "Boston Police Strike."
8. *Boston Globe*, September 10, 1919.
9. Citizens' Committee, *Report*, Appendix 18.
10. Ibid., Appendix 20.
11. Coolidge, *Autobiography*, 131.
12. *Boston Globe*, September 10, 1919; Koss," The Boston Police Strike," 179.
13. *Boston Globe*, September 11, 1919.
14. *Boston Globe*, September 11, 1919; Koss, "The Boston Police Strike," 195.
15. Coolidge, *Autobiography*, 131.
16. *Boston Herald*, September 10, 1919; Koss, "The Boston Police Strike," 193.
17. Citizens' Committee, *Report*, Appendix 26.
18. Ibid.
19. Ibid.
20. Ibid.
21. Shlaes, *Coolidge*, 158.
22. Ibid.
23. Citizens' Committee, *Report*, Appendix 21.
24. *Boston Globe*, September 10, 1919; Koss, "The Boston Police Strike," 195.
25. *Boston Herald*, September 10, 1919; *Boston Globe*, September 11, 1919.
26. Coolidge, *Autobiography*, 132.
27. Russell, *A City in Terror*, 150.
28. *Boston Globe*, September 11, 1919.
29. Shlaes, *Coolidge*, 160.
30. Ibid.
31. Ibid.
32. *Boston Herald*, September 10, 1919; Koss, "The Boston Police Strike," 194.
33. *Boston Globe*, September 10, 1919.
34. Ibid.

35. Ibid.
36. Ibid.
37. Ibid.
38. *Boston Globe*, September 11, 1919.
39. Ibid.
40. *Boston Globe*, September 10, 1919.
41. *Boston Globe*, September 10, 1919; *Boston Herald*, September 10, 1919.
42. *Boston Globe*, September 11, 1919.
43. Ibid.
44. Ibid.
45. Ibid.
46. *Boston Evening Globe*, September 10, 1919.
47. Ibid.
48. *Boston Globe*, September 10, 1919.
49. *Boston Globe*, September 11, 1919.
50. *Boston Evening Globe*, September 10, 1919; Russell, *A City in Terror*, 151.
51. Koss, "The Boston Police Strike," 198.
52. *Boston Herald*, September 11, 1919.
53. Russell, *A City in Terror*, 152–53.
54. *Boston Herald*, September 11, 1919.
55. Ibid.
56. Ibid.
57. Rezneck, "An Innocent Abroad," 442.
58. *Boston Globe*, September 11, 1919.
59. Ibid.
60. *Boston Evening Globe*, September 10, 1919.
61. *Boston Globe*, September 10, 1919.
62. *Boston Evening Globe*, September 10, 1919.
63. Ibid.
64. Ibid.
65. *Boston Globe*, September 11, 1919.
66. *Boston Evening Globe*, September 10, 1919.
67. *Boston Evening Transcript*, September 12, 1919.
68. *Boston Evening Globe*, September 10, 1919.
69. Ibid.
70. *Boston Globe*, September 11, 1919.
71. Koss, "The Boston Police Strike," 179.
72. *Boston Evening Globe*, September 10, 1919.
73. Koss, "The Boston Police Strike," 179.
74. *Boston Globe*, September 11, 1919.
75. Russell, *A City in Terror*, 156.
76. *Boston Globe*, September 11, 1919.
77. Ibid.
78. Ibid.
79. *Boston Globe*, September 11, 1919; *Boston Herald*, September 11, 1919.

80. *Boston Globe*, September 10, 1919.
81. *Boston Evening Globe*, September 10, 1919.
82. *Boston Globe*, September 11, 1919.
83. D Company, *D of the Tenth*, 28.
84. D Company, *D of the Tenth*, 28; Russell, *A City in Terror*, 153.
85. D Company, *D of the Tenth*, 28; Russell, *A City in Terror*, 160.
86. D Company, *D of the Tenth*, 28.
87. Ibid., 28–29.
88. Ibid., 29.
89. Ibid., 29.
90. *Boston Globe*, September 12, 1919.
91. D Company, *D of the Tenth*, 29.
92. Ibid., 29.
93. Ibid.
94. Ibid., 31.
95. Ibid.
96. Ibid.
97. A Company, *Dates*, 7.
98. Ibid.
99. Ibid.
100. Ibid.
101. *Boston Globe*, September 11, 1919.
102. A Company, *Dates*, 8.
103. Ibid.
104. A Company, *Dates*, 8; Russell, *A City in Terror*, 155.
105. A Company, *Dates*, 10.
106. Ibid., 8.
107. *Boston Globe*, September 11, 1919.
108. Ibid.
109. Ibid.
110. Ibid.
111. Ibid.
112. Ibid.
113. *Boston Globe*, September 11, 1919; Russell, *A City in Terror*, 158.
114. *Boston Globe*, September 11, 1919; Koss, "The Boston Police Strike," 200.
115. *Boston Herald*, September 11, 1919.
116. *Boston Herald*, September 11, 1919; Russell, *A City in Terror*, 161.
117. *Boston Globe*, September 11, 1919.
118. D Company, *D of the Tenth*, 31.
119. Ibid.
120. Ibid., 32.
121. Ibid.
122. *Boston Globe*, September 11, 1919.
123. Ibid.

124. Russell, *A City in Terror*, 161.
125. *Boston Globe*, September 11, 1919; *Boston Evening Globe*, September 12, 1919.
126. Ibid.
127. *Boston Globe*, September 11, 1919.
128. Russell, *A City in Terror*, 162–63.
129. *Boston Globe*, September 11, 1919.
130. Ibid.
131. *Boston Globe*, September 12, 1919.
132. Ibid.
133. Ibid.
134. *Boston Globe*, September 11, 1919.
135. Ibid.
136. Ibid.
137. Ibid.
138. Ibid.
139. *Boston Globe*, September 13, 1919.
140. Ibid.
141. *Boston Globe*, September 11, 1919.
142. *Boston Globe*, September 11, 1919; Russell, *A City in Terror*, 164.
143. *Boston Globe*, September 11, 1919.
144. Ibid.
145. Ibid.
146. A Company, *Dates*, 11.
147. New England Historical Society, "Before Dunkin'."

Chapter 11. Quelling the Violence

1. *Boston Globe*, September 12, 1919.
2. Ibid.
3. UMASS Boston, *1919 Boston Police Strike Project*.
4. Ibid.
5. *Boston Evening Globe*, September 11, 1919.
6. UMASS Boston, *1919 Boston Police Strike Project*.
7. Ibid.
8. Ibid.
9. *Boston Evening Globe*, September 11, 1919.
10. Ibid.
11. Ibid.
12. Russell, *A City in Terror*, 165.
13. *Boston Globe*, September 12, 1919.
14. *Boston Evening Globe*, September 11, 1919.
15. Ibid.

16. *Boston Globe*, September 12, 1919.
17. *Boston Evening Globe*, September 11, 1919.
18. Ibid.
19. *Boston Globe*, September 12, 1919.
20. UMASS Boston, *1919 Boston Police Strike Project*.
21. Ibid.
22. Russell, *A City in Terror*, 166.
23. *Boston Evening Globe*, September 11, 1919.
24. Ibid.
25. *Boston Globe*, September 12, 1919.
26. Ibid.
27. Ibid.
28. *Boston Evening Globe*, September 11, 1919; Russell, *A City in Terror*, 167.
29. *Boston Globe*, September 12, 1919.
30. Ibid.
31. Ibid.
32. *Boston Evening Globe*, September 11, 1919.
33. Ibid.
34. *Boston Globe*, September 12, 1919.
35. *Boston Evening Globe*, September 11, 1919.
36. Ibid.
37. *Boston Evening Globe*, September 11, 1919; *Boston Herald*, September 12, 1919.
38. *Boston Evening Globe*, September 11, 1919.
39. Ibid.
40. Ibid.
41. D Company, *D of the Tenth*.
42. *Boston Evening Globe*, September 11, 1919.
43. Ibid.
44. Ibid.
45. *Boston Evening Globe*, September 11, 1919; Russell, *A City in Terror*, 172.
46. *Boston Evening Globe*, September 11, 1919.
47. Friedheim, *Seattle*.
48. *Boston Globe*, September 12, 1919.
49. Ibid.
50. Ibid.
51. Shlaes, *Coolidge*, 165.
52. *Boston Globe*, September 12, 1919; Russell, *A City in Terror*, 174.
53. *Boston Evening Globe*, September 11, 1919.
54. Koss, "Boston Police Strike," 221; Russell, *A City in Terror*, 167.
55. Coolidge, *The Autobiography*, 132.
56. Shlaes, *Coolidge*, 164–65.
57. Coolidge, *The Autobiography*, 132.
58. Koss, "The Boston Police Strike," 220.
59. Coolidge, *The Autobiography*, 132; Russell, *A City in Terror*, 173.

60. Shlaes, *Coolidge*, 164–65.
61. Boston Police Department, *Police Records; Boston Globe*, September 12, 1919.
62. Citizens' Committee, *Report*, Appendix 27.
63. Coolidge, *The Autobiography*, 132.
64. Russell, *A City in Terror*, 174–75; Koss, "The Boston Police Strike," 218.
65. Koss, "The Boston Police Strike," 218.
66. Shlaes, *Coolidge*, 164–65.
67. Fuess, *Calvin Coolidge*, 222; Koss, "The Boston Police Strike," 218.
68. *Boston Herald*, September 12, 1919.
69. *Boston Globe*, September 12, 1919.
70. Lyons, "The Boston Police Strike."
71. Coolidge, *The Autobiography*, 132.
72. *Boston Globe*, September 12, 1919.
73. Ibid.
74. Ibid.
75. Citizens' Committee, *Report*, Appendix 28.
76. *Boston Herald*, September 12, 1919; *Boston Post*, September 12, 1919.
77. *Boston Globe*, September 12, 1919.
78. Ibid.
79. Ibid.
80. *Boston Evening Globe*, September 11, 1919.
81. Ibid.
82. Ibid.
83. Ibid.
84. *Boston Globe*, September 12, 1919.
85. Ibid.
86. Ibid.
87. *Boston Evening Globe*, September 11, 1919.
88. *Boston Globe*, September 12, 1919; Russell, *A City in Terror*, 173.
89. Koss, "The Boston Police Strike," 226–27.
90. *Boston Globe*, September 12, 1919.
91. Ibid.
92. Russell, *A City in Terror*, 170.
93. *Boston Globe*, September 12, 1919.
94. *Boston Evening Globe*, September 11, 1919; Russell, *A City in Terror*, 165.
95. *Boston Globe*, September 12, 1919.
96. Ibid.
97. Ibid.
98. Ibid.
99. *Boston Herald*, September 12, 1919; Koss, "The Boston Police Strike."
100. *Boston Globe*, September 12, 1919.
101. Ibid.
102. *Boston Evening Globe*, September 11, 1919.
103. *Boston Globe*, September 12, 1919.

104. Ibid.
105. D Company, *D of the Tenth*, 33.
106. Ibid.
107. *Boston Globe*, September 12, 1919.
108. Ibid.
109. Ibid.
110. *Boston Herald*, September 12, 1919.
111. *Boston Globe*, September 12, 1919.
112. Marx, "Thomas G. Plant."
113. *Boston Globe*, September 14, 1919.
114. Ibid.
115. Ibid.
116. Ibid.
117. *Boston Globe*, September 12, 1919; Boston Herald, September 12, 1919.
118. *Boston Globe*, September 14, 1919.
119. Ibid.
120. *Boston Globe*, September 12, 1919.
121. *Boston Globe*, September 14, 1919.
122. Ibid.
123. *Boston Evening Globe*, September 12, 1919.

Chapter 12. Coolidge Takes Charge

1. *Boston Evening Globe*, September 12, 1919.
2. Ibid.
3. Ibid.
4. Ibid.
5. Ibid.
6. Boston, *City Records* Vol. 6 (1914), 1189.
7. *Boston Evening Globe*, September 12, 1919.
8. Ibid.
9. Koss, "The Boston Police Strike"; *Boston Traveler*, September 13, 1919.
10. *Boston Evening Globe*, September 12, 1919.
11. D Company, *D of the Tenth*.
12. Ibid., 34.
13. *Boston Evening Globe*, September 12, 1919.
14. Ibid.
15. Ibid.
16. Ibid.
17. *Boston Globe*, September 13, 1919.
18. *Boston Evening Globe*, September 12, 1919.
19. Ibid.
20. Shlaes, *Coolidge*, 167.

21. Ibid.
22. Ibid.
23. Ibid.
24. Coolidge, *The Autobiography*, 132.
25. *Boston Evening Globe*, September 12, 1919; Koss, "The Boston Police Strike."
26. *Boston Evening Globe*, September 12, 1919; *Boston Herald*, September 13, 1919.
27. *Boston Evening Globe*, September 12, 1919.
28. Ibid.
29. Ibid.
30. Ibid.
31. Ibid.
32. Ibid.
33. Ibid.
34. Ibid.
35. Ibid.
36. Koss, "The Boston Police Strike," 234.
37. Ibid.
38. Russell, *A City in Terror*, 181.
39. *Boston Globe*, September 13, 1919.
40. Koss, "The Boston Police Strike," 229.
41. *Boston Herald*, September 12, 1919; Russell, *A City in Terror*, 180.
42. *Boston Herald*, September 12, 1919.
43. *Boston Evening Globe*, September 12, 1919; Russell, *A City in Terror*, 180.
44. *Boston Evening Globe*, September 12, 1919.
45. Koss, "The Boston Police Strike," 230.
46. *Boston Herald*, September 13, 1919.
47. *Boston Herald*, September 13, 1919; Koss, "The Boston Police Strike," 231.
48. Koss, "The Boston Police Strike."
49. Ibid.
50. Ibid., 232.
51. *Boston Evening Globe*, September 12, 1919.
52. *Boston Herald*, September 13, 1919; Koss, "The Boston Police Strike," 232.
53. Koss, "The Boston Police Strike," 231.
54. *Boston Evening Globe*, September 13, 1919.
55. *Boston Globe*, September 13, 1919.
56. Ibid.
57. *Boston Evening Globe*, September 12, 1919.
58. Ibid.
59. Ibid.
60. *Boston Globe*, September 13, 1919.
61. Ibid.

62. *Boston Evening Globe*, September 13, 1919.
63. Ibid., 1919.
64. *Boston Evening Globe*, September 12, 1919.
65. Ibid., 1919.
66. *Boston Traveler*, September 13, 1919; Koss, "The Boston Police Strike,"
232.
67. *Boston Globe*, September 13, 1919.
68. Ibid.
69. Koss, "The Boston Police Strike."
70. *Boston Globe*, September 13, 1919.
71. Ibid.

Chapter 13. Firing and Hiring a Police Department

1. *Boston Globe*, September 14, 1919.
2. Ibid.
3. *Boston Globe*, September 13, 1919.
4. Koss, "The Boston Police Strike," 236.
5. Ibid.
6. Ibid.
7. Koss, "The Boston Police Strike," 236–37; Russell, *A City in Terror*, 182.
8. Koss, "The Boston Police Strike," 236–37.
9. Russell, *A City in Terror*, 182.
10. *Boston Globe*, September 13, 1919; Russell, *A City in Terror*, 183.
11. *Boston Globe*, September 13, 1919.
12. Ibid.
13. Russell, *A City in Terror*, 183.
14. *Boston Herald*, September 14, 1919; Koss, "The Boston Police Strike,"
236.
15. *Boston Evening Globe*, September 13, 1919.
16. Ibid.
17. Ibid.
18. Ibid.
19. Russell, *A City in Terror*, 183.
20. *Boston Globe*, September 14, 1919.
21. Ibid.
22. *Boston Evening Globe*, September 13, 1919.
23. Ibid.
24. Ibid.
25. Boston Police Commissioner, *Police Records*.
26. UMASS, *1919 Boston Police Strike Project*.
27. *Boston Evening Globe*, September 13, 1919.
28. *Boston Herald*, September 14, 1919.

29. *Boston Globe*, September 13, 1919; Russell, *A City in Terror*, 190.
30. Russell, *A City in Terror*, 184.
31. Initially, the newspapers incorrectly spelled his last name "Geist."
32. *Boston Globe*, September 14, 1919.
33. *Boston Globe*, September 14, 1919; *Boston Evening Globe*, September 13, 1919.
34. Ibid.
35. *Boston Globe*, September 14, 1919.
36. *Boston Evening Globe*, September 13, 1919.
37. *Boston Globe*, September 14, 1919.
38. *Boston Globe*, September 14, 1919.
39. *Boston Evening Globe*, September 13, 1919.
40. Ibid.
41. Ibid.
42. *Boston Globe*, September 14, 1919.
43. Ibid.
44. *Boston Globe*, September 14, 1919; Russell, *A City in Terror*, 188.
45. *Boston Globe*, September 14, 1919.
46. Ibid.
47. Ibid.
48. *Boston Evening Globe*, September 13, 1919.
49. Ibid.
50. *Boston Globe*, September 14, 1919.
51. *Boston Globe*, September 14, 1919; Russell, *A City in Terror*, 190–91.
52. Ibid.
53. Ibid.; Note: Russell, like the newspapers, refers to him as Geist.
54. *Boston Globe*, September 14, 1919.
55. Ibid.
56. *Boston Globe*, September 14, 1919; Russell, *A City in Terror*, 184.
57. *Boston Globe*, September 14, 1919.
58. Ibid.
59. *Boston Globe*, September 15, 1919.
60. *Boston Globe*, September 14, 1919.
61. Ibid.

Chapter 14. . . . Is Paved with Good Intentions

1. Shlaes, *Coolidge*.
2. *Boston Globe*, September 15, 1919.
3. Ibid.
4. Ibid.
5. *Boston Sunday Post*, September 14, 1919.
6. Coolidge, *The Autobiography*, 134.

7. *Boston Globe*, September 15, 1919; Russell, *A City in Terror*, 191.
8. *Boston Globe*, September 14, 1919; Russell, *A City in Terror*, 191.
9. *Boston Globe*, September 15, 1919; Russell, *A City in Terror*, 191.
10. *Boston Globe*, September 14, 1919; Russell, *A City in Terror*, 191.
11. *Boston Globe*, September 15, 1919; Russell, *A City in Terror*, 191.
12. Koss, "The Boston Police Strike," 244.
13. *Boston Globe*, September 15, 1919.
14. Russell, *A City in Terror*, 192.
15. Shlaes, *Coolidge*, 174; see also Koss, "The Boston Police Strike," 207.
16. Coolidge, *The Autobiography*, 134.
17. *Boston Globe*, September 15, 1919.
18. O'Connor, *The Boston Irish*, 192–93.
19. Sobel, *Coolidge*, 148.
20. Russell, *A City in Terror*, 200.
21. Lyons, "The Boston Police Strike," 165; see also Boston Police Commissioner, *14th Annual Report*.
22. Ibid.
23. Boston Police Commissioner, *14th Annual Report*, 20.
24. Ibid.
25. Ibid., 23.
26. Ibid., 15.
27. Ibid., 19.
28. *Boston Herald*, September 9, 1919.
29. Coolidge, *The Autobiography*, 131.
30. Ibid.
31. D Company, *D of the Tenth*.
32. A Company, *Dates*, 5.
33. Lyons, "The Boston Police Strike," 166.
34. Tager, *Boston Riots*, 170.
35. Sobel, *Coolidge*, 147.
36. Boston Police Commissioner, *14th Annual Report*, 19–20, 27.
37. *Boston Globe*, March 29, 1922.
38. Slater, "Public Workers."
39. 1920 Census, "John McInnes"; Russell, *A City in Terror*, 217.
40. *Boston Globe*, May 17, 1924; UMASS Boston, *1919 Boston Police Strike Project*.
41. *Boston Globe*, May 17, 1924.
42. UMASS Boston, *1919 Boston Police Strike Project*.
43. Ibid.
44. Ibid.
45. Pattullo, "The National Crisis."
46. Ibid.
47. Ibid.
48. Ibid.
49. Ibid.

50. Ibid.
51. White, "A Triumph," 205.
52. Fogelson, *Big-City*, 81.
53. Reppetto, *American Police*, 118.
54. Reppetto, *American Police*, 118; see also Russell, *A City in Terror*, 234–35; Walker, *A Critical History of Police Reform*, 110, 119.
55. Shlaes, *Coolidge*, 174.
56. Sobel, *Coolidge*, 145.
57. Sobel, *Coolidge*, 150; Russell, *A City in Terror*, 212.
58. Sobel, *Coolidge*, 136.
59. *Boston Herald*, November 6, 1919.
60. Green, "Coolidge," 487.
61. Ibid.
62. Coolidge, *The Autobiography*, 141.
63. Ibid., 173–74.
64. Ibid.
65. Russell, "Coolidge," 403.
66. Murray, *Red Scare*; Outlook, "The Boston Strike," "The Right of the People"; Youth's Companion, "Striking Policemen."
67. Green, "Coolidge and the Police Strike."
68. Sobel, *Coolidge*; Fraser and Freeman, "In the Rearview Mirror"; Slater, "Public Workers."
69. Koss, "The Boston Police Strike"; Russell, *A City in Terror*; White, "A Triumph of Bureaucracy."
70. Koss, "The Boston Police Strike"; Russell, *A City in Terror*.
71. Versions of this quote have been heard many times by the author, including by playwright Peter Shaffer, and most recently by John Campbell Jr. on the Old Time Radio show *Exploring Tomorrow*.
72. Matthew 6:24.

Epilogue

1. Reagan, *An American Life*, 244.
2. Ibid.
3. Brands, *Reagan*.
4. Reagan, *The Reagan Diaries*, 26; see also Reagan, *An American Life*, 282.
5. Reagan, "Remarks and a Question-and-Answer Session."
6. Ibid.
7. Ibid.
8. Coolidge, *The Autobiography*, 134.
9. Brands, *Reagan*, 311.

Bibliography

Abbott, Edith. "The Civil War and the Crime Wave of 1865–70." *Social Service Review*, 1 (June 1927): 212–34.

Ackerman, Kenneth D. *Young J. Edgar: Hoover, The Red Scare, and the Assault on Civil Liberties*. New York: Carroll & Graf Publishers, 2007.

A Company. *Dates, Data and Ditties: Tour of Duty A Company, 11th Regiment Infantry, Massachusetts State Guard During the Strike of the Boston Police*. Boston: A Company, 11th Infantry, M.S.G., 1920.

Ainely, Leslie G. *Boston Mahatma*. Boston: Bruce Humphries Inc. Publishers, 1949.

American Experience. "A Letter from Camp Devens." PBS. Accessed November 5, 2020. www.pbs.org/wgbh/americanexperience/features/influenza-letter/#:~:text=Camp%20Devens%20is%20near%20Boston,up%20till%20it%20has%20passed.

American Federation of Labor. *Report of Proceedings of the Thirty-Seventh Annual Convention of the American Federation of Labor*. Washington, DC: The American Federation of Labor, 1917.

———. *Report of Proceedings of the Thirty-Ninth Annual Convention of the American Federation of Labor*. Washington, DC: The American Federation of Labor, 1919.

American Jurist and Law Magazine, The. "Codification of the Common Law in Massachusetts." *The American Jurist and Law Magazine*, 15 (April & July 1836): 111–28.

Amory, Cleveland. *The Proper Bostonians*. New York: E.P. Dutton & Co. Inc., 1947.

Anonymous. *Dates, Data, and Ditties: Tour of Duty "A" Company, 11th Regiment Infantry Massachusetts State Guard, Boston Police Strike, Nineteen Hundred and Nineteen.* Boston: A Company, 11th Infantry, M.S.G., 1920.

Armory, Thomas C. *The Metropolitan Police Bill for Boston, 1863.* Boston: J. E. Farwell and Company, 1863.

Arnold Arboretum, The. "Our History." *The Arnold Arboretum of Harvard University.* Accessed January 27, 2021. https://arboretum.harvard.edu/about/our-history/.

Asinof, Eliot. *1919: America's Loss of Innocence.* New York: Donald I. Fine Inc., 1990.

Augustus, John. *A Report of the Labors of John Augustus for the Last Ten Years, in Aid of the Unfortunate.* Boston: Wright & Hasty, 1852.

Barry, John M. *The Great Influenza: The Epic Story of the Deadliest Plague in History.* New York: Penguin Books, 2004.

Bartlett, Randolph. "Anarchy in Boston." *The American Mercury* 36 (December 1935): 456–63.

Bean, Ron. "Police Unrest, Unionization and the 1919 Strike in Liverpool." *Journal of Contemporary History* 15, no. 4 (October 1980): 633–53.

Beattie, J. M. *The First English Detectives: The Bow Street Runners and the Policing of London, 1750–1840.* New York: Oxford University Press, 2012.

Beatty, Jack. *The Rascal King: The Life and Times of James Michael Curley.* Cambridge: De Cap Press, 2000.

Bopp, William J., and Donald O. Schultz. *A Short History of American Law Enforcement.* Springfield: Charles C. Thomas, 1972.

Boston Citizens' Committee. *Report of the Citizens' Committee Appointed by Mayor Peters to Consider the Police Situation.* Boston: City of Boston, 1920.

Boston City Council. *Ordinances and Rules and Orders of the City of Boston: Together with the General and Special Statutes of the Massachusetts Legislature Relating to the City.* Boston: Alfred Mudge and Son Printers, 1869.

Boston, City of. "A Brief History of the B.P.D." *City of Boston.* May 4, 2012. https://web.archive.org/web/20120304222909/; www.cityof boston.gov/police/about/history.asp.

———. *Documents of the City of Boston,* No. 15. Boston: City of Boston, 1837.

———. *Documents of the City of Boston,* Volume XV. Boston: City of Boston, 1837.

———. *Documents of the City of Boston*, six volumes. Boston: Rockwell and Churchill, City Printers, 1895.

———. *First Annual Report of the Board of Police for the City of Boston*. Boston: Wright & Potter Printing Co., 1886.

———. *The Inaugural Addresses of the Mayors of Boston, Vol. 1, 1822–51*. Boston: Rockwell and Churchill, 1894.

———. *Reports of the Special Committee Appointed to Investigate the Official Conduct of the Members of the Board of Police Commissioners, 1881*. Boston: City of Boston, 1881.

———. "Symbols of the City of Boston." *City of Boston*. July 16, 2016. www.boston.gov/departments/tourism-sports-and-entertainment/symbols-city-boston.

Boston Fire Historical Society. "Great Boston Fire of 1872." *Boston Fire Historical Society*. Accessed January 14, 2021. https://bostonfirehistory.org/fires/great-boston-fire-of-1872/.

Boston Police Commissioner. *Fourteenth Annual Report of the Police Commission for the City of Boston, Year Ending November 30, 1919*. Boston: Wright & Potter Printing Company, 1920.

———. *Police Records*, 56 (January 1, 1919, to December 31, 1919). Boston: Boston Police Department.

———. *Sixth Annual Report of the Police Commissioner for the City of Boston, Year Ending November 30, 1911*. Boston: Wright and Potter Printing Company, 1912.

———. *Third Annual Report of the Police Commissioner for the City of Boston, Year Ending November 30, 1908*. Boston: Wright and Potter Printing Company, 1909.

———. *Twelfth Annual Report of the Police Commissioner for the City of Boston, December 1906*. Boston: Wright & Potter Printing Co., 1907.

Boston Police Department. "History." *BPDnews.com*. Accessed February 11, 2020. https://bpdnews.com/history.

Bourne, Randolph. *The War and the Intellectuals*. New York: American Union Against Militarism, 1917.

Brands, H. W. *Reagan: The Life*. New York: Doubleday, 2015.

Burrows, Edwin G., and Mike Wallace. *Gotham: A History of New York City to 1898*. New York: Oxford University Press, 1999.

Byrnes, Thomas. *Professional Criminals of America*. New York: G. W. Dillingham Publisher, 1895.

Centers for Disease Control and Prevention. "1918 Pandemic (H1N1 Virus)." Centers for Disease Control and Prevention. Accessed December 3, 2020. www.cdc.gov/flu/pandemic-resources/1918-pandemic-h1n1.html.

Chernev, Borislav. *Twilight of Empire: The Brest-Litovsk Conference and the Remaking of the East-Central Europe, 1917–1918.* Toronto: University of Toronto Press, 2017.

Citizens' Committee. *Report of Citizens' Committee Appointed by Mayor Peters to Consider the Police Situation.* Boston: Citizens' Committee, 1919.

Connolly, James J. *The Triumph of Ethnic Progressivism: Urban Political Culture in Boston, 1900–1920.* Cambridge: Harvard University Press, 1998.

Coolidge, Calvin. *The Autobiography of Calvin Coolidge.* New York: Cosmopolitan Book Corporation, 1929.

Coolidge, Grace. *Grace Coolidge: An Autobiography,* edited by Lawrence E. Wikander and Robert H. Ferrell. Worland, WY: High Plains Publishing Company, 1992.

Coolidge, Louis A. "Edwin Upton Curtis: The Tribute of a Friend." *National Magazine* 50, no. 12 (May 1922): 536.

Cromwell, Adelaide M. *The Other Brahmins: Boston's Black Upper Class, 1750–1950.* Fayetteville: University of Arkansas Press, 1994.

Curley, James Michael. *I'd Do It Again.* New York: Prentice Hall, 1957.

Current Opinion. "Coolidge, A Governor Who Makes No Mistakes and Never Lost an Election." *Current Opinion* 68, no. 1 (January 1920): 35–38.

D Company. *D of the Tenth.* Boston: D. Co., 10th Regiment Infantry, Massachusetts State Guard, 1921.

Davis, David Brion. *Inhuman Bondage: The Rise and Fall of Slavery in the New World.* New York: Oxford University Press, 2006.

DeGregorio, William A. *The Complete Book of U.S. Presidents.* New York: Gramercy Books, 2002.

Diamond, Jared. *Guns, Germs, and Steel: The Fates of Human Societies.* New York: W. W. Norton & Company, 2017.

Dilworth, Donald C. (ed). *The Blue and the Brass: American Policing: 1890–1910.* Gaithersburg, MD: International Association of Chiefs of Police, 1976.

Douglas, Paul H. *Real Wages in the United States: 1890–1926.* Boston: Houghton Mifflin, 1930.

Eliot, Samuel A. "Being Mayor of Boston a Hundred Years Ago." *Proceedings of the Massachusetts Historical Society,* 66 (1936): 154–73.

Ellis, Charles M. *The Argument of Charles M. Ellis, in Favor of the Metropolitan Police Act, 1863.* Boston: Wright & Potter, Printers, 1863.

Ellis, Mark. "J. Edgar Hoover and the 'Red Summer' of 1919." *Journal of American Studies* 28, no. 1 (April 1994): 39–59.

Emsley, Clive, and Haia Shpayer-Makov. *Police Detectives in History, 1750–1950.* New York: Routledge, 2017.

Epstein, S. R., and Maarten Prak. *Guilds, Innovation, and the European Economy, 1400–1800.* New York: Cambridge University Press, 2008.

Fairlie, John. A. "Police Administration." *Political Science Quarterly* 16, no. 1 (March 1901): 1–23.

Farmer, Brian. "The Boston Police Strike of 1919." *New American* 27 (July 18, 2011): 36–40.

Federal Bureau of Investigation. "Palmer Raids." *Federal Bureau of Investigation History,* Accessed October 29, 2020. www.fbi.gov/his tory/famous-cases/palmer-raids#:~:text=On%20June%202%2C%20 1919%2C%20a,the%20bomb%20exploded%20too%20early.

Ferdinand, Theodore N. *Boston's Lower Criminal Courts, 1814–1850.* Newark: University of Delaware Press, 1992.

———. "The Criminal Patterns of Boston since 1849." *American Journal of Sociology* 73, no. 1 (July 1967): 84–99.

Fitzgerald, Charles. "The Boston Police Strike of September 1919." Thesis, Boston College, 1952.

Fogelson, Robert M. *Big-City Police.* Cambridge: Harvard University Press, 1977.

Foner, Philip. *History of the Labor Movement in the United States,* vol. 4. New York: International Publishers, 1965.

Fosdick, Raymond B. *American Police Systems.* New York: The Century Co., 1920.

Franklin, Benjamin. *The Autobiography of Benjamin Franklin.* Rockville: Arc Manor, 1788/2008.

Fraser, Steve, and Joshua B. Freeman. "In the Rearview Mirror: When Congress Roared." *New Labor Reform* 19, no. 1 (February 2010): 90–92.

Fried, Rebecca A. "No Irish Need Deny: Evidence for the Historicity of NINA Restrictions in Advertisements and Signs." *Journal of Social History* 49, no. 4 (Summer 2016): 829–54.

Friedheim, Robert L. *The Seattle General Strike.* Seattle: University of Washington Press, 2018.

Friedman, Lawrence M. *Crime and Punishment in American History.* New York: Basic Books, 1993.

Fuess, Claude M. *Amherst: The Story of a New England College.* Boston: Little, Brown, and Company, 1935.

———. *Calvin Coolidge—the Man from Vermont.* New York: The Atlantic Monthly Press Books, 1940.

Gage, Beverly. *The Day Wall Street Exploded: A Story of America in Its First Age of Terror*. New York: Oxford University Press, 2009.

Galvin, John. T. "The Dark Ages of Boston City Politics." *Proceedings of the Massachusetts Historical Society* 89 (1977): 88–111.

Gately, Ian. *Drink: A Cultural History of Alcohol*. London: Gotham Books, 2009.

Gies, Frances, and Joseph Gies. *Cathedral, Forge, and Waterwheel: Technology and Invention in the Middle Ages*. New York: HarperCollins, 1994.

Gompers, Samuel. *Seventy Years of Life and Labor: An Autobiography*. New York: E. P. Dutton & Company, 1925.

Goodman, Jonathan. *The Passing of Starr Faithfull*. Kent: The Kent State University Press, 1996.

Green, Horace. "Coolidge and the Police Strike." *Forum* 71, no. 4 (April 1924): 479–87.

Green, James. *Death in the Haymarket: A Story of Chicago, the First Labor Movement and the Bombing that Divided Gilded Age America*. New York: Pantheon Books, 2006.

Gusfield, Joseph R. *Symbolic Crusade: Status Politics and the American Temperance Movement*. Urbana: University of Illinois Press, 1963.

Gutman, Herbert G. 1977. *Work, Culture, and Society in Industrializing America: Essays in American Working-Class and Social History*. New York: Alfred A. Knopf, 1976.

Handlin, Oscar. *Boston's Immigrants: A Study in Acculturation*. Cambridge, MA: Belknap Press, 1959.

Hanna, William F. "The Boston Draft Riot." *Civil War History* Vol. 36 (September 1990): 262–73.

Harding, Alan. *England in the Thirteenth Century*. New York: Cambridge University Press, 1993.

Harding, Warren G. "Inaugural Address of Warren G. Harding, Friday March 4, 1921." *The Avalon Project*. Accessed November 19, 2020. https://avalon.law.yale.edu/20th_century/harding.asp.

Harrison, Leonard Vance. *Police Administration in Boston*. Cambridge: Harvard University Press, 1934.

Hart, Albert Bushnell. *Commonwealth History of Massachusetts*. New York: States History Company, 1930.

Harvard College. "Edwin Upton Curtis." In *Harvard College Class of 1895: Twenty-Fifth Anniversary Report*, edited by Class Committee, 361–62. Cambridge: Harvard College, 1920.

Herron, R. "The Police Strike of 1918." *The Bulletin* 17, (1989): 181–94.

Hill, Clement Hugh. *Argument Made Before a Joint Committee of the Legislature of Massachusetts, May 17, 1869, Against the Establishment of a State Police in the City of Boston.* Boston: Alfred Mudge & Son, 1869.

History News Network. "Racial Violence and a Pandemic: How the Red Summer of 1919 Relates to 2020." *History News Network.* https://historynewsnetwork.org/article/176081.

Hoogenboom, Ari Arthur. *Outlawing the Spoils: A History of the Civil Service Reform Movement, 1865–1883.* Champaign: University of Illinois Press, 1961.

Hopkins, Ernest Jerome. *Our Lawless Police: A Study of the Unlawful Enforcement of the Law.* New York: The Viking Press, 1931.

Ireland, Merritt W., ed. *Medical Department of the United States Army in the World War, Communicable Diseases,* vol. 9. Washington, DC: U.S. Army, 1928.

Jaher, Frederic Cople. *The Urban Establishment: Upper Strata in Boston, New York, Charleston, Chicago, and Los Angeles.* Urbana: University of Illinois Press, 1982.

Jeffers, H. Paul. *Commissioner Roosevelt: The Story of Theodore Roosevelt and the New York City Police, 1895–1897.* New York: John Wiley & Sons Inc., 1994.

Jensen, Richard. "'No Irish Need Apply': A Myth of Victimization." *Journal of Social History* 36, no. 2 (Winter 2002): 36–57.

Johnson, James Weldon. *Along This Way: The Autobiography of James Weldon Johnson.* New York: Penguin Classics, 1990.

Juris, Henry A., and Peter Feuille. *Police Unionism: Power and Impact in Public-Sector Bargaining.* Lanham: Lexington Books, 1973.

Kappeler, Victor. E., Richard D. Sluder, and Geoffrey P. Alpert. *Forces of Deviance: Understanding the Dark Side of Policing.* Prospect Heights: Waveland Press Inc., 1994.

Kennedy, David M. *Over Here: The First World War and American Society. Twenty-Fifth Anniversary Edition.* New York: Oxford University Press, 2004.

King, Joseph F. "Police Strikes of 1918 and 1919 in the United Kingdom and Boston and Their Effects." PhD diss., City University of New York, 1999.

Kirkland, Edward C. "Boston During the Civil War." *Proceedings of the Massachusetts Historical Society, Third Series* Vol. 71 (October 1953 to May 1957): 194–203.

Kleinfelder, Henry C. *D of the Tenth.* Boston: D. Co., 10th Regiment Infantry, Massachusetts State Guard, 1921.

Koss, Frederick M. "The Boston Police Strike of 1919." PhD diss., Columbia University, 1966.

Lane, Roger. *Policing the City: Boston, 1822–1885.* Cambridge: Harvard University Press, 1967.

———. "Urban Police and Crime in Nineteenth-Century America." *Crime and Justice* 15 (1992): 1–50.

Levy, Leonard W. "The 'Abolition Riot': Boston's First Slave Rescue." *The New England Quarterly*, 25, no. 1 (1952): 85–93.

Lorwin, Lewis L. *The American Federation of Labor: History, Policies, and Prospects.* Washington, DC: The Brookings Institution, 1933.

Lurie, Melvin. "Government Regulation and Union Power: A Case Study of the Boston Transit Industry." *The Journal of Law & Economics* 3 (Oct. 1960): 118–35.

Lynch, Shawn M. "'Red Riots' and the Origins of the Civil Liberties Union of Massachusetts, 1915–1930." *Historical Journal of Massachusetts* 38, no. 1 (Spring 2010): 61–81.

Lyons, Richard L. "The Boston Police Strike of 1919." *New England Quarterly* 20, no. 2 (June 1947): 147–68.

Mandel, Bernard. *Samuel Gompers: A Biography.* Yellow Springs: The Antioch Press, 1963.

Marx, Walter H. "Thomas G. Plant Shoe Factory Fire." *Jamaica Plain Historical Society*, Accessed November 15, 2021. www.jphs.org/locales/2004/1/5/thomas-g-plant-shoe-factory-fire.html.

McCaffrey, George H. "The Boston Police Department." *Journal of the American Institute of Criminal Law and Criminology* 2, no. 5 (1912): 672–90.

McCoy, Donald R. *Calvin Coolidge: The Quiet President.* New York: Macmillan, 1967.

Migration Policy Institute. "U.S. Immigration Trends." *Migration Policy Institute.* Accessed December 10, 2020. www.migrationpolicy.org/programs/data-hub/us-immigration-trends.

Miller, Wilbur B. *Cops and Bobbies: Police Authority in New York and London, 1830–1870.* 2nd edition. Columbus: Ohio State University Press, 1999.

Monkkonen, Eric H. "History of Urban Police." *Crime and Justice* 15 (1992): 547–80.

———. *Police in Urban America 1860–1920.* Cambridge: Cambridge University Press, 1981.

Morris, William Alfred. *The Frankpledge System.* New York: Longmans, Green, and Co., 1910.

———. *The Medieval English Sheriff to 1300*. New York: Barnes & Noble Inc., 1927.

Morton, James. *The First Detective: The Life and Revolutionary Times of Eugène-François Vidocq, Criminal Spy and Private Eye*. London: Ebury Press, 2004.

Munsey's Magazine. "In the Public Eye." *Munsey's Magazine* 15 (July 1896): 481–88.

Murray, Robert K. *Red Scare: A Study in National Hysteria, 1919–1920*. Minneapolis: University of Minnesota Press, 1955.

———. "The Outer World and the Inner Light: A Case Study." *Pennsylvania History: A Journal of Mid-Atlantic Studies*, 36 (July 1969): 265–89.

National Commission on Law Observance and Enforcement (Wickersham Commission. *Report on Lawlessness in Law Enforcement*. Washington, DC: U.S. GPO, 1931.

National Lancers. "Our History." *National Lancers*. Accessed October 8, 2020. www.nationallancers.org/aboutus.html.

National Park Service. "From the Great Migration to Boston's Charlestown Navy Yard." *National Park Service*. Accessed November 12, 2020. www.nps.gov/articles/great-migration-to-charlestown-navy-yard.htm.

New England Historical Society. "Before Dunkin', New England Had the Waldorf Lunch System." *New England Historical Society*, Accessed September 2, 2021. www.newenglandhistoricalsociety.com/before-dunkin-new-england-had-the-waldorf-lunch-system/.

New England Magazine. "Edwin Upton Curtis." *New England Magazine* 43 (September 1910): 113.

O'Connor, Thomas H. *The Boston Irish: A Political History*. Boston: Northeastern University Press, 1995.

———. *Civil War Boston*. Boston: Northeastern University Press, 1979.

Officer Down Memorial Page. "Captain Hugh J. Lee." *Officer Down Memorial Page*. Accessed December 16, 2020. www.odmp.org/officer/21154-captain-hugh-j-lee.

Ogilvie, Sheilagh. *Institutions and European Trade: Merchant Guilds, 1000–1800*. New York: Cambridge University Press, 2011.

Oliver, Willard M., and James F. Hilgenberg Jr. *A History of Crime and Criminal Justice in America*. 3rd ed. Durham: Carolina Academic Press, 2018.

Panzarella, Robert. "Theory and Practice of Probation on Bail in the Report of John Augustus." *Federal Probation* 66, no. 2 (September 2002): 38–42.

Pattullo, George. "The National Crisis in Boston." *The Saturday Evening Post*, November 15, 1919. Accessed September 1, 2021. www.saturdayeveningpost.com/2016/09/national-crisis-boston/.

Pearl, Matthew. "Into the Shadows." *Boston Globe Magazine*. Accessed July 30, 2020. www.bostonglobe.com/magazine/2016/04/28/the-incredible-untold-story-america-first-police-detectives/jewdTrdVz-kQZJuVZEEc9TJ/story.html.

Pendergrass, Drew C. "The Boys in Crimson: Boston's Police Strike-breakers." *The Crimson*. Accessed January 14, 2020. www.thecrimson.com/article/2016/11/10/boston-strikebreakers/.

Peters, Andrew J. *Inaugural Address of Andrew J. Peters, Mayor of Boston, to the City Council*. Boston: City of Boston, 1918.

Peterson, Mark. *The City-State of Boston: The Rise and Fall of an Atlantic Power, 1630–1865*. Princeton: Princeton University Press, 2019.

Phillips, Wendell. *Wendell Phillips, Esq. on a Metropolitan Police, 1863*. Boston: City of Boston, 1863.

Pringle, Patrick. *Hue and Cry: The Story of Henry and John Fielding and Their Bow Street Runners*. Suffolk: William Morrow, 2005.

Prioli, Carmine A. "The Ursuline Outrage." *American Heritage* 33 (Feb./Mar. 1982): 100–105.

Puleo, Stephen. *Dark Tide: The Great Molasses Flood of 1919*. Boston: Beacon Press, 2003.

Quincy, Josiah. *A Municipal History of the Town and City of Boston During Two Centuries from September 17, 1630, to September 17, 1830*. Boston: Charles C. Little and James Brown, 1852.

Reagan, Ronald. *The Reagan Diaries*. New York: Harper Perennial, 2009.

———. "Remarks and a Question-and-Answer Session with Reporters on the Air Traffic Controllers Strike." *The American Presidency Project*. www.presidency.ucsb.edu/documents/remarks-and-question-and-answer-session-with-reporters-the-air-traffic-controllers-strike.

Reagan, Ronald. *Ronald Reagan: An American Life*. New York: Simon & Schuster, 1990.

Reppetto, Thomas. *American Police: The Blue Parade, 1845–1945*. New York: Enigma Books, 2010–2011.

Reynolds, Gerald W., and Anthony Judge. *The Night the Police Went on Strike*. London: Weidenfeld & Nicolson, 1968.

Rezneck, Daniel A. "An Innocent Abroad: My Father's Diary." *American Scholar*, 60, no. 3 (1991): 441–45.

Roth, Mitchel P. *Historical Dictionary of Law Enforcement*. Westport: Greenwood Press, 2001.

———. *A History of Crime and the American Criminal Justice System.* 3rd ed. New York: Routledge, 2019.

Round, John Horace. *Feudal England: Historical Studies on the XIth and XIIth Centuries.* London: Sonnenschein & Co., 1909.

Rowland, Thomas J. "Irish-American Catholics and the Quest for Respectability in the Coming of the Great War, 1900–1917." *Journal of American Ethnic History* 15, no. 2 (Winter 1996): 3–31.

Russell, Francis. *A City in Terror: Calvin Coolidge and the 1919 Boston Police Strike.* Boston: Beacon Press, 1975.

———. "Coolidge and the Boston Police Strike." *The Antioch Review* 16, no. 4 (Winter 1956): 403–15.

———. "The Strike That Made a President." *American Heritage,* 14, Number 6 (October 1963): 44–50.

Ryan, Dennis P. *Beyond the Ballot Box: A Social History of the Boston Irish, 1845–1917.* Amherst: University of Massachusetts Press, 1989.

Savage, Edward H. *A Chronological History of the Boston Watch and Police from 1631 to 1865.* Boston: J. E. Farwell and Company, 1865.

———. *Police Records and Recollections or, Boston by Daylight and Gaslight for Two Hundred and Forty Years.* Boston: John P. Dale & Company, 1873.

Schultz, Nancy Lusignan. *Fire and Roses: The Burning of the Charlestown Convent.* New York: The Free Press, 2000.

Semi-Weekly Atlas. Boston, Massachusetts, 1844–1857.

Shakespeare, William. *Much Ado About Nothing.* New York: Oxford University Press, 1999.

Shlaes, Amity. *Coolidge.* New York: Harper Perennial, 2013.

Silverman, Kenneth. *Edgar A. Poe: Mournful and Never-Ending Remembrance.* New York: Harper Perennial, 1991.

Slater, Joseph. "Public Workers: Labor and the Boston Police Strike of 1919." *Labor History* 38, no. 1 (Winter 1976): 7–27.

Smith, John S. "Organized Labor and Government in the Wilson Era; 1913–1921: Some Conclusions." *Labor History* 3, no. 3 (Fall 1962): 265–86.

Sobel, Robert. *Coolidge: An American Enigma.* Washington, DC: Regnery Publishing Inc., 1998.

Stevens, Peter F. *Hidden History of the Boston Irish.* Charleston: The History Press, 2008.

Story, Ronald. "Harvard and the Boston Brahmins: A Study in Institutional and Class Development, 1800–1865." *Journal of Social History* 8, no. 3 (Spring 1975): 94–121.

Sykley, Anatole. "Boston at War." *Over the Top: Magazine of the World War I Centennial.* Accessed October 8, 2020. www.worldwar1centen nial.org/images/massachusetts/boston-at-War-text-draft-5.pdf.

Taaffe, Peter, and Tony Mulhearn. *Liverpool: A City That Dared to Fight.* Minneapolis: Fortress Press, 1988.

Tager, Jack. *Boston Riots: Three Centuries of Social Violence.* Boston: Northeastern University Press, 2001. www.iwp.edu/articles/2020/10/01/the-boston-police-strike-a-harbinger-for-today/.

Tomes, Nancy. "'Destroyer and Teacher': Managing the Masses During the 1918–1919 Influenza Pandemic." *Public Health Reports* 125, no. 3 (Supplement 3, 2010): 48–125.

UMASS, Boston. *1919 Boston Police Strike Project.* Boston: Joseph P. Healy Library at the University of Massachusetts, Boston. www.bpstrike1919.org/.

United States World War One Centennial Commission. "Immigrants." *The United States World War One Centennial Commission.* Accessed October 15, 2020. www.worldwar1centennial.org/index.php/edu-home/edu-topics/588-americans-at-war/4993-immigrants.html#:~:text=During%20World%20War%20I%2C%20nearly,arrived%20in%20the%20United%20States.

US House of Representatives. *Attorney General A. Mitchell Palmer on Charges Made Against Department of Justice by Louis F. Post and Others.* Washington, DC: US GPO, 1920.

US House of Representatives. *Sedition, Syndicalism, Sabotage, and Anarchy: Hearings Before the Committee on the Judiciary, December 11 and 16, 1919.* Washington, DC: US GPO, 1919.

Von Hoffman, Alexander. "An Officer of the Neighborhood: A Boston Patrolman on the Beat in 1895." *Journal of Social History* 26, no. 2 (Winter 1992): 309–30.

Walker, Samuel. *A Critical History of Police Reform.* Lexington: Lexington Books, 1977.

———. *Popular Justice: A History of American Criminal Justice.* 2nd edition. New York: Oxford University Press, 1998.

Walling, George W. *Recollections of a New York Chief of Police.* Montclair, NJ: Patterson Smith, 1972.

Walworth, Arthur. *Woodrow Wilson.* Boston: Houghton Mifflin, 1965.

Watson, Bruce. *Sacco & Vanzetti: The Men, the Murders, and the Judgement of Mankind.* New York: Viking, 2007.

Wells, Donna M. *Boston Police Department.* Portsmouth, NH: Arcadia Publishing, 2003.

White, Jonathan. "A Triumph of Bureaucracy: The Boston Police Strike and the Ideological Origins of the American Police Structure." PhD diss., Michigan State University, 1982.

———. "Violence during the 1919 Boston Police Strike: An Analysis of the Crime Control Myth." *Criminal Justice Review* 13, no. 2 (Spring 1988): 61–68.

White, William Allen. *A Puritan in Babylon: The Story of Calvin Coolidge.* New York: Macmillan, 1938.

Whiting, Edward Elwell. *President Coolidge: A Contemporary Estimate.* Boston: Atlantic Monthly Press, 1923.

Wilkerson, Isabel. *The Warmth of Other Suns: The Epic Story of America's Great Migration.* New York: Vintage Books, 2010.

Wilson, Woodrow Wilson. "War Message to Congress." 65th Cong., 1st Sess. Senate Doc. No. 5, Serial No. 7264, Washington, DC, 1917, 3–8.

Winthrop, John (Edited by J. Franklin Jameson). *Winthrop's Journal, 1630–1649.* Vol. 1. New York: Charles Scribner's Sons, 1908.

Wood, Charles G. *Reds and Lost Wages.* New York: Harper and Brothers Publishers, 1930.

Youth's Companion, The. "Striking Policemen." *The Youth's Companion* 93, no. 41 (October 9, 1919): 542.

Zacks, Richard. *Island of Vice: Theodore Roosevelt's Doomed Quest to Clean Up Sin-Loving New York.* New York: Doubleday, 2012.

Ziskind, David. *One Thousand Strikes of Government Employees.* New York: Columbia University Press, 1940.

Index

About the Author

Willard M. Oliver is a professor of criminal justice at Sam Houston State University in Huntsville, Texas. He received his PhD and MA in political science from West Virginia University, and his BS and MS in criminal justice from Radford University. His areas of research interest include policing, criminal justice history, and crime/criminal justice policy, especially where the three intersect. He has authored two dozen books, including *The Birth of the FBI: Teddy Roosevelt, the Secret Service, and the Fight Over America's Premier Law Enforcement Agency* (Rowman & Littlefield 2019). Oliver is a retired major in the US Army Reserves and a former police officer. He resides in Huntsville, Texas, with his family.

www.ingramcontent.com/pod-product-compliance
Lightning Source LLC
Chambersburg PA
CBHW030255100426
42812CB00002B/439